GACE

Middle Grades
Social Science
Secrets Study Guide

DEAR FUTURE EXAM SUCCESS STORY

First of all, **THANK YOU** for purchasing Mometrix study materials!

Second, congratulations! You are one of the few determined test-takers who are committed to doing whatever it takes to excel on your exam. **You have come to the right place.** We developed these study materials with one goal in mind: to deliver you the information you need in a format that's concise and easy to use.

In addition to optimizing your guide for the content of the test, we've outlined our recommended steps for breaking down the preparation process into small, attainable goals so you can make sure you stay on track.

We've also analyzed the entire test-taking process, identifying the most common pitfalls and showing how you can overcome them and be ready for any curveball the test throws you.

Standardized testing is one of the biggest obstacles on your road to success, which only increases the importance of doing well in the high-pressure, high-stakes environment of test day. Your results on this test could have a significant impact on your future, and this guide provides the information and practical advice to help you achieve your full potential on test day.

Your success is our success

We would love to hear from you! If you would like to share the story of your exam success or if you have any questions or comments in regard to our products, please contact us at **800-673-8175** or **support@mometrix.com**.

Thanks again for your business and we wish you continued success!

Sincerely,
The Mometrix Test Preparation Team

> **Need more help? Check out our flashcards at:**
> **http://MometrixFlashcards.com/GACE**

TABLE OF CONTENTS

Introduction

Thank you for purchasing this resource! You have made the choice to prepare yourself for a test that could have a huge impact on your future, and this guide is designed to help you be fully ready for test day. Obviously, it's important to have a solid understanding of the test material, but you also need to be prepared for the unique environment and stressors of the test, so that you can perform to the best of your abilities.

For this purpose, the first section that appears in this guide is the **Secret Keys**. We've devoted countless hours to meticulously researching what works and what doesn't, and we've boiled down our findings to the five most impactful steps you can take to improve your performance on the test. We start at the beginning with study planning and move through the preparation process, all the way to the testing strategies that will help you get the most out of what you know when you're finally sitting in front of the test.

We recommend that you start preparing for your test as far in advance as possible. However, if you've bought this guide as a last-minute study resource and only have a few days before your test, we recommend that you skip over the first two Secret Keys since they address a long-term study plan.

If you struggle with **test anxiety**, we strongly encourage you to check out our recommendations for how you can overcome it. Test anxiety is a formidable foe, but it can be beaten, and we want to make sure you have the tools you need to defeat it.

Secret Key #1 – Plan Big, Study Small

There's a lot riding on your performance. If you want to ace this test, you're going to need to keep your skills sharp and the material fresh in your mind. You need a plan that lets you review everything you need to know while still fitting in your schedule. We'll break this strategy down into three categories.

Information Organization

Start with the information you already have: the official test outline. From this, you can make a complete list of all the concepts you need to cover before the test. Organize these concepts into groups that can be studied together, and create a list of any related vocabulary you need to learn so you can brush up on any difficult terms. You'll want to keep this vocabulary list handy once you actually start studying since you may need to add to it along the way.

Time Management

Once you have your set of study concepts, decide how to spread them out over the time you have left before the test. Break your study plan into small, clear goals so you have a manageable task for each day and know exactly what you're doing. Then just focus on one small step at a time. When you manage your time this way, you don't need to spend hours at a time studying. Studying a small block of content for a short period each day helps you retain information better and avoid stressing over how much you have left to do. You can relax knowing that you have a plan to cover everything in time. In order for this strategy to be effective though, you have to start studying early and stick to your schedule. Avoid the exhaustion and futility that comes from last-minute cramming!

Study Environment

The environment you study in has a big impact on your learning. Studying in a coffee shop, while probably more enjoyable, is not likely to be as fruitful as studying in a quiet room. It's important to keep distractions to a minimum. You're only planning to study for a short block of time, so make the most of it. Don't pause to check your phone or get up to find a snack. It's also important to **avoid multitasking**. Research has consistently shown that multitasking will make your studying dramatically less effective. Your study area should also be comfortable and well-lit so you don't have the distraction of straining your eyes or sitting on an uncomfortable chair.

 The time of day you study is also important. You want to be rested and alert. Don't wait until just before bedtime. Study when you'll be most likely to comprehend and remember. Even better, if you know what time of day your test will be, set that time aside for study. That way your brain will be used to working on that subject at that specific time and you'll have a better chance of recalling information.

Finally, it can be helpful to team up with others who are studying for the same test. Your actual studying should be done in as isolated an environment as possible, but the work of organizing the information and setting up the study plan can be divided up. In between study sessions, you can discuss with your teammates the concepts that you're all studying and quiz each other on the details. Just be sure that your teammates are as serious about the test as you are. If you find that your study time is being replaced with social time, you might need to find a new team.

Secret Key #2 – Make Your Studying Count

You're devoting a lot of time and effort to preparing for this test, so you want to be absolutely certain it will pay off. This means doing more than just reading the content and hoping you can remember it on test day. It's important to make every minute of study count. There are two main areas you can focus on to make your studying count.

Retention

It doesn't matter how much time you study if you can't remember the material. You need to make sure you are retaining the concepts. To check your retention of the information you're learning, try recalling it at later times with minimal prompting. Try carrying around flashcards and glance at one or two from time to time or ask a friend who's also studying for the test to quiz you.

To enhance your retention, look for ways to put the information into practice so that you can apply it rather than simply recalling it. If you're using the information in practical ways, it will be much easier to remember. Similarly, it helps to solidify a concept in your mind if you're not only reading it to yourself but also explaining it to someone else. Ask a friend to let you teach them about a concept you're a little shaky on (or speak aloud to an imaginary audience if necessary). As you try to summarize, define, give examples, and answer your friend's questions, you'll understand the concepts better and they will stay with you longer. Finally, step back for a big picture view and ask yourself how each piece of information fits with the whole subject. When you link the different concepts together and see them working together as a whole, it's easier to remember the individual components.

Finally, practice showing your work on any multi-step problems, even if you're just studying. Writing out each step you take to solve a problem will help solidify the process in your mind, and you'll be more likely to remember it during the test.

Modality

Modality simply refers to the means or method by which you study. Choosing a study modality that fits your own individual learning style is crucial. No two people learn best in exactly the same way, so it's important to know your strengths and use them to your advantage.

For example, if you learn best by visualization, focus on visualizing a concept in your mind and draw an image or a diagram. Try color-coding your notes, illustrating them, or creating symbols that will trigger your mind to recall a learned concept. If you learn best by hearing or discussing information, find a study partner who learns the same way or read aloud to yourself. Think about how to put the information in your own words. Imagine that you are giving a lecture on the topic and record yourself so you can listen to it later.

For any learning style, flashcards can be helpful. Organize the information so you can take advantage of spare moments to review. Underline key words or phrases. Use different colors for different categories. Mnemonic devices (such as creating a short list in which every item starts with the same letter) can also help with retention. Find what works best for you and use it to store the information in your mind most effectively and easily.

3

Secret Key #3 – Practice the Right Way

Your success on test day depends not only on how many hours you put into preparing, but also on whether you prepared the right way. It's good to check along the way to see if your studying is paying off. One of the most effective ways to do this is by taking practice tests to evaluate your progress. Practice tests are useful because they show exactly where you need to improve. Every time you take a practice test, pay special attention to these three groups of questions:

- The questions you got wrong
- The questions you had to guess on, even if you guessed right
- The questions you found difficult or slow to work through

This will show you exactly what your weak areas are, and where you need to devote more study time. Ask yourself why each of these questions gave you trouble. Was it because you didn't understand the material? Was it because you didn't remember the vocabulary? Do you need more repetitions on this type of question to build speed and confidence? Dig into those questions and figure out how you can strengthen your weak areas as you go back to review the material.

 Additionally, many practice tests have a section explaining the answer choices. It can be tempting to read the explanation and think that you now have a good understanding of the concept. However, an explanation likely only covers part of the question's broader context. Even if the explanation makes perfect sense, **go back and investigate** every concept related to the question until you're positive you have a thorough understanding.

As you go along, keep in mind that the practice test is just that: practice. Memorizing these questions and answers will not be very helpful on the actual test because it is unlikely to have any of the same exact questions. If you only know the right answers to the sample questions, you won't be prepared for the real thing. **Study the concepts** until you understand them fully, and then you'll be able to answer any question that shows up on the test.

It's important to wait on the practice tests until you're ready. If you take a test on your first day of study, you may be overwhelmed by the amount of material covered and how much you need to learn. Work up to it gradually.

On test day, you'll need to be prepared for answering questions, managing your time, and using the test-taking strategies you've learned. It's a lot to balance, like a mental marathon that will have a big impact on your future. Like training for a marathon, you'll need to start slowly and work your way up. When test day arrives, you'll be ready.

Start with the strategies you've read in the first two Secret Keys—plan your course and study in the way that works best for you. If you have time, consider using multiple study resources to get different approaches to the same concepts. It can be helpful to see difficult concepts from more than one angle. Then find a good source for practice tests. Many times, the test website will suggest potential study resources or provide sample tests.

Practice Test Strategy

If you're able to find at least three practice tests, we recommend this strategy:

UNTIMED AND OPEN-BOOK PRACTICE

Take the first test with no time constraints and with your notes and study guide handy. Take your time and focus on applying the strategies you've learned.

TIMED AND OPEN-BOOK PRACTICE

Take the second practice test open-book as well, but set a timer and practice pacing yourself to finish in time.

TIMED AND CLOSED-BOOK PRACTICE

Take any other practice tests as if it were test day. Set a timer and put away your study materials. Sit at a table or desk in a quiet room, imagine yourself at the testing center, and answer questions as quickly and accurately as possible.

Keep repeating timed and closed-book tests on a regular basis until you run out of practice tests or it's time for the actual test. Your mind will be ready for the schedule and stress of test day, and you'll be able to focus on recalling the material you've learned.

Secret Key #4 – Pace Yourself

Once you're fully prepared for the material on the test, your biggest challenge on test day will be managing your time. Just knowing that the clock is ticking can make you panic even if you have plenty of time left. Work on pacing yourself so you can build confidence against the time constraints of the exam. Pacing is a difficult skill to master, especially in a high-pressure environment, so **practice is vital**.

Set time expectations for your pace based on how much time is available. For example, if a section has 60 questions and the time limit is 30 minutes, you know you have to average 30 seconds or less per question in order to answer them all. Although 30 seconds is the hard limit, set 25 seconds per question as your goal, so you reserve extra time to spend on harder questions. When you budget extra time for the harder questions, you no longer have any reason to stress when those questions take longer to answer.

Don't let this time expectation distract you from working through the test at a calm, steady pace, but keep it in mind so you don't spend too much time on any one question. Recognize that taking extra time on one question you don't understand may keep you from answering two that you do understand later in the test. If your time limit for a question is up and you're still not sure of the answer, mark it and move on, and come back to it later if the time and the test format allow. If the testing format doesn't allow you to return to earlier questions, just make an educated guess; then put it out of your mind and move on.

On the easier questions, be careful not to rush. It may seem wise to hurry through them so you have more time for the challenging ones, but it's not worth missing one if you know the concept and just didn't take the time to read the question fully. Work efficiently but make sure you understand the question and have looked at all of the answer choices, since more than one may seem right at first.

Even if you're paying attention to the time, you may find yourself a little behind at some point. You should speed up to get back on track, but do so wisely. Don't panic; just take a few seconds less on each question until you're caught up. Don't guess without thinking, but do look through the answer choices and eliminate any you know are wrong. If you can get down to two choices, it is often worthwhile to guess from those. Once you've chosen an answer, move on and don't dwell on any that you skipped or had to hurry through. If a question was taking too long, chances are it was one of the harder ones, so you weren't as likely to get it right anyway.

On the other hand, if you find yourself getting ahead of schedule, it may be beneficial to slow down a little. The more quickly you work, the more likely you are to make a careless mistake that will affect your score. You've budgeted time for each question, so don't be afraid to spend that time. Practice an efficient but careful pace to get the most out of the time you have.

Secret Key #5 – Have a Plan for Guessing

When you're taking the test, you may find yourself stuck on a question. Some of the answer choices seem better than others, but you don't see the one answer choice that is obviously correct. What do you do?

The scenario described above is very common, yet most test takers have not effectively prepared for it. Developing and practicing a plan for guessing may be one of the single most effective uses of your time as you get ready for the exam.

In developing your plan for guessing, there are three questions to address:

- When should you start the guessing process?
- How should you narrow down the choices?
- Which answer should you choose?

When to Start the Guessing Process

Unless your plan for guessing is to select C every time (which, despite its merits, is not what we recommend), you need to leave yourself enough time to apply your answer elimination strategies. Since you have a limited amount of time for each question, that means that if you're going to give yourself the best shot at guessing correctly, you have to decide quickly whether or not you will guess.

Of course, the best-case scenario is that you don't have to guess at all, so first, see if you can answer the question based on your knowledge of the subject and basic reasoning skills. Focus on the key words in the question and try to jog your memory of related topics. Give yourself a chance to bring the knowledge to mind, but once you realize that you don't have (or you can't access) the knowledge you need to answer the question, it's time to start the guessing process.

It's almost always better to start the guessing process too early than too late. It only takes a few seconds to remember something and answer the question from knowledge. Carefully eliminating wrong answer choices takes longer. Plus, going through the process of eliminating answer choices can actually help jog your memory.

Summary: Start the guessing process as soon as you decide that you can't answer the question based on your knowledge.

How to Narrow Down the Choices

The next chapter in this book (**Test-Taking Strategies**) includes a wide range of strategies for how to approach questions and how to look for answer choices to eliminate. You will definitely want to read those carefully, practice them, and figure out which ones work best for you. Here though, we're going to address a mindset rather than a particular strategy.

Your odds of guessing an answer correctly depend on how many options you are choosing from.

Number of options left	5	4	3	2	1
Odds of guessing correctly	20%	25%	33%	50%	100%

You can see from this chart just how valuable it is to be able to eliminate incorrect answers and make an educated guess, but there are two things that many test takers do that cause them to miss out on the benefits of guessing:

- Accidentally eliminating the correct answer
- Selecting an answer based on an impression

We'll look at the first one here, and the second one in the next section.

To avoid accidentally eliminating the correct answer, we recommend a thought exercise called **the $5 challenge**. In this challenge, you only eliminate an answer choice from contention if you are willing to bet $5 on it being wrong. Why $5? Five dollars is a small but not insignificant amount of money. It's an amount you could afford to lose but wouldn't want to throw away. And while losing

$5 once might not hurt too much, doing it twenty times will set you back $100. In the same way, each small decision you make—eliminating a choice here, guessing on a question there—won't by itself impact your score very much, but when you put them all together, they can make a big difference. By holding each answer choice elimination decision to a higher standard, you can reduce the risk of accidentally eliminating the correct answer.

The $5 challenge can also be applied in a positive sense: If you are willing to bet $5 that an answer choice *is* correct, go ahead and mark it as correct.

Summary: Only eliminate an answer choice if you are willing to bet $5 that it is wrong.

8

Which Answer to Choose

You're taking the test. You've run into a hard question and decided you'll have to guess. You've eliminated all the answer choices you're willing to bet $5 on. Now you have to pick an answer. Why do we even need to talk about this? Why can't you just pick whichever one you feel like when the time comes?

The answer to these questions is that if you don't come into the test with a plan, you'll rely on your impression to select an answer choice, and if you do that, you risk falling into a trap. The test writers know that everyone who takes their test will be guessing on some of the questions, so they intentionally write wrong answer choices to seem plausible. You still have to pick an answer though, and if the wrong answer choices are designed to look right, how can you ever be sure that you're not falling for their trap? The best solution we've found to this dilemma is to take the decision out of your hands entirely. Here is the process we recommend:

Once you've eliminated any choices that you are confident (willing to bet $5) are wrong, select the first remaining choice as your answer.

Whether you choose to select the first remaining choice, the second, or the last, the important thing is that you use some preselected standard. Using this approach guarantees that you will not be enticed into selecting an answer choice that looks right, because you are not basing your decision on how the answer choices look.

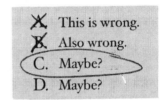

This is not meant to make you question your knowledge. Instead, it is to help you recognize the difference between your knowledge and your impressions. There's a huge difference between thinking an answer is right because of what you know, and thinking an answer is right because it looks or sounds like it should be right.

Summary: To ensure that your selection is appropriately random, make a predetermined selection from among all answer choices you have not eliminated.

Test-Taking Strategies

This section contains a list of test-taking strategies that you may find helpful as you work through the test. By taking what you know and applying logical thought, you can maximize your chances of answering any question correctly!

It is very important to realize that every question is different and every person is different: no single strategy will work on every question, and no single strategy will work for every person. That's why we've included all of them here, so you can try them out and determine which ones work best for different types of questions and which ones work best for you.

Question Strategies

☑ READ CAREFULLY

Read the question and the answer choices carefully. Don't miss the question because you misread the terms. You have plenty of time to read each question thoroughly and make sure you understand what is being asked. Yet a happy medium must be attained, so don't waste too much time. You must read carefully and efficiently.

☑ CONTEXTUAL CLUES

Look for contextual clues. If the question includes a word you are not familiar with, look at the immediate context for some indication of what the word might mean. Contextual clues can often give you all the information you need to decipher the meaning of an unfamiliar word. Even if you can't determine the meaning, you may be able to narrow down the possibilities enough to make a solid guess at the answer to the question.

☑ PREFIXES

If you're having trouble with a word in the question or answer choices, try dissecting it. Take advantage of every clue that the word might include. Prefixes can be a huge help. Usually, they allow you to determine a basic meaning. *Pre-* means before, *post-* means after, *pro-* is positive, *de-* is negative. From prefixes, you can get an idea of the general meaning of the word and try to put it into context.

☑ HEDGE WORDS

Watch out for critical hedge words, such as *likely, may, can, sometimes, often, almost, mostly, usually, generally, rarely,* and *sometimes*. Question writers insert these hedge phrases to cover every possibility. Often an answer choice will be wrong simply because it leaves no room for exception. Be on guard for answer choices that have definitive words such as *exactly* and *always*.

☑ SWITCHBACK WORDS

Stay alert for *switchbacks*. These are the words and phrases frequently used to alert you to shifts in thought. The most common switchback words are *but, although,* and *however*. Others include *nevertheless, on the other hand, even though, while, in spite of, despite,* and *regardless of*. Switchback words are important to catch because they can change the direction of the question or an answer choice.

10

☑ FACE VALUE

When in doubt, use common sense. Accept the situation in the problem at face value. Don't read too much into it. These problems will not require you to make wild assumptions. If you have to go beyond creativity and warp time or space in order to have an answer choice fit the question, then you should move on and consider the other answer choices. These are normal problems rooted in reality. The applicable relationship or explanation may not be readily apparent, but it is there for you to figure out. Use your common sense to interpret anything that isn't clear.

Answer Choice Strategies

☑ ANSWER SELECTION

The most thorough way to pick an answer choice is to identify and eliminate wrong answers until only one is left, then confirm it is the correct answer. Sometimes an answer choice may immediately seem right, but be careful. The test writers will usually put more than one reasonable answer choice on each question, so take a second to read all of them and make sure that the other choices are not equally obvious. As long as you have time left, it is better to read every answer choice than to pick the first one that looks right without checking the others.

☑ ANSWER CHOICE FAMILIES

An answer choice family consists of two (in rare cases, three) answer choices that are very similar in construction and cannot all be true at the same time. If you see two answer choices that are direct opposites or parallels, one of them is usually the correct answer. For instance, if one answer choice says that quantity x increases and another either says that quantity x decreases (opposite) or says that quantity y increases (parallel), then those answer choices would fall into the same family. An answer choice that doesn't match the construction of the answer choice family is more likely to be incorrect. Most questions will not have answer choice families, but when they do appear, you should be prepared to recognize them.

☑ ELIMINATE ANSWERS

Eliminate answer choices as soon as you realize they are wrong, but make sure you consider all possibilities. If you are eliminating answer choices and realize that the last one you are left with is also wrong, don't panic. Start over and consider each choice again. There may be something you missed the first time that you will realize on the second pass.

☑ AVOID FACT TRAPS

Don't be distracted by an answer choice that is factually true but doesn't answer the question. You are looking for the choice that answers the question. Stay focused on what the question is asking for so you don't accidentally pick an answer that is true but incorrect. Always go back to the question and make sure the answer choice you've selected actually answers the question and is not merely a true statement.

☑ EXTREME STATEMENTS

In general, you should avoid answers that put forth extreme actions as standard practice or proclaim controversial ideas as established fact. An answer choice that states the "process should be used in certain situations, if..." is much more likely to be correct than one that states the "process should be discontinued completely." The first is a calm rational statement and doesn't even make a definitive, uncompromising stance, using a hedge word *if* to provide wiggle room, whereas the second choice is far more extreme.

⊘ Benchmark

As you read through the answer choices and you come across one that seems to answer the question well, mentally select that answer choice. This is not your final answer, but it's the one that will help you evaluate the other answer choices. The one that you selected is your benchmark or standard for judging each of the other answer choices. Every other answer choice must be compared to your benchmark. That choice is correct until proven otherwise by another answer choice beating it. If you find a better answer, then that one becomes your new benchmark. Once you've decided that no other choice answers the question as well as your benchmark, you have your final answer.

⊘ Predict the Answer

Before you even start looking at the answer choices, it is often best to try to predict the answer. When you come up with the answer on your own, it is easier to avoid distractions and traps because you will know exactly what to look for. The right answer choice is unlikely to be word-for-word what you came up with, but it should be a close match. Even if you are confident that you have the right answer, you should still take the time to read each option before moving on.

General Strategies

⊘ Tough Questions

If you are stumped on a problem or it appears too hard or too difficult, don't waste time. Move on! Remember though, if you can quickly check for obviously incorrect answer choices, your chances of guessing correctly are greatly improved. Before you completely give up, at least try to knock out a couple of possible answers. Eliminate what you can and then guess at the remaining answer choices before moving on.

⊘ Check Your Work

Since you will probably not know every term listed and the answer to every question, it is important that you get credit for the ones that you do know. Don't miss any questions through careless mistakes. If at all possible, try to take a second to look back over your answer selection and make sure you've selected the correct answer choice and haven't made a costly careless mistake (such as marking an answer choice that you didn't mean to mark). This quick double check should more than pay for itself in caught mistakes for the time it costs.

⊘ Pace Yourself

It's easy to be overwhelmed when you're looking at a page full of questions; your mind is confused and full of random thoughts, and the clock is ticking down faster than you would like. Calm down and maintain the pace that you have set for yourself. Especially as you get down to the last few minutes of the test, don't let the small numbers on the clock make you panic. As long as you are on track by monitoring your pace, you are guaranteed to have time for each question.

⊘ Don't Rush

It is very easy to make errors when you are in a hurry. Maintaining a fast pace in answering questions is pointless if it makes you miss questions that you would have gotten right otherwise. Test writers like to include distracting information and wrong answers that seem right. Taking a little extra time to avoid careless mistakes can make all the difference in your test score. Find a pace that allows you to be confident in the answers that you select.

⊘ KEEP MOVING

Panicking will not help you pass the test, so do your best to stay calm and keep moving. Taking deep breaths and going through the answer elimination steps you practiced can help to break through a stress barrier and keep your pace.

Final Notes

The combination of a solid foundation of content knowledge and the confidence that comes from practicing your plan for applying that knowledge is the key to maximizing your performance on test day. As your foundation of content knowledge is built up and strengthened, you'll find that the strategies included in this chapter become more and more effective in helping you quickly sift through the distractions and traps of the test to isolate the correct answer.

Now that you're preparing to move forward into the test content chapters of this book, be sure to keep your goal in mind. As you read, think about how you will be able to apply this information on the test. If you've already seen sample questions for the test and you have an idea of the question format and style, try to come up with questions of your own that you can answer based on what you're reading. This will give you valuable practice applying your knowledge in the same ways you can expect to on test day.

Good luck and good studying!

14

United States and Georgia: Historical, Geographic, Economic, and Civic Understanding

American History Pre-Columbian to 1789

WELL-KNOWN NATIVE AMERICANS

The following are five well-known Native Americans and their roles in early US history:

1. **Squanto**, an Algonquian, helped early English settlers survive the hard winter by teaching them the native methods of planting corn, squash, and pumpkins.
2. **Pocahontas**, also Algonquian, became famous as a liaison with John Smith's Jamestown colony in 1607.
3. **Sacagawea**, a Shoshone, served a vital role in the Lewis and Clark expedition when the two explorers hired her as their guide in 1805.
4. **Crazy Horse** and **Sitting Bull** led Sioux and Cheyenne troops in the Battle of the Little Bighorn in 1876, soundly defeating George Armstrong Custer.
5. **Chief Joseph**, a leader of the Nez Perce who supported peaceful interaction with white settlers, attempted to relocate his tribe to Canada rather than move them to a reservation.

MAJOR REGIONAL NATIVE AMERICAN GROUPS

The major regional Native American groups and the major traits of each are as follows:

- The **Algonquians** in the eastern part of the United States lived in wigwams. The northern tribes subsisted on hunting and gathering, while those who were farther south grew crops such as corn.
- The **Iroquois**, also an east coast tribe, spoke a different language from the Algonquians and lived in rectangular longhouses.
- The **Plains tribes** lived between the Mississippi River and the Rocky Mountains. These nomadic tribes lived in teepees and followed the buffalo herds. Plains tribes included the Sioux, Cheyenne, Comanche, and Blackfoot.
- **Pueblo tribes** included the Zuni, Hopi, and Acoma. They lived in the Southwest deserts in homes made of stone or adobe. They domesticated animals and cultivated corn and beans.
- On the Pacific coast, tribes such as the **Tlingit**, **Chinook**, and **Salish** lived on fish, deer, native berries, and roots. Their rectangular homes housed large family groups, and they used totem poles.
- In the far north, the **Aleuts** and **Inuit** lived in skin tents or igloos. Talented fishermen, they built kayaks and umiaks and also hunted caribou, seals, whales, and walrus.

> **Review Video: Major Regional Native American Groups**
> Visit mometrix.com/academy and enter code: 550136

AGE OF EXPLORATION

The Age of Exploration is also called the **Age of Discovery**. It is generally considered to have begun in the early 15th century and continued into the 17th century. Major developments of the **Age of Exploration** included technological advances in navigation, mapmaking, and shipbuilding. These

15

advances led to expanded European exploration of the rest of the world. Explorers set out from several European countries, including Portugal, Spain, France, and England, seeking new routes to Asia. These efforts led to the discovery of new lands, as well as colonization in India, Asia, Africa, and North America.

> **Review Video: Age of Exploration**
> Visit mometrix.com/academy and enter code: 612972

IMPACT OF TECHNOLOGICAL ADVANCES IN NAVIGATION AND SEAFARING EXPLORATION

For long ocean journeys, it was important for sailors to be able to find their way home even when their vessels sailed far out to sea. A variety of navigational tools enabled them to launch ambitious journeys over long distances. The **compass** and **astrolabe** were particularly important advancements. Chinese navigators used the magnetic compass in approximately 200 BC, and knowledge of the astrolabe came to Europe from Arab navigators and traders who had refined designs developed by the ancient Greeks. The Portuguese developed a ship called a **caravel** in the 1400s that incorporated navigational advancements with the ability to make long sea journeys. Equipped with this advanced vessel, the Portuguese achieved a major goal of the Age of Exploration by discovering a **sea route** from Europe to Asia in 1498.

SIGNIFICANCE OF CHRISTOPHER COLUMBUS'S VOYAGE

In 1492, Columbus, a Genoan explorer, obtained financial backing from King Ferdinand and Queen Isabella of Spain to seek a sea route to Asia. He sought a trade route with the Asian Indies to the west. With three ships, the *Niña*, the *Pinta*, and the *Santa Maria*, he eventually landed in the **West Indies**. While Columbus failed in his effort to discover a western route to Asia, he is credited with the discovery of the **Americas**.

> **Review Video: Christopher Columbus**
> Visit mometrix.com/academy and enter code: 496598

FRENCH, SPANISH, DUTCH, AND BRITISH GOALS IN COLONIZATION OF THE AMERICAS

France, Spain, the Netherlands, and England each had specific goals in the colonization of the Americas:

- Initial **French colonies** were focused on expanding the fur trade. Later, French colonization led to the growth of plantations in Louisiana, which brought numerous African slaves to the New World.
- **Spanish colonists** came to look for wealth and to convert the natives to Christianity. For some, the desire for gold led to mining in the New World, while others established large ranches.
- The **Dutch** were also involved in the fur trade and imported slaves as the need for laborers increased.
- **British colonists** arrived with various goals. Some were simply looking for additional income, while others were fleeing Britain to escape religious persecution.

> **Review Video: Colonization of the Americas**
> Visit mometrix.com/academy and enter code: 438412

NEW ENGLAND COLONIES

The New England colonies were New Hampshire, Connecticut, Rhode Island and Massachusetts. These colonies were founded largely to escape **religious persecution** in England. The beliefs of the

Puritans, who migrated to America in the 1600s, significantly influenced the development of these colonies. Situated in the northeast coastal areas of America, the New England colonies featured numerous harbors as well as dense forests. The soil, however, was rocky and had a very short growing season, so was not well suited for agriculture. The economy of New England during the colonial period centered around fishing, shipbuilding and trade along with some small farms and lumber mills. Although some groups congregated in small farms, life centered mainly in towns and cities where **merchants** largely controlled the trade economy. Coastal cities such as Boston grew and thrived.

Review Video: The Massachusetts Bay Colony Visit mometrix.com/academy and enter code: 407058

MIDDLE OR MIDDLE ATLANTIC COLONIES

The Middle or Middle Atlantic Colonies were New York, New Jersey, Pennsylvania, and Delaware. Unlike the New England colonies, where most colonists were from England and Scotland, the Middle Colonies founders were from various countries, including the Netherlands and Sweden. Various factors led these colonists to America. More fertile than New England, the Middle Colonies became major producers of **crops**, including rye, oats, potatoes, wheat, and barley. Some particularly wealthy inhabitants owned large farms and/or businesses. Farmers, in general, were able to produce enough to have a surplus to sell. Tenant farmers also rented land from larger landowners.

SOUTHERN COLONIES

The Southern Colonies were Maryland, Virginia, North Carolina, South Carolina, and Georgia. Of the Southern Colonies, Virginia was the first permanent English colony and Georgia the last. The warm climate and rich soil of the south encouraged **agriculture**, and the growing season was long. As a result, economy in the south was based largely on labor-intensive **plantations**. Crops included tobacco, rice, and indigo, all of which became valuable cash crops. Most land in the south was controlled by wealthy plantation owners and farmers. Labor on the farms came in the form of indentured servants and African slaves. The first of these **African slaves** arrived in Virginia in 1619.

Review Video: Southern Colonies: An Overview Visit mometrix.com/academy and enter code: 703830 **Review Video: The English Colony of Virginia** Visit mometrix.com/academy and enter code: 537399

SIGNIFICANCE OF THE FRENCH AND INDIAN WARS

The **British defeat of the Spanish Armada** in 1588 led to the decline of Spanish power in Europe. This, in turn, led the British and French into battle several times between 1689 and 1748. These wars were:

- King William's War, or the Nine Years War, 1689-1697. This war was fought largely in Flanders.
- The War of Spanish Succession, or Queen Anne's War, 1702-1713
- War of Austrian Succession, or King George's War, 1740-1748

The fourth and final war, the **French and Indian War** (1754-1763), was fought largely in the North American territory and resulted in the end of France's reign as a colonial power in North America.

Although the French held many advantages, including more cooperative colonists and numerous Indian allies, the strong leadership of **William Pitt** eventually led the British to victory. Costs incurred during the wars eventually led to discontent in the colonies and helped spark the **American Revolution**.

> **Review Video: French and Indian War**
> Visit mometrix.com/academy and enter code: 502183

NAVIGATION ACTS

The Navigation Acts, enacted in 1651, were an attempt by Britain to dominate international trade. Aimed largely at the Dutch, the acts banned foreign ships from transporting goods to the British colonies and from transporting goods to Britain from elsewhere in Europe. While the restrictions on trade angered some colonists, these acts were helpful to other American colonists who, as members of the British Empire, were legally able to provide ships for Britain's growing trade interests and use the ships for their own trading ventures. By the time the French and Indian War had ended, one-third of British merchant ships were built in the American colonies. Many colonists amassed fortunes in the shipbuilding trade.

BRITAIN'S TAXATION OF THE AMERICAN COLONIES AFTER THE FRENCH AND INDIAN WAR

The French and Indian War created circumstances for which the British desperately needed more revenue. These needs included:

- Paying off the war debt
- Defending the expanding empire
- Governing Britain's 33 far-flung colonies, including the American colonies

To meet these needs, the British passed additional laws, increasing revenues from the colonies. Because they had spent so much money to defend the American colonies, the British felt it was appropriate to collect considerably higher **taxes** from them. The colonists felt this was unfair, and many were led to protest the increasing taxes. Eventually, protest led to violence.

TRIANGULAR TRADE

Triangular trade began in the colonies with ships setting off for **Africa**, carrying rum. In Africa, the rum was traded for gold or slaves. Ships then went from Africa to the **West Indies**, trading slaves for sugar, molasses, or money. To complete the triangle, the ships returned to the **colonies** with sugar or molasses to make more rum, as well as stores of gold and silver. This trade triangle violated the Molasses Act of 1733, which required the colonists to pay high duties to Britain on molasses acquired from French, Dutch, and Spanish colonies. The colonists ignored these duties, and the British government adopted a policy of salutary neglect by not enforcing them.

EFFECTS OF NEW LAWS ON BRITISH-COLONIAL RELATIONS

While earlier revenue-generating acts such as the Navigation Acts brought money to the colonists, the new laws after 1763 required colonists to pay money back to **Britain**. The British felt this was fair since the colonists were British subjects and since they had incurred debt protecting the Colonies. The colonists felt it was not only unfair but illegal.

The development of **local government** in America had given the colonists a different view of the structure and role of government. This made it difficult for the British to understand the colonists' protests against what the British felt was a fair and reasonable solution to the mother country's financial problems.

FACTORS THAT LED TO INCREASING DISCONTENT IN THE AMERICAN COLONIES

More and more colonists were born on American soil, decreasing any sense of kinship with the far-away British rulers. Their new environment had led to new ideas of government and a strong view of the colonies as a separate entity from Britain. Colonists were allowed to **self-govern** in domestic issues, but **Britain** controlled international issues. In fact, the American colonies were largely left to form their own local government bodies, giving them more freedom than any other colonial territory. This gave the colonists a sense of **independence**, which led them to resent control from Britain. Threats during the French and Indian War led the colonists to call for unification in order to protect themselves.

COLONIAL GOVERNMENT AND BRITISH GOVERNMENT DIFFERENCES THAT LED TO "NO TAXATION WITHOUT REPRESENTATION"

As new towns and other legislative districts developed in America, the colonists began to practice **representative government**. Colonial legislative bodies were made up of elected representatives chosen by male property owners in the districts. These individuals represented the interests of the districts from which they had been elected.

By contrast, in Britain, the **Parliament** represented the entire country. Parliament was not elected to represent individual districts. Instead, they represented specific classes. Because of this drastically different approach to government, the British did not understand the colonists' statement that they had no representation in the British Parliament.

ACTS OF BRITISH PARLIAMENT THAT OCCURRED AFTER THE FRENCH AND INDIAN WARS

After the French and Indian Wars, the British Parliament passed four major acts:

1. The **Sugar Act**, 1764—this act not only required taxes to be collected on molasses brought into the colonies but gave British officials the right to search the homes of anyone suspected of violating it.
2. The **Stamp Act**, 1765—this act taxed printed materials such as newspapers and legal documents. Protests led the Stamp Act to be repealed in 1766, but the repeal also included the Declaratory Act, which stated that Parliament had the right to govern the colonies.
3. The **Quartering Act**, 1765—this act required colonists to provide accommodations and supplies for British troops. In addition, colonists were prohibited from settling west of the Appalachians until given permission by Britain.
4. The **Townshend Acts**, 1767—these acts taxed paper, paint, lead, and tea that came into the colonies. Colonists led boycotts in protest, and in Massachusetts leaders like Samuel and John Adams began to organize resistance against British rule.

FACTORS THAT LED TO THE BOSTON MASSACRE

With the passage of the **Stamp Act**, nine colonies met in New York to demand its repeal. Elsewhere, protest arose in New York City, Philadelphia, Boston, and other cities. These protests sometimes escalated into violence, often targeting ruling British officials. The passage of the **Townshend Acts** in 1767 led to additional tension in the colonies. The British sent troops to New York City and Boston. On March 5, 1770, protesters began to taunt the British troops, throwing snowballs. The soldiers responded by firing into the crowd. This clash between protesters and soldiers led to five deaths and eight injuries, and was christened the **Boston Massacre**. Shortly thereafter, Britain repealed the majority of the Townshend Acts.

TEA ACT THAT LED TO THE BOSTON TEA PARTY

The majority of the **Townshend Acts** were repealed after the Boston Massacre in 1770, but Britain kept the tax on tea. In 1773, the **Tea Act** was passed. This allowed the East India Company to sell tea for much lower prices and also allowed them to bypass American distributors, selling directly to shopkeepers instead. Colonial tea merchants saw this as a direct assault on their business. In December of 1773, the **Sons of Liberty** boarded ships in Boston Harbor and dumped 342 chests of tea into the sea in protest of the new laws. This act of protest came to be known as the **Boston Tea Party**.

COERCIVE ACTS PASSED AFTER THE BOSTON TEA PARTY

The Coercive Acts passed by Britain in 1774 were meant to punish Massachusetts for defying British authority. The following were also known as the **Intolerable Acts**:

- Shut down ports in Boston until the city paid back the value of the tea destroyed during the Boston Tea Party
- Required that local government officials in Massachusetts be appointed by the governor rather than being elected by the people
- Allowed trials of British soldiers to be transferred to Britain rather than being held in Massachusetts
- Required locals to provide lodging for British soldiers any time there was a disturbance, even if lodging required them to stay in private homes

These acts led to the assembly of the First Continental Congress in Philadelphia on September 5, 1774. Fifty-five delegates met, representing 12 of the American colonies. They sought compromise with England over England's increasingly harsh efforts to control the colonies.

FIRST CONTINENTAL CONGRESS

The goal of the First Continental Congress was to achieve a peaceful agreement with Britain. Made up of delegates from 12 of the 13 colonies, the Congress affirmed loyalty to Britain and the power of Parliament to dictate foreign affairs in the colonies. However, they demanded that the **Intolerable Acts** be repealed, and instituted a trade embargo with Britain until this came to pass.

In response, George III of England declared that the American colonies must submit or face military action. The British sought to end assemblies that opposed their policies. These assemblies gathered weapons and began to form militias. On April 19, 1775, the British military was ordered to disperse a meeting of the Massachusetts Assembly. A battle ensued on Lexington Common as the armed colonists resisted. The resulting battles became the **Battle of Lexington and Concord**—the first battles of the **American Revolution**.

SIGNIFICANCE OF THE SECOND CONTINENTAL CONGRESS

The Second Continental Congress met in Philadelphia on May 10, 1775, a month after Lexington and Concord. Their discussions centered on the defense of the American colonies and how to conduct the growing war, as well as local government. The delegates also discussed declaring independence from Britain, with many members in favor of this drastic move. They established an army, and on June 15, named **George Washington** as its commander in chief. By 1776, it was obvious that there was no turning back from full-scale war with Britain. The colonial delegates of the Continental Congress signed the **Declaration of Independence** on July 4, 1776.

> **Review Video: The First and Second Continental Congress**
> Visit mometrix.com/academy and enter code: 835211

ORIGINS AND BASIC IDEAS OF THE DECLARATION OF INDEPENDENCE

Penned by Thomas Jefferson and signed on July 4, 1776, the **Declaration of Independence** stated that King George III had violated the rights of the colonists and was establishing a tyrannical reign over them. Many of Jefferson's ideas of natural rights and property rights were shaped by 17th-century philosopher **John Locke**. Jefferson asserted all people's rights to "life, liberty and the pursuit of happiness." Locke's comparable idea asserted "life, liberty, and private property." Both felt that the purpose of government was to protect the rights of the people, and that individual rights were more important than individuals' obligations to the state.

> **Review Video: Declaration of Independence**
> Visit mometrix.com/academy and enter code: 256838

BATTLES OF THE REVOLUTIONARY WAR

The following are five major battles of the Revolutionary War and their significance:

- The **Battle of Lexington and Concord** (April 1775) is considered the first engagement of the Revolutionary War.
- The **Battle of Bunker Hill** (June 1775) was one of the bloodiest of the entire war. Although American troops withdrew, about half of the British army was lost. The colonists proved they could stand against professional British soldiers. In August, Britain declared that the American colonies were officially in a state of rebellion.
- The first colonial victory occurred in Trenton, New Jersey, when Washington and his troops **crossed the Delaware River** on Christmas Day, 1776, for a December 26 surprise attack on British and Hessian troops.
- The **Battle of Saratoga** effectively ended a plan to separate the New England colonies from their Southern counterparts. The surrender of British general John Burgoyne led to France joining the war as allies of the Americans and is generally considered a turning point of the war.
- On October 19, 1781, General Cornwallis surrendered after a defeat in the **Battle of Yorktown**, ending the Revolutionary War.

> **Review Video: The Revolutionary War**
> Visit mometrix.com/academy and enter code: 935282

SIGNIFICANCE OF THE TREATY OF PARIS

The Treaty of Paris was signed on September 3, 1783, bringing an official end to the Revolutionary War. In this document, Britain officially recognized the United States of America as an **independent nation**. The treaty established the Mississippi River as the country's western border. The treaty also restored Florida to Spain, while France reclaimed African and Caribbean colonies seized by the British in 1763. On November 25, 1783, the last British troops departed from the newly born United States of America.

SIGNIFICANCE OF THE ARTICLES OF CONFEDERATION

A precursor to the Constitution, the **Articles of Confederation** represented the first attempt of the newly independent colonies to establish the basics of government. The Continental Congress approved the Articles on November 15, 1777. They went into effect on March 1, 1781, following ratification by the thirteen states. The articles prevented a central government from gaining too much power, instead giving power to a **congressional body** made up of **delegates** from all thirteen states. However, the individual states retained final authority.

Without a strong central **executive**, though, this weak alliance among the new states proved ineffective in settling disputes or enforcing laws. The idea of a weak central government needed to be revised. Recognition of these weaknesses eventually led to the drafting of a new document, the **Constitution**.

> **Review Video: Articles of Confederation**
> Visit mometrix.com/academy and enter code: 927401

INITIAL PROPOSITION AND DRAFT OF THE CONSTITUTION

Delegates from twelve of the thirteen states (Rhode Island was not represented) met in Philadelphia in May of 1787, initially intending to revise the Articles of Confederation. However, it quickly became apparent that a simple revision would not provide the workable governmental structure the newly formed country needed. After vowing to keep all the proceedings secret until the final document was completed, the delegates set out to draft what would eventually become the **Constitution of the United States of America**. By keeping the negotiations secret, the delegates were able to present a completed document to the country for ratification, rather than having every small detail hammered out by the general public.

GENERAL STRUCTURE OF GOVERNMENT PROPOSED BY THE DELEGATES

The delegates agreed that the new nation required a **strong central government** but that its overall power should be **limited**. The various branches of the government should have **balanced power**, so that no one group could control the others. Final power belonged to the **citizens** who voted officials into office based on who would provide the best representation.

SIGNIFICANCE OF THE VIRGINIA PLAN, THE NEW JERSEY PLAN, AND THE GREAT COMPROMISE

Disagreement immediately occurred between delegates from large states and those from smaller states. James Madison and Edmund Randolph (the governor of Virginia) felt that representation in Congress should be based on state population. This was the **Virginia Plan**. The **New Jersey Plan**, presented by William Paterson from New Jersey, proposed that each state should have equal representation. Finally, Roger Sherman from Connecticut formulated the **Connecticut Compromise**, also called the Great Compromise. The result was the familiar structure we have today. Each state has the equal representation of two Senators in the Senate, with the number of representatives in the House of Representatives based on population. This is called a **bicameral congress**. Both houses may draft bills, but financial matters must originate in the House of Representatives.

EFFECTS OF THE THREE-FIFTHS COMPROMISE AND THE NUMBER OF REPRESENTATIVES FOR EACH STATE

During debate on the US Constitution, a disagreement arose between the Northern and Southern states involving how **slaves** should be counted when determining a state's quota of representatives. In the South, large numbers of slaves were commonly used to run plantations. Delegates wanted slaves to be counted to determine the number of representatives but not counted to determine the amount of taxes the states would pay. The Northern states wanted exactly the opposite arrangement. The final decision was to count three-fifths of the slave population both for tax purposes and to determine representation. This was called the **Three-fifths Compromise**.

PROVISIONS OF THE COMMERCE COMPROMISE

The Commerce Compromise also resulted from a North/South disagreement. In the North, the economy was centered on **industry and trade**. The Southern economy was largely **agricultural**.

22

The Northern states wanted to give the new government the ability to regulate exports as well as trade between the states. The South opposed this plan. Another compromise was in order. In the end, Congress received regulatory power over all trade, including the ability to collect **tariffs** on exported goods. In the South, this raised another red flag regarding the slave trade, as they were concerned about the effect on their economy if tariffs were levied on slaves. The final agreement allowed importing slaves to continue for twenty years without government intervention. Import taxes on slaves were limited, and after the year 1808, Congress could decide whether to allow continued imports of slaves.

OBJECTIONS AGAINST THE CONSTITUTION

Once the Constitution was drafted, it was presented for approval by the states. Nine states needed to approve the document for it to become official. However, debate and discussion continued. Major **concerns** included:

- There was nobill of rights to protect individual freedoms.
- States felt too much power was being handed over to the central government.
- Voters wanted more control over their elected representatives.

Discussion about necessary changes to the Constitution was divided into two camps: Federalists and Anti-Federalists. **Federalists** wanted a strong central government. **Anti-Federalists** wanted to prevent a tyrannical government from developing if a central government held too much power.

MAJOR PLAYERS IN THE FEDERALIST AND ANTI-FEDERALIST CAMPS

Major Federalist leaders included Alexander Hamilton, John Jay, and James Madison. They wrote a series of letters, called the **Federalist Papers**, aimed at convincing the states to ratify the Constitution. These were published in New York papers. Anti-Federalists included Thomas Jefferson and Patrick Henry. They argued against the Constitution as it was originally drafted in a series of **Anti-Federalist Papers**.

The final compromise produced a strong central government controlled by checks and balances. A **Bill of Rights** was also added, becoming the first ten amendments to the Constitution. These amendments protected rights such as freedom of speech, freedom of religion, and other basic rights. Aside from various amendments added throughout the years, the United States Constitution has remained unchanged.

INDIVIDUALS WHO FORMED THE FIRST ADMINISTRATION OF THE NEW GOVERNMENT

The individuals who formed the first administration of the new government were:

- **George Washington**—elected as the first President of the United States in 1789
- **John Adams**—finished second in the election and became the first Vice President
- **Thomas Jefferson**—appointed by Washington as Secretary of State
- **Alexander Hamilton**—appointed Secretary of the Treasury

American History 1790 to 1898

ALIEN AND SEDITION ACTS

When **John Adams** became president, a war was raging between Britain and France. While Adams and the **Federalists** backed the British, Thomas Jefferson and the **Republican Party** supported the French. The United States nearly went to war with France during this time period, while France worked to spread its international standing and influence under the leadership of **Napoleon Bonaparte**. The **Alien and Sedition Acts** grew out of this conflict and made it illegal to speak in a hostile fashion against the existing government. They also allowed the president to deport anyone in the US who was not a citizen and who was suspected of treason or treasonous activity. When Jefferson became the third president in 1800, he repealed these four laws and pardoned anyone who had been convicted under them.

DEVELOPMENT OF POLITICAL PARTIES IN EARLY US GOVERNMENT

Many in the US were against political parties after seeing the way parties, or factions, functioned in Britain. The factions in Britain were more interested in personal profit than the overall good of the country, and they did not want this to happen in the US.

However, the differences of opinion between Thomas Jefferson and Alexander Hamilton led to the formation of **political parties**. Hamilton favored a stronger central government, while Jefferson felt that more power should remain with the states. Jefferson was in favor of strict Constitutional interpretation, while Hamilton believed in a more flexible approach. As others joined the two camps, Hamilton backers began to call themselves **Federalists**, while those supporting Jefferson became identified as **Democratic-Republicans**.

DEVELOPMENT OF THE WHIG, THE DEMOCRATIC, AND THE REPUBLICAN PARTIES

Thomas Jefferson was elected president in 1800 and again in 1804. The **Federalist Party** began to decline, and its major figure, Alexander Hamilton, died in a duel with Aaron Burr in 1804. By 1816, the Federalist Party had virtually disappeared.

New parties sprang up to take its place. After 1824, the **Democratic-Republican Party** suffered a split. The **Whigs** rose, backing John Quincy Adams and industrial growth. The new Democratic Party formed in opposition to the Whigs, and their candidate, Andrew Jackson, was elected as president in 1828.

By the 1850s, issues regarding slavery led to the formation of the **Republican Party**, which was anti-slavery, while the Democratic Party, with a larger interest in the South, favored slavery. This Republican/Democrat division formed the basis of today's **two-party system**.

SIGNIFICANCE OF MARBURY V. MADISON

The main duty of the Supreme Court today is **judicial review**. This power was largely established by **Marbury v. Madison**. When John Adams was voted out of office in 1800, he worked during his final days in office to appoint Federalist judges to Supreme Court positions, knowing Jefferson, his replacement, held opposing views. As late as March 3, the day before Jefferson was to take office, Adams made last-minute appointments referred to as "Midnight Judges." One of the late appointments was William Marbury. The next day, March 4, Jefferson ordered his Secretary of State, James Madison, not to deliver Marbury's commission. This decision was backed by Chief Justice Marshall, who determined that the **Judiciary Act of 1789**, which granted the power to deliver

24

commissions, was illegal in that it gave the Judicial Branch powers not granted in the Constitution. This case set precedent for the Supreme Court to nullify laws it found to be **unconstitutional**.

Review Video: Marbury v Madison
Visit mometrix.com/academy and enter code: 573964

McCulloch v. Maryland

Judicial review was further exercised by the Supreme Court in **McCulloch v. Maryland**. When Congress chartered a national bank, the **Second Bank of the United States**, Maryland voted to tax any bank business dealing with banks chartered outside the state, including the federally chartered bank. Andrew McCulloch, an employee of the Second Bank of the US in Baltimore, refused to pay this tax. The resulting lawsuit from the State of Maryland went to the Supreme Court for judgment.

John Marshall, Chief Justice of the Supreme Court, stated that Congress was within its rights to charter a national bank. In addition, the State of Maryland did not have the power to levy a tax on the federal bank or on the federal government in general. In cases where state and federal government collided, precedent was set for the **federal government** to prevail.

Effect of the Treaty of Paris on Native Americans

After the Revolutionary War, the **Treaty of Paris**, which outlined the terms of surrender of the British to the Americans, granted large parcels of land to the US that were occupied by Native Americans. The new government attempted to claim the land, treating the natives as a conquered people. This approach proved unenforceable.

Next, the government tried purchasing the land from the Indians via a series of **treaties** as the country expanded westward. In practice, however, these treaties were not honored, and Native Americans were simply dislocated and forced to move farther and farther west, often with military action, as American expansion continued.

Indian Removal Act of 1830 and the Treaty of New Echota

The Indian Removal Act of 1830 gave the new American government power to form treaties with Native Americans. In theory, America would claim land east of the Mississippi in exchange for land west of the Mississippi, to which the natives would relocate voluntarily. In practice, many tribal leaders were forced into signing the treaties, and relocation at times occurred by force.

The **Treaty of New Echota** in 1835 was supposedly a treaty between the US government and Cherokee tribes in Georgia. However, the treaty was not signed by tribal leaders but rather by a small portion of the represented people. The leaders protested and refused to leave, but President Martin Van Buren enforced the treaty by sending soldiers. During their forced relocation, more than 4,000 Cherokee Indians died on what became known as the **Trail of Tears**.

Review Video: Indian Removal Act
Visit mometrix.com/academy and enter code: 666738

Development of Economic Trends as the US Continued to Grow

In the Northeast, the economy mostly depended on **manufacturing, industry, and industrial development**. This led to a dichotomy between rich business owners and industrial leaders and the much poorer workers who supported their businesses. The South continued to depend on **agriculture**, especially on large-scale farms or plantations worked mostly by slaves and indentured servants. In the West, where new settlements had begun to develop, the land was largely wild.

Growing communities were essentially **agricultural**, raising crops and livestock. The differences between regions led each to support different interests both politically and economically.

POLITICAL MOTIVATIONS BEHIND FRANCE SELLING THE LOUISIANA PURCHASE

With tension still high between France and Britain, Napoleon was in need of money to support his continuing war efforts. To secure necessary funds, he decided to sell the **Louisiana Territory** to the US. President **Thomas Jefferson** wanted to buy New Orleans, feeling US trade was made vulnerable to both Spain and France at that port. Instead, Napoleon sold him the entire territory for the bargain price of $15 million. The Louisiana Territory was larger than all the rest of the United States put together, and it eventually became 15 additional states.

Federalists in Congress were opposed to the purchase. They feared that the Louisiana Purchase would extend slavery, and that further western growth would weaken the power of the northern states.

MAJOR IDEAS DRIVING AMERICAN FOREIGN POLICY

The three major ideas driving American foreign policy during its early years were:

- **Isolationism**—the early US government did not intend to establish colonies, though they did plan to grow larger within the bounds of North America.
- **No entangling alliances**—both George Washington and Thomas Jefferson were opposed to forming any permanent alliances with other countries or becoming involved in other countries' internal issues.
- **Nationalism**—a positive patriotic feeling about the United States blossomed quickly among its citizens, particularly after the War of 1812, when the US once again defeated Britain. The Industrial Revolution also sparked increased nationalism by allowing even the most far-flung areas of the US to communicate with each other via telegraph and the expanding railroad.

CAUSES AND RESULT OF THE WAR OF 1812

The War of 1812 grew out of the continuing tension between France and Great Britain. Napoleon continued striving to conquer Britain, while the US continued trade with both countries but favored France and the French colonies. Because of what Britain saw as an alliance between America and France, they determined to bring an end to trade between the two nations.

With the British preventing US trade with the French and the French preventing trade with the British, James Madison's presidency introduced acts to **regulate international trade**. If either Britain or France removed their restrictions, America would not trade with the other country. Napoleon acted first, and Madison prohibited trade with England. England saw this as the US formally siding with the French, and war ensued in 1812.

The **War of 1812** has been called the **Second American Revolution**. It established the superiority of the US naval forces and reestablished US independence from Britain and Europe.

The British had two major objections to America's continued trade with France. First, they saw the US as helping France's war effort by providing supplies and goods. Second, the United States had grown into a competitor, taking trade and money away from British ships and tradesmen. In its attempts to end American trade with France, the British put into effect the **Orders in Council**, which made any and all French-owned ports off-limits to American ships. They also began to seize American ships and conscript their crews.

MAJOR MILITARY EVENTS OF THE WAR OF 1812

Two major naval battles, at **Lake Erie** and **Lake Champlain**, kept the British from invading the US via Canada. American attempts to conquer Canadian lands were not successful.

In another memorable British attack, the British invaded Washington, DC and burned the White House on August 24, 1814. Legend has it that **Dolley Madison**, the First Lady, salvaged the portrait of George Washington from the fire. On Christmas Eve, 1814, the **Treaty of Ghent** officially ended the war. However, Andrew Jackson, unaware that the war was over, managed another victory at New Orleans on January 8, 1815. This victory improved American morale and led to a new wave of national pride and support known as the "**Era of Good Feelings**."

MONROE DOCTRINE

On December 2, 1823, President Monroe delivered a message to Congress in which he introduced the **Monroe Doctrine**. In this address, he stated that any attempts by European powers to establish new colonies on the North American continent would be considered interference in American politics. The US would stay out of European matters, and expected Europe to offer America the same courtesy. This approach to foreign policy stated in no uncertain terms that America would not tolerate any new European colonies in the New World, and that events occurring in Europe would no longer influence the policies and doctrines of the US.

LEWIS AND CLARK EXPEDITION

The purchase of the **Louisiana Territory** from France in 1803 more than doubled the size of the United States. President Thomas Jefferson wanted to have the area mapped and explored, since much of the territory was wilderness. He chose Meriwether Lewis and William Clark to head an expedition into the Louisiana Territory. After two years, Lewis and Clark returned, having traveled all the way to the Pacific Ocean. They brought maps, detailed journals, and a multitude of information about the wide expanse of land they had traversed. The **Lewis and Clark Expedition** opened up the west in the Louisiana Territory and beyond for further exploration and settlement.

EFFECTS OF MANIFEST DESTINY ON AMERICAN POLITICS

In the 1800s, many believed America was destined by God to expand west, bringing as much of the North American continent as possible under the umbrella of the US government. With the Northwest Ordinance and the Louisiana Purchase, over half of the continent became American. However, the rapid and relentless expansion brought conflict with the Native Americans, Great Britain, Mexico, and Spain. One result of "**Manifest Destiny**" was the **Mexican-American War** from 1846 to 1848. By the end of the war, Texas, California, and a large portion of what is now the American Southwest joined the growing nation. Conflict also arose over the **Oregon Territory**, shared by the US and Britain. In 1846, President James Polk resolved this problem by compromising with Britain, establishing a US boundary south of the 49th parallel.

Review Video: What is the Manifest Destiny?
Visit mometrix.com/academy and enter code: 957409

MEXICAN-AMERICAN WAR

Spain had held colonial interests in America since the 1540s—earlier even than Great Britain. In 1810, **Mexico** revolted against Spain, becoming a free nation in 1821. **Texas** followed suit, declaring its independence after an 1836 revolution. In 1844, the Democrats pressed President Tyler to annex Texas. Unlike his predecessor, Andrew Jackson, Tyler agreed to admit Texas into the Union, and in 1845, Texas became a state.

During Mexico's war for independence, the nation incurred $4.5 million in war debts to the US. Polk offered to forgive the debts in return for New Mexico and Upper California, but Mexico refused. In 1846, war was declared in response to a Mexican attack on American troops along the southern border of Texas. Additional conflict arose in Congress over the **Wilmot Proviso**, which stated that slavery was prohibited in any territory the US acquired from Mexico as a result of the **Mexican-American War**. The war ended in 1848.

Review Video: When was the Mexican-American War?
Visit mometrix.com/academy and enter code: 271216

Review Video: Sectional Crisis: The Wilmot Proviso
Visit mometrix.com/academy and enter code: 974842

GADSDEN PURCHASE AND THE 1853 POST-WAR TREATY WITH MEXICO

After the Mexican-American war, a **second treaty** in 1853 determined hundreds of miles of America's southwest borders. In 1854, the **Gadsden Purchase** was finalized, providing even more territory to aid in the building of the transcontinental railroad. This purchase added what would eventually become the southernmost regions of Arizona and New Mexico to the growing nation. The modern outline of the United States was by this time nearly complete.

INFLUENCE OF THE AMERICAN SYSTEM ON AMERICAN ECONOMICS

Spurred by the trade conflicts of the War of 1812 and supported by Henry Clay among others, the **American System** set up tariffs to help protect American interests from competition with overseas products. Reducing competition led to growth in employment and an overall increase in American industry. The higher tariffs also provided funds for the government to pay for various improvements. Congress passed high tariffs in 1816 and also chartered a federal bank. The **Second Bank of the United States** was given the job of regulating America's money supply.

JACKSONIAN DEMOCRACY VS. PRECEDING POLITICAL CLIMATE

Jacksonian Democracy is largely seen as a shift from politics favoring the wealthy to politics favoring the common man. The right to vote was given to all free white males, not just property owners, as had been the case previously. Jackson's approach favored the patronage system, laissez-faire economics, and relocation of the Indian tribes from the Southeast portion of the country. Jackson opposed the formation of a federal bank and allowed the Second Bank of the United States to collapse by vetoing a bill to renew the charter. Jackson also faced the challenge of the **Nullification Crisis** when South Carolina claimed that it could ignore or nullify any federal law it considered unconstitutional. Jackson sent troops to the state to enforce the protested tariff laws, and a compromise engineered by Henry Clay in 1833 settled the matter for the time being.

MAJOR EVENTS AND DEVELOPMENTS THAT BROUGHT THE NORTH AND SOUTH INTO CONFLICT

The conflict between the North and South coalesced around the issue of **slavery**, but other elements contributed to the growing disagreement. Though most farmers in the South worked small farms with little or no slave labor, the huge plantations run by the South's rich depended on slaves or indentured servants to remain profitable. They had also become more dependent on **cotton**, with slave populations growing in concert with the rapid increase in cotton production. In the North, a more diverse agricultural economy and the growth of **industry** made slaves rarer. The **abolitionist movement** grew steadily, with Harriet Beecher Stowe's *Uncle Tom's Cabin* giving many an idea to rally around. A collection of anti-slavery organizations formed, with many actively working to free slaves in the South, often bringing them to the northern states or Canada.

ANTI-SLAVERY ORGANIZATIONS

Five anti-slavery organizations and their significance are:

- **American Colonization Society**—Protestant churches formed this group, aimed at returning black slaves to Africa. Former slaves subsequently formed Liberia, but the colony did not do well, as the region was not well-suited for agriculture.
- **American Anti-Slavery Society**—William Lloyd Garrison, a Quaker, was the major force behind this group and its newspaper, *The Liberator*.
- **Philadelphia Female Anti-Slavery Society**—this women-only group was formed by Margaretta Forten because women were not allowed to join the Anti-Slavery Society formed by her father.
- **Anti-Slavery Convention of American Women**—this group continued meeting even after pro-slavery factions burned down their original meeting place.
- **Female Vigilant Society**—this organization raised funds to help the Underground Railroad, as well as slave refugees.

ATTITUDES TOWARD EDUCATION IN THE EARLY 19TH CENTURY

Horace Mann, among others, felt that schools could help children become better citizens, keep them away from crime, prevent poverty, and help American society become more unified. His *Common School Journal* brought his ideas of the importance of education into the public consciousness and proposed his suggestions for an improved American education system. Increased literacy led to increased awareness of current events, Western expansion, and other major developments of the time period. Public interest and participation in the arts and literature also increased. By the end of the 19th century, all children had access to a **free public elementary education**.

DEVELOPMENTS IN TRANSPORTATION

As America expanded its borders, it also developed new technology to travel the rapidly growing country. Roads and railroads traversed the nation, with the **Transcontinental Railroad** eventually allowing travel from one coast to the other. Canals and steamboats simplified water travel and made shipping easier and less expensive. The **Erie Canal** (1825) connected the Great Lakes to the Hudson River. Other canals connected other major waterways, further facilitating transportation and the shipment of goods.

With growing numbers of settlers moving into the West, **wagon trails** developed, including the Oregon Trail, California Trail, and the Santa Fe Trail. The most common vehicles seen along these westbound trails were covered wagons, also known as **prairie schooners**.

INDUSTRIAL ACTIVITY BEFORE AND AFTER 1800

During the 18th century, goods were often manufactured in houses or small shops. With increased technology allowing for the use of machines, **factories** began to develop. In factories, a large volume of salable goods could be produced in a much shorter amount of time. Many Americans, including increasing numbers of **immigrants**, found jobs in these factories, which were in constant need of labor. Another major invention was the **cotton gin**, which significantly decreased the processing time of cotton and was a major factor in the rapid expansion of cotton production in the South.

DEVELOPMENT OF LABOR MOVEMENTS IN THE 1800S

In 1751, a group of bakers held a protest in which they stopped baking bread. This was technically the first American **labor strike**. In the 1830s and 1840s, labor movements began in earnest. Boston's masons, carpenters, and stoneworkers protested the length of the workday, fighting to reduce it to ten hours. In 1844, a group of women in the textile industry also fought to reduce their workday to ten hours, forming the **Lowell Female Labor Reform Association**. Many other protests occurred and organizations developed through this time period with the same goal in mind.

SECOND GREAT AWAKENING

Led by Protestant evangelical leaders, the **Second Great Awakening** occurred between 1800 and 1830. Several missionary groups grew out of the movement, including the **American Home Missionary Society**, which formed in 1826. The ideas behind the Second Great Awakening focused on personal responsibility, both as an individual and in response to injustice and suffering. The **American Bible Society** and the **American Tract Society** provided literature, while various traveling preachers spread the word. New denominations arose, including the Latter-day Saints and Seventh-day Adventists.

Another movement associated with the Second Great Awakening was the **temperance movement**, focused on ending the production and use of alcohol. One major organization behind the temperance movement was the **Society for the Promotion of Temperance**, formed in 1826 in Boston.

EARLY LEADERS IN THE WOMEN'S RIGHTS MOVEMENT

The women's rights movement began in the 1840s, with leaders including Elizabeth Cady Stanton, Sojourner Truth, Ernestine Rose, and Lucretia Mott. In 1869, Elizabeth Cady Stanton and Susan B. Anthony formed the **National Woman Suffrage Association**, fighting for women's right to vote.

In 1848, in Seneca Falls, the first women's rights convention was held, with about 300 attendees. The two-day **Seneca Falls Convention** discussed the rights of women to vote (suffrage) as well as equal treatment in careers, legal proceedings, etc. The convention produced a "Declaration of Sentiments," which outlined a plan for women to attain the rights they deserved. **Frederick**

Douglass supported the women's rights movement, as well as the abolition movement. In fact, women's rights and abolition movements often went hand-in-hand during this time period.

> **Review Video: What was the Women's Rights Movement in America?**
> Visit mometrix.com/academy and enter code: 987734

EFFECTS OF THE MISSOURI COMPROMISE ON THE TENSIONS BETWEEN THE NORTH AND SOUTH

By 1819, the United States had developed a tenuous balance between slave and free states, with exactly 22 senators in Congress from each faction. However, Missouri was ready to join the union. As a slave state, it would tip the balance in Congress. To prevent this imbalance, the **Missouri Compromise** brought the northern part of Massachusetts into the union as Maine, establishing it as a free state to balance the admission of Missouri as a slave state. In addition, the remaining portion of the Louisiana Purchase was to remain free north of **latitude 36°30'**. Since cotton did not grow well this far north, this limitation was acceptable to congressmen representing the slave states.

However, the proposed Missouri constitution presented a problem, as it outlawed immigration of free blacks into the state. Another compromise was in order, this time proposed by **Henry Clay**. According to this new compromise, Missouri would never pass a law that prevented anyone from entering the state. Through this and other work, Clay earned his title of the "**Great Compromiser.**"

> **Review Video: What was the Missouri Compromise?**
> Visit mometrix.com/academy and enter code: 848091

POPULAR SOVEREIGNTY AND THE COMPROMISE OF 1850

In addition to the pro-slavery and anti-slavery factions, a third group rose, who felt that each individual state should decide whether to allow or permit slavery within its borders. The idea that a state could make its own choices was referred to as **popular sovereignty**.

When California applied to join the union in 1849, the balance of congressional power was again threatened. The **Compromise of 1850** introduced a group of laws meant to bring an end to the conflict:

- California's admittance as a free state
- The outlaw of the slave trade in Washington, DC
- An increase in efforts to capture escaped slaves
- The right of New Mexico and Utah territories to decide individually whether to allow slavery

In spite of these measures, debate raged each time a new state prepared to enter the union.

KANSAS-NEBRASKA ACT TRIGGER OF ADDITIONAL CONFLICT

With the creation of the Kansas and Nebraska territories in 1854, another debate began. Congress allowed popular sovereignty in these territories, but slavery opponents argued that the Missouri Compromise had already made slavery illegal in this region. In Kansas, two separate governments arose, one pro-slavery and one anti-slavery. Conflict between the two factions rose to violence, leading Kansas to gain the nickname of "**Bleeding Kansas.**"

> **Review Video: Sectional Crisis: The Kansas-Nebraska Act**
> Visit mometrix.com/academy and enter code: 982119

DRED SCOTT DECISION

Abolitionist factions coalesced around the case of **Dred Scott**, using his case to test the country's laws regarding slavery. Scott, a slave, had been taken by his owner from Missouri, which was a slave state. He then traveled to Illinois, a free state, then on to the Minnesota Territory, also free based on the Missouri Compromise. After several years, he returned to Missouri, and his owner subsequently died. Abolitionists took Scott's case to court, stating that Scott was no longer a slave but free, since he had lived in free territory. The case went to the Supreme Court.

The Supreme Court stated that, because Scott, as a slave, was not a US citizen, his time in free states did not change his status. He also did not have the right to sue. In addition, the Court determined that the **Missouri Compromise** was unconstitutional, stating that Congress had overstepped its bounds by outlawing slavery in the territories.

> **Review Video: What was the Dred Scott Decision?**
> Visit mometrix.com/academy and enter code: 364838

INCIDENTS AT HARPER'S FERRY AND JOHN BROWN'S ROLE

John Brown, an abolitionist, had participated in several anti-slavery activities, including killing five pro-slavery men in retaliation, after the sacking of Lawrence, Kansas, an anti-slavery town. He and other abolitionists also banded together to pool their funds and build a runaway slave colony.

In 1859, Brown seized a federal arsenal in **Harper's Ferry**, located in what is now West Virginia. Brown intended to seize guns and ammunition and lead a slave rebellion. **Robert E. Lee** captured Brown and 21 followers, who were subsequently tried and hanged. While Northerners took the executions as an indication that the government supported slavery, Southerners were of the opinion that most of the North supported Brown and were, in general, anti-slavery.

PRESIDENTIAL CANDIDATES FOR THE 1860 ELECTION

The 1860 presidential candidates represented four different parties, each with a different opinion on slavery:

- **John Breckinridge**, representing the Southern Democrats, was pro-slavery but urged compromise to preserve the Union.
- **Abraham Lincoln**, of the Republican Party, was anti-slavery.
- **Stephen Douglas**, of the Northern Democrats, felt that the issue should be determined locally, on a state-by-state basis.
- **John Bell**, of the Constitutional Union Party, focused primarily on keeping the Union intact.

In the end, Abraham Lincoln won both the popular and electoral election. Southern states, who had sworn to secede from the Union if Lincoln was elected, did so, led by South Carolina. Shortly thereafter, the Civil War began when Confederate shots were fired on **Fort Sumter** in Charleston.

NORTH VS. SOUTH IN THE CIVIL WAR

The Northern states had significant advantages, including:

- **Larger population**—the North consisted of 24 states, while the South had 11.
- **Better transportation and finances**—with railroads primarily in the North, supply chains were much more dependable, as was overseas trade.
- **Raw materials**—the North held the majority of America's gold, as well as iron, copper, and other minerals vital to wartime.

The South's advantages included the following:

- **Better-trained military officers**—many of the Southern officers were West Point trained and had commanded in the Mexican and Indian wars.
- **Familiarity with weapons**—the climate and lifestyle of the South meant most of the people were experienced with both guns and horses. The industrial North had less extensive experience.
- **Defensive position**—the South felt that victory was guaranteed, since they were protecting their own lands, while the North would be invading.
- **Well-defined goals**—the South fought an ideological war to be allowed to govern themselves and preserve their way of life. The North originally fought to preserve the Union and later to free the slaves.

> **Review Video: The Civil War: A North vs South Overview**
> Visit mometrix.com/academy and enter code: 370788

BENEFIT OF THE EMANCIPATION PROCLAMATION ON THE UNION'S MILITARY STRATEGY

The Emancipation Proclamation, issued by President Lincoln on January 1, 1863, freed all slaves in **Confederate states** that were still in rebellion against the Union. While the original proclamation did not free any slaves in the states actually under Union control, it did set a precedent for the emancipation of slaves as the war progressed.

The **Emancipation Proclamation** worked in the Union's favor, as many freed slaves and other black troops joined the **Union Army**. Almost 200,000 blacks fought in the Union army, and over 10,000 served in the navy. By the end of the war, over 4 million slaves had been freed, and in 1865 slavery was abolished in the **13th amendment** to the Constitution.

> **Review Video: The Civil War: The Emancipation Proclamation**
> Visit mometrix.com/academy and enter code: 181778

MAJOR EVENTS OF THE CIVIL WAR

Six major events of the Civil War and their outcomes or significance are:

- The **First Battle of Bull Run** (July 21, 1861)—this was the first major land battle of the war. Observers, expecting to enjoy an entertaining skirmish, set up picnics nearby. Instead, they found themselves witness to a bloodbath. Union forces were defeated, and the battle set the course of the Civil War as long, bloody, and costly.
- The **Capture of Fort Henry** by Ulysses S. Grant—this battle in February of 1862 marked the Union's first major victory.

33

- The **Battle of Gettysburg** (July 1-3, 1863)—often seen as the turning point of the war, Gettysburg also saw the largest number of casualties of the war, with over 50,000 dead, wounded, or missing. Robert E. Lee was defeated, and the Confederate army, significantly crippled, withdrew.
- The **Overland Campaign** (May and June of 1864)—Grant, now in command of all the Union armies, led this high casualty campaign that eventually positioned the Union for victory.
- **Sherman's March to the Sea**—William Tecumseh Sherman, in May of 1864, conquered Atlanta. He then continued to Savannah, destroying vast amounts of property as he went.
- Following Lee's defeat at the Appomattox Courthouse, General Grant accepted **Lee's surrender** in the home of Wilmer McLean in Appomattox, Virginia on April 9, 1865.

CIRCUMSTANCES OF LINCOLN'S ASSASSINATION

The Civil War ended with the surrender of the South on April 9, 1865. Five days later, Lincoln and his wife, Mary, went to the play *Our American Cousin* at the Ford Theater. John Wilkes Booth, who did not know that the war was over, did his part in a plot to help the Confederacy by shooting Lincoln. He was carried from the theater to a nearby house, where he died the next morning. Booth was tracked down and killed by Union soldiers twelve days later.

> **Review Video: Overview of the Civil War**
> Visit mometrix.com/academy and enter code: 239557

GOALS OF RECONSTRUCTION AND THE FREEDMEN'S BUREAU

In the aftermath of the Civil War, the South was left in chaos. From 1865 to 1877, government on all levels worked to help restore order to the South, ensure civil rights to the freed slaves, and bring the Confederate states back into the Union. This became known as the **Reconstruction period**. In 1866, Congress passed the **Reconstruction Acts**, placing former Confederate states under military rule and stating the grounds for readmission into the Union.

The **Freedmen's Bureau** was formed to help freedmen both with basic necessities like food and clothing and also with employment and finding of family members who had been separated during the war. Many in the South felt the Freedmen's Bureau worked to set freed slaves against their former owners. The Bureau was intended to help former slaves become self-sufficient, and to keep them from falling prey to those who would take advantage of them. It eventually closed due to lack of funding and to violence from the **Ku Klux Klan**.

POLICIES OF THE RADICAL AND MODERATE REPUBLICANS

The **Radical Republicans** wished to treat the South quite harshly after the war. **Thaddeus Stevens**, the House Leader, suggested that the Confederate states be treated as if they were territories again, with ten years of military rule and territorial government before they would be readmitted. He also wanted to give all black men the right to vote. Former Confederate soldiers would be required to swear they had never supported the Confederacy (knows as the "Ironclad Oath") in order to be granted full rights as American citizens.

In contrast, the **moderate Republicans** wanted only black men who were literate or who had served as Union troops to be able to vote. All Confederate soldiers except troop leaders would also be able to vote. Before his death, **Lincoln** had favored a more moderate approach to Reconstruction, hoping this approach might bring some states back into the Union before the end of the war.

BLACK CODES AND THE CIVIL RIGHTS BILL

The Black Codes were proposed to control freed slaves. They would not be allowed to bear arms, assemble, serve on juries, or testify against whites. Schools would be segregated, and unemployed blacks could be arrested and forced to work. The **Civil Rights Act** countered these codes, providing much wider rights for the freed slaves.

Andrew Johnson, who became president after Lincoln's death, supported the Black Codes and vetoed the Civil Rights Act in 1865 and again in 1866. The second time, Congress overrode his veto, and it became law.

Two years later, Congress voted to **impeach** Johnson, the culmination of tensions between Congress and the president. He was tried and came within a single vote of being convicted, but ultimately was acquitted and finished his term in office.

PURPOSE OF THE THIRTEENTH, FOURTEENTH, AND FIFTEENTH AMENDMENTS

The Thirteenth, Fourteenth and Fifteenth Amendments were all passed shortly after the end of the Civil War:

- The **Thirteenth Amendment** was ratified by the states on December 6, 1865. This amendment prohibited slavery in the United States.
- The **Fourteenth Amendment** overturned the Dred Scott decision and was ratified July 9, 1868. American citizenship was redefined: a citizen was any person born or naturalized in the US, with all citizens guaranteed equal legal protection by all states. It also guaranteed citizens of any race the right to file a lawsuit or serve on a jury.
- The **Fifteenth Amendment** was ratified on February 3, 1870. It states that no citizen of the United States can be denied the right to vote based on race, color, or previous status as a slave.

> **Review Video: What is the 13th Amendment?**
> Visit mometrix.com/academy and enter code: 800185
>
> **Review Video: What is the 14th Amendment?**
> Visit mometrix.com/academy and enter code: 851325
>
> **Review Video: What is the 15th Amendment?**
> Visit mometrix.com/academy and enter code: 287199

PHASES OF RECONSTRUCTION

The three phases of Reconstruction are:

- **Presidential Reconstruction**—largely driven by President Andrew Johnson's policies, the presidential phase of Reconstruction was lenient on the South and allowed continued discrimination against and control over blacks.
- **Congressional Reconstruction**—Congress, controlled largely by Radical Republicans, took a different stance, providing a wider range of civil rights for blacks and greater control over Southern government. Congressional Reconstruction is marked by military control of the former Confederate States.
- **Redemption**—gradually, the Confederate states were readmitted into the Union. During this time, white Democrats took over the government of most of the South. In 1877, President Rutherford Hayes withdrew the last federal troops from the South.

CARPETBAGGERS AND SCALAWAGS

The chaos in the South attracted a number of people seeking to fill the power vacuums and take advantage of the economic disruption. **Scalawags** were southern whites who aligned with freedmen to take over local governments. Many in the South who could have filled political offices refused to take the necessary oath required to grant them the right to vote, leaving many opportunities for Scalawags and others. **Carpetbaggers** were Northerners who traveled to the South for various reasons. Some provided assistance, while others sought to make money or to acquire political power during this chaotic period.

TRANSCONTINENTAL RAILROAD

In 1869, the **Union Pacific Railroad** completed the first section of a planned **transcontinental railroad**. This section went from Omaha, Nebraska to Sacramento, California. Ninety percent of the workers were Chinese, working in very dangerous conditions for very low pay. With the rise of the railroad, products were much more easily transported across the country. While this was positive overall for industry throughout the country, it was often damaging to family farmers, who found themselves paying high shipping costs for smaller supply orders while larger companies received major discounts.

MEASURES TO LIMIT IMMIGRATION IN THE 19TH CENTURY

In 1870, the **Naturalization Act** put limits on US citizenship, allowing full citizenship only to whites and those of African descent. The **Chinese Exclusion Act of 1882** put limits on Chinese immigration. The **Immigration Act of 1882** taxed immigrants, charging 50 cents per person. These funds helped pay administrative costs for regulating immigration. **Ellis Island** opened in 1892 as a processing center for those arriving in New York. The year 1921 saw the **Emergency Quota Act** passed, also known as the **Johnson Quota Act**, which severely limited the number of immigrants allowed into the country.

AGRICULTURE IN THE 19TH CENTURY
TECHNOLOGICAL ADVANCES IN AGRICULTURAL CHANGES

During the mid-1800s, irrigation techniques improved significantly. Advances occurred in cultivation and breeding, as well as fertilizer use and crop rotation. In the Great Plains, also known as the Great American Desert, the dense soil was finally cultivated with steel plows. In 1892, gasoline-powered tractors arrived, and they were widely used by 1900. Other advancements in agriculture's toolset included barbed wire fences, combines, silos, deep-water wells, and the cream separator.

MAJOR ACTIONS THAT HELPED IMPROVE AGRICULTURE

Four major government actions that helped improve US agriculture in the 19th century are:

- The **Department of Agriculture** came into being in 1862, working for the interests of farmers and ranchers across the country.
- The **Morrill Land-Grant Acts** were a series of acts passed between 1862 and 1890, allowing land-grant colleges.
- In conjunction with land-grant colleges, the **Hatch Act of 1887** brought agriculture experiment stations into the picture, helping discover new farming techniques.
- In 1914, the **Smith-Lever Act** provided cooperative programs to help educate people about food, home economics, community development, and agriculture. Related agriculture extension programs helped farmers increase crop production to feed the rapidly growing nation.

INVENTORS FROM THE 1800S

Major inventors from the 1800s and their inventions include:

- Alexander Graham Bell—the telephone
- Orville and Wilbur Wright—the airplane
- Richard Gatling—the machine gun
- Walter Hunt, Elias Howe, and Isaac Singer—the sewing machine
- Nikola Tesla—alternating current motor
- George Eastman—the Kodak camera
- Thomas Edison—light bulbs, motion pictures, the phonograph
- Samuel Morse—the telegraph
- Charles Goodyear—vulcanized rubber
- Cyrus McCormick—the reaper
- George Westinghouse—the transformer, the air brake

This was an active period for invention, with about 700,000 patents registered between 1860 and 1900.

GILDED AGE

The time period from the end of the Civil War to the beginning of the First World War is often referred to as the **Gilded Age**, or the **Second Industrial Revolution**. The US was changing from an agricultural-based economy to an **industrial economy**, with rapid growth accompanying the shift. In addition, the country itself was expanding, spreading into the seemingly unlimited west.

This time period saw the beginning of banks, department stores, chain stores, and trusts—all familiar features of the modern-day landscape. Cities also grew rapidly, and large numbers of immigrants arrived in the country, swelling the urban ranks.

> **Review Video: The Gilded Age: An Overview**
> Visit mometrix.com/academy and enter code: 684770
>
> **Review Video: The Gilded Age: Chinese Immigration**
> Visit mometrix.com/academy and enter code: 624166

FACTORS LEADING TO THE DEVELOPMENT OF THE POPULIST PARTY

A major **recession** struck the United States during the 1890s, with crop prices falling dramatically. **Drought** compounded the problems, leaving many American farmers in crippling debt. The **Farmers' Alliance** formed in 1875, drawing the rural poor into a single political entity.

Recession also affected the more industrial parts of the country. The **Knights of Labor**, formed in 1869 by **Uriah Stephens**, was able to unite workers into a union to protect their rights. Dissatisfied by views espoused by industrialists, the Farmers Alliance and the Knights of Labor, joined to form the **Populist Party**, also known as the People's Party, in 1892. Some of the elements of the party's platform included:

- National currency
- Graduated income tax
- Government ownership of railroads as well as telegraph and telephone systems
- Secret ballots for voting

- Immigration restriction
- Single-term limits for president and vice-president

The Populist Party was in favor of decreasing elitism and making the voice of the common man more easily heard in the political process.

GROWTH OF THE LABOR MOVEMENT THROUGH THE LATE 19TH CENTURY

One of the first large, well-organized strikes occurred in 1892. Called the **Homestead Strike**, it occurred when the Amalgamated Association of Iron and Steel Workers struck against the Carnegie Steel Company. Gunfire ensued, and Carnegie was able to eliminate the plant's union. In 1894, workers in the American Railway Union, led by Eugene Debs, initiated the **Pullman Strike** after the Pullman Palace Car Co. cut their wages by 28 percent. President Grover Cleveland called in troops to break up the strike on the grounds that it interfered with mail delivery. Mary Harris "Mother" Jones organized the **Children's Crusade** to protest child labor. A protest march proceeded to the home of President Theodore Roosevelt in 1903. Jones also worked with the United Mine Workers of America and helped found the **Industrial Workers of the World**.

PANIC OF 1893

Far from a US-centric event, the **Panic of 1893** was an economic crisis that affected most of the globe. As a response, President Grover Cleveland repealed the **Sherman Silver Purchase Act**, afraid it had caused the downturn rather than boosting the economy as intended. The Panic led to bankruptcies, with banks and railroads going under and factory unemployment rising as high as 25 percent. In the end, the **Republican Party** regained power due to the economic crisis.

PROGRESSIVE ERA

From the 1890s to the end of the First World War, **Progressives** set forth an ideology that drove many levels of society and politics. The Progressives were in favor of workers' rights and safety and wanted measures taken against waste and corruption. They felt science could help improve society and that the government could—and should—provide answers to a variety of social problems. Progressives came from a wide variety of backgrounds but were united in their desire to improve society.

> **Review Video: The Progressive Era**
> Visit mometrix.com/academy and enter code: 722394

MUCKRAKERS AND THE PROGRESSIVE MOVEMENT

"Muckrakers" was a term used to identify aggressive investigative journalists who exposed scandals, corruption, and many other wrongs in late 19th-century society. Among these intrepid writers were:

- **Ida Tarbell**—she exposed John D. Rockefeller's Standard Oil Trust.
- **Jacob Riis**—a photographer, he brought the living conditions of the poor in New York to the public's attention.
- **Lincoln Steffens**—he worked to expose political corruption in municipal government.
- **Upton Sinclair**—his book *The Jungle* led to reforms in the meat-packing industry.

Through the work of these journalists, many new policies came into being, including workmen's compensation, child labor laws, and trust-busting.

GOVERNMENT DEALINGS WITH NATIVE AMERICANS THROUGH THE END OF THE 19TH CENTURY

America's westward expansion led to conflict and violent confrontations with Native Americans such as the **Battle of Little Bighorn**. In 1876, the American government ordered all Indians to relocate to reservations. Lack of compliance led to the **Dawes Act** in 1887, which ordered assimilation rather than separation: Native Americans were offered American citizenship and a piece of their tribal land if they would accept the lot chosen by the government and live on it separately from the tribe. This act remained in effect until 1934. Reformers also forced Indian children to attend **Indian Boarding Schools**, where they were not allowed to speak their native language and were immersed into a Euro-American culture and religion. Children were often abused in these schools and were indoctrinated to abandon their identity as Native Americans.

In 1890, the massacre at **Wounded Knee**, accompanied by Geronimo's surrender, led the Native Americans to work to preserve their culture rather than fight for their lands.

> **Review Video: Government Dealings with Native Americans Through the End of the 19th Century**
> Visit mometrix.com/academy and enter code: 635645

ROLE OF NATIVE AMERICANS IN WARTIME THROUGH THE BEGINNING OF THE 20TH CENTURY

The **Spanish-American War** (1898) saw a number of Native Americans serving with Teddy Roosevelt in the Rough Riders. Apache scouts accompanied General John J. Pershing to Mexico, hoping to find **Pancho Villa**. More than 17,000 Native Americans were drafted into service for **World War I**, though at the time, they were not considered legal citizens. In 1924, Indians were finally granted official citizenship by the **Indian Citizenship Act**.

After decades of relocation, forced assimilation, and genocide, the number of Native Americans in the US has greatly declined. Though many Native Americans have chosen—or have been forced—to assimilate, about 300 reservations exist today, with most of their inhabitants living in abject poverty.

> **Review Video: Role of Native Americans in Wartime Through the Beginning of the 20th Century**
> Visit mometrix.com/academy and enter code: 419128

EVENTS LEADING UP TO THE SPANISH-AMERICAN WAR

Spain had controlled **Cuba** since the 15th century. Over the centuries, the Spanish had quashed a variety of revolts. In 1886, slavery ended in Cuba, and another revolt was rising.

In the meantime, the US had expressed interest in Cuba, offering Spain $130 million for the island in 1853, during Franklin Pierce's presidency. In 1898, the Cuban revolt was underway. In spite of various factions supporting the Cubans, the US President, William McKinley, refused to recognize the rebellion, preferring negotiation over involvement in war. Then, the *Maine*, a US battleship in Havana Harbor, was blown up, killing 266 crew members. The US declared war two months later, and the war ended with a **Spanish surrender** in less than four months.

American History 1899 to Present

PROVISIONS OF THE SIXTEENTH, SEVENTEENTH, EIGHTEENTH, AND NINETEENTH AMENDMENTS

The early 20th century saw several amendments made to the US Constitution:

- The **Sixteenth Amendment** (1913) established a federal income tax.
- The **Seventeenth Amendment** (1913) allowed popular election of senators.
- The **Eighteenth Amendment** (1919) prohibited the sale, production, and transportation of alcohol. This amendment was later repealed by the Twenty-first Amendment.
- The **Nineteenth Amendment** (1920) gave women the right to vote.

These amendments largely grew out of the Progressive Era, as many citizens worked to improve American society.

ROLE OF THE FEDERAL TRADE COMMISSION IN ELIMINATING TRUSTS

Muckrakers such as Ida Tarbell and Lincoln Steffens brought to light the damaging trend of trusts—huge corporations working to monopolize areas of commerce so they could control prices and distribution. The **Sherman Antitrust Act** and the **Clayton Antitrust Act** set out guidelines for competition among corporations and set out to eliminate these trusts. The **Federal Trade Commission** was formed in 1914 in order to enforce antitrust measures and ensure that companies were operated fairly and did not create controlling monopolies.

IMPORTANCE OF THE PANAMA CANAL

Initial work began on the **Panama Canal** in 1881, though the idea had been discussed since the 1500s. The canal greatly reduces the length and time needed to sail from one ocean to the other by connecting the Atlantic to the Pacific through the Isthmus of Panama, which joins South America to North America. Before the canal was built, travelers had to sail around the entire perimeter of South America to reach the West Coast of the US. The French began the work after successfully completing the **Suez Canal**, which connected the Mediterranean Sea to the Red Sea. However, due to disease and high expense, the work moved slowly, and after eight years, the company went bankrupt, suspending work. The US purchased the holdings, and the first ship sailed through the canal in 1914. The Panama Canal was constructed as a lock-and-lake canal, with ships lifted on locks to travel from one lake to another over the rugged, mountainous terrain. In order to maintain control of the Canal Zone, the US assisted Panama in its battle for independence from **Columbia**.

INFLUENCE OF BIG STICK DIPLOMACY ON AMERICAN FOREIGN POLICY IN LATIN AMERICA

Theodore Roosevelt's famous quote, "Speak softly and carry a big stick," is supposedly of African origins, at least according to Roosevelt. He used this proverb to justify expanded involvement in foreign affairs during his tenure as President. The US military was deployed to protect American interests in **Latin America**. Roosevelt also worked to maintain an equal or greater influence in Latin America than those held by European interests. As a result, the US Navy grew larger, and the US generally became more involved in foreign affairs. Roosevelt felt that if any country was left vulnerable to control by Europe due to economic issues or political instability, the US had not only a right to intervene but was **obligated** to do so. This led to US involvement in Cuba, Nicaragua, Haiti, and the Dominican Republic over several decades leading into the First and Second World Wars.

TAFT'S DOLLAR DIPLOMACY VS. ROOSEVELT'S DIPLOMATIC THEORIES

During William Howard Taft's presidency, Taft instituted "**Dollar Diplomacy**." This approach was America's effort to influence Latin America and East Asia through economic rather than military means. Taft saw past efforts in these areas to be political and warlike, while his efforts focused on peaceful economic goals. His justification of the policy was to protect the **Panama Canal**, which was vital to US trade interests.

In spite of Taft's assurance that Dollar Diplomacy was a peaceful approach, many interventions proved violent. During Latin American revolts, such as those in **Nicaragua**, the US sent troops to settle the revolutions. Afterward, bankers moved in to help support the new leaders through loans. Dollar Diplomacy continued until 1913, when Woodrow Wilson was elected president.

Wilson's Approach to International Diplomacy

Turning away from Taft's "Dollar Diplomacy," Wilson instituted a foreign policy he referred to as "**moral diplomacy**." This approach still influences American foreign policy today.

Wilson felt that **representative government and democracy** in all countries would lead to worldwide stability. Democratic governments, he felt, would be less likely to threaten American interests. He also saw the US and Great Britain as the great role models in this area, as well as champions of world peace and self-government. Free trade and international commerce would allow the US to speak out regarding world events.

Main elements of Wilson's policies included:

- Maintaining a strong military
- Promoting democracy throughout the world
- Expanding international trade to boost the American economy

Major Events of World War I

World War I occurred from 1914 to 1918 and was fought largely in Europe. Triggered by the assassination of Austrian Archduke Franz Ferdinand, the war rapidly escalated. At the beginning of the conflict, Woodrow Wilson declared the US neutral. Major events influencing US involvement included:

- **Sinking of the *Lusitania***—the British passenger liner RMS *Lusitania* was sunk by a German U-boat in 1915. Among the 1,000 civilian victims were over 100 American citizens. Outraged by this act, many Americans began to push for US involvement in the war, using the *Lusitania* as a rallying cry.
- **German U-boat aggression**—Wilson continued to keep the US out of the war, using as his 1916 reelection slogan, "He kept us out of war." While he continued to work toward an end of the war, German U-boats began to indiscriminately attack American and Canadian merchant ships carrying supplies to Germany's enemies in Europe.
- **Zimmerman Telegram** —the final event that brought the US into World War I was the interception of the Zimmerman Telegram (also known as the Zimmerman Note). In this telegram, Germany proposed forming an alliance with Mexico if the US entered the war.

Efforts in the US During World War I Supporting the War Effort

American **railroads** came under government control in December 1917. The widespread system was consolidated into a single system, with each region assigned a director. This greatly increased the efficiency of the railroad system, allowing the railroads to supply both domestic and military needs. Control returned to private ownership in 1920. In 1918, **telegraph, telephone, and cable services** also came under Federal control, to be returned to private management the next year. The **American Red Cross** supported the war effort by knitting clothes for Army and Navy troops. They also helped supply hospital and refugee clothing and surgical dressings. Over 8 million people participated in this effort. To generate wartime funds, the US government sold **Liberty Bonds**. In four issues, they sold nearly $25 billion—more than one-fifth of Americans purchased them. After the war, a fifth bond drive was held but sold "**Victory Liberty Bonds**."

> **Review Video: WWI Overview**
> Visit mometrix.com/academy and enter code: 659767

INFLUENCE OF WILSON'S FOURTEEN POINTS ON THE FINAL PEACE TREATIES THAT ENDED WORLD WAR I

President Woodrow Wilson proposed **Fourteen Points** as the basis for a peace settlement to end the war. Presented to the US Congress in January 1918, the Fourteen Points included:

- Five points outlining **general ideals**
- Eight points to resolve **immediate problems** of political and territorial nature
- One point proposing an **organization of nations** (the League of Nations) with the intent of maintaining world peace

In November of that same year, Germany agreed to an **armistice**, assuming the final treaty would be based on the Fourteen Points. However, during the peace conference in Paris 1919, there was much disagreement, leading to a final agreement that punished Germany and the other Central Powers much more than originally intended. Henry Cabot Lodge, who had become the Foreign Relations Committee chairman in 1918, wanted an unconditional surrender from Germany and was concerned about the article in the **Treaty of Versailles** that gave the League of Nations power to declare war without a vote from the US Congress. A **League of Nations** was included in the Treaty of Versailles at Wilson's insistence. The Senate rejected the Treaty of Versailles, and in the end, Wilson refused to concede to Lodge's demands. As a result, the US did not join the League of Nations.

MAJOR CHANGES AND EVENTS THAT TOOK PLACE IN AMERICA DURING THE 1920S

The post-war 1920s saw many Americans moving from the farm to the city, with growing prosperity in the US. The **Roaring Twenties**, or the **Jazz Age**, was driven largely by growth in the automobile and entertainment industries. Individuals like Charles Lindbergh, the first aviator to make a solo flight across the Atlantic Ocean, added to the American admiration of individual accomplishment. Telephone lines, distribution of electricity, highways, the radio, and other inventions brought great changes to everyday life.

> **Review Video: 1920's**
> Visit mometrix.com/academy and enter code: 124996

MAJOR CULTURAL MOVEMENTS OF THE 1920S INFLUENCED BY AFRICAN AMERICANS

The **Harlem Renaissance** saw a number of African-American artists settling in Harlem in New York. This community produced a number of well-known artists and writers, including Langston Hughes, Nella Larsen, Zora Neale Hurston, Claude McKay, Countee Cullen, and Jean Toomer. The growth of jazz, also largely driven by African Americans, defined the **Jazz Age**. Its unconventional, improvisational style matched the growing sense of optimism and exploration of the decade. Originating as an offshoot of the blues, jazz began in New Orleans. Some significant jazz musicians were Duke Ellington, Louis Armstrong, and Jelly Roll Morton. **Big Band** and **Swing Jazz** also developed in the 1920s. Well-known musicians of this movement included Bing Crosby, Frank Sinatra, Count Basie, Benny Goodman, Billie Holiday, Ella Fitzgerald, and The Dorsey Brothers.

Provisions and Importance of the National Origins Act of 1924

The National Origins Act (Johnson-Reed Act) placed limitations on **immigration**. The number of immigrants allowed into the US was based on the population of each nationality of immigrants who were living in the country in 1890. Only two percent of each nationality's 1890 population numbers were allowed to immigrate. This led to great disparities between immigrants from various nations, and Asian immigration was not allowed at all. Some of the impetus behind the Johnson-Reed Act came as a result of paranoia following the **Russian Revolution**. Fear of communist influences in the US led to a general fear of immigrants.

Origins of the Red Scare

World War I created many jobs, but after the war ended, these jobs disappeared, leaving many unemployed. In the wake of these employment changes, the **International Workers of the World** and the **Socialist Party**, headed by Eugene Debs, became more and more visible. Workers initiated strikes in an attempt to regain the favorable working conditions that had been put into place before the war. Unfortunately, many of these strikes became violent, and the actions were blamed on "Reds," or Communists, for trying to spread their views into America. With the recent Bolshevik Revolution in Russia, many Americans feared a similar revolution might occur in the US. The **Red Scare** ensued, with many individuals jailed for supposedly holding communist, anarchist, or socialist beliefs.

Growth of Civil Rights for African Americans

Marcus Garvey founded the **Universal Negro Improvement Association and African Communities League (UNIA-ACL)**, which became a large and active organization focused on building black nationalism. In 1909, the **National Association for the Advancement of Colored People (NAACP)** came into being, working to defeat Jim Crow laws. The NAACP also helped prevent racial segregation from becoming federal law, fought against lynchings, helped black soldiers in WWI become officers, and helped defend the Scottsboro Boys, who were unjustly accused of rape.

Ku Klux Klan

In 1866, Confederate Army veterans came together to fight against Reconstruction in the South, forming a group called the **Ku Klux Klan (KKK)**. With white supremacist beliefs, including anti-Semitism, nativism, anti-Catholicism, and overt racism, this organization relied heavily on violence to get its message across. In 1915, they grew again in power, using a film called *The Birth of a Nation*, by D.W. Griffith, to spread their ideas. In the 1920s, the reach of the KKK spread far into the north and midwest, and members controlled a number of state governments. Its membership and power began to decline during the Great Depression but experienced a resurgence later.

American Civil Liberties Union

In 1866, Confederate Army veterans came together to fight against Reconstruction in the South, forming a group called the Ku Klux Klan (KKK). With white supremacist beliefs, including anti-Semitism, nativism, anti-Catholicism, and overt racism, this organization relied heavily on violence to get its message across. In 1915, they grew again in power, using a film called The Birth of a Nation, by D.W. Griffith, to spread their ideas. In the 1920s, the reach of the KKK spread far into the north and midwest, and members controlled a number of state governments. Its membership and power began to decline during the Great Depression but experienced a resurgence later.

GOALS OF THE ANTI-DEFAMATION LEAGUE

In 1913, the Anti-Defamation League was formed to prevent anti-Semitic behavior and practices. Its actions also worked to prevent all forms of racism and to prevent individuals from being discriminated against for any reason involving their race. They spoke against the Ku Klux Klan, as well as other racist or anti-Semitic organizations. This organization still works to fight discrimination against all minorities.

ROOSEVELT'S NEW DEAL

The **Great Depression**, which began in 1929 with the stock market crash, grew out of several factors that had developed over the previous years, including:

- Growing economic disparity between the rich and middle classes, with the rich amassing wealth much more quickly than the lower classes
- Disparity in economic distribution in industries
- Growing use of credit, leading to an inflated demand for some goods
- Government support of new industries rather than agriculture
- Risky stock market investments, leading to the stock market crash

Additional factors contributing to the Depression also included the **Labor Day Hurricane** in the Florida Keys (1935) and the **Great Hurricane of 1938** in New England, along with the **Dust Bowl** in the Great Plains, which destroyed crops and resulted in the displacement of as many as 2.5 million people.

> **Review Video: What Caused the Great Depression?**
> Visit mometrix.com/academy and enter code: 635912

Franklin D. Roosevelt was elected president in 1932 with his promise of a "**New Deal**" for Americans. His goals were to provide government work programs to provide jobs, wages, and relief to numerous workers throughout the beleaguered US. Congress gave Roosevelt almost free rein to produce relief legislation. The goals of this legislation were:

- **Relief**—creating jobs for the high numbers of unemployed
- **Recovery**—stimulating the economy through the National Recovery Administration
- **Reform**—passing legislation to prevent future, similar economic crashes

The Roosevelt Administration also passed legislation regarding ecological issues, including the Soil Conservation Service, aimed at preventing another Dust Bowl.

ROOSEVELT'S ALPHABET ORGANIZATIONS

So-called "alphabet organizations" set up during Roosevelt's administration included:

- **Civilian Conservation Corps** (CCC)—provided jobs in the forestry service
- **Agricultural Adjustment Administration** (AAA)—increased agricultural income by adjusting both production and prices
- **Tennessee Valley Authority** (TVA)—organized projects to build dams in the Tennessee River for flood control and production of electricity, resulting in increased productivity for industries in the area, and easier navigation of the Tennessee River

- **Public Works Administration** (PWA) and Civil Works Administration (CWA)—provided a multitude of jobs, initiating over 34,000 projects
- **Works Progress Administration** (WPA)—helped unemployed persons to secure employment on government work projects or elsewhere

ACTIONS TAKEN DURING THE ROOSEVELT ADMINISTRATION TO PREVENT FUTURE CRASHES

The Roosevelt administration passed several laws and established several institutions to initiate the "reform" portion of the New Deal, including:

- **Glass-Steagall Act**—separated investment from commercial banking
- **Securities Exchange Commission (SEC)**—helped regulate Wall Street investment practices, making them less dangerous to the overall economy
- **Wagner Act**—provided worker and union rights to improve relations between employees and employers
- **Social Security Act of 1935**—provided pensions as well as unemployment insurance

Other actions focused on insuring bank deposits and adjusting the value of American currency. Most of these regulatory agencies and government policies and programs still exist today.

MAJOR REGULATIONS REGARDING LABOR AFTER THE GREAT DEPRESSION

Three major regulations regarding labor that were passed after the Great Depression are:

- The **Wagner Act** (1935)—also known as the National Labor Relations Act, it established that unions were legal, protected members of unions, and required collective bargaining. This act was later amended by the Taft-Hartley Act of 1947 and the Landrum-Griffin Act of 1959, which further clarified certain elements.
- **Davis-Bacon Act** (1931)—provided fair compensation for contractors and subcontractors.
- **Walsh-Healey Act** (1936)—established a minimum wage, child labor laws, safety standards, and overtime pay.

ACCOMPLISHMENTS OF THE LYNDON B. JOHNSON PRESIDENCY

Kennedy's vice president, **Lyndon Johnson**, assumed the presidency after Kennedy's **assassination**. He supported civil rights bills, tax cuts, and other wide-reaching legislation that Kennedy had also supported. Johnson saw America as a "**Great Society**," and enacted legislation to fight disease and poverty, renew urban areas, and support education and environmental conservation. Medicare and Medicaid were instituted under his administration. He continued Kennedy's support of space exploration, and he is also known, although less positively, for his handling of the **Vietnam War**.

FACTORS THAT LED TO THE GROWTH OF THE CIVIL RIGHTS MOVEMENT

In the 1950s, post-war America was experiencing a rapid growth in prosperity. However, African-Americans found themselves left behind. Following the lead of **Mahatma Gandhi**, who led similar class struggles in India, African-Americans began to demand equal rights. Major figures in this struggle included:

- **Rosa Parks**—often called the "mother of the Civil Rights Movement," her refusal to give up her seat on the bus to a white man served as a seed from which the movement grew.
- **Martin Luther King, Jr.**—the best-known leader of the movement, King drew on Gandhi's beliefs and encouraged non-violent opposition. He led a march on Washington in 1963, received the Nobel Peace Prize in 1964, and was assassinated in 1968.
- **Malcolm X**—espousing less peaceful means of change, Malcolm X became a Black Muslim and supported black nationalism.

IMPACT OF STOKELY CARMICHAEL, ADAM CLAYTON POWELL, AND JESSE JACKSON ON THE CIVIL RIGHTS MOVEMENT

- **Stokely Carmichael**—Carmichael originated the term "Black Power" and served as head of the Student Nonviolent Coordinating Committee. He believed in black pride and black culture and felt separate political and social institutions should be developed for blacks.
- **Adam Clayton Powell**—chairman of the Coordinating Committee for Employment, he led rent strikes and other actions, as well as a bus boycott, to increase the hiring of blacks.
- **Jesse Jackson**—Jackson was selected to head the Chicago Operation Breadbasket in 1966, and went on to organize boycotts and other actions. He also had an unsuccessful run for president.

EVENTS OF THE CIVIL RIGHTS MOVEMENT

Three major events of the Civil Rights Movement are:

- **Montgomery Bus Boycott**—in 1955, Rosa Parks refused to give her seat on the bus to a white man. As a result, she was tried and convicted of disorderly conduct and of violating local ordinances. A 381-day bus boycott ensued, protesting segregation on public buses.
- **Desegregation of Little Rock**—in 1957, after the Supreme Court decision on Brown v. Board of Education, which declared "separate but equal" unconstitutional, the Arkansas school board voted to desegregate their schools. Even though Arkansas was considered progressive, its governor brought in the Arkansas National Guard to prevent nine black students from entering Central High School in Little Rock. President Eisenhower responded by federalizing the National Guard and ordering them to stand down.
- **Birmingham Campaign**—protestors organized a variety of actions such as sit-ins and an organized march to launch a voting campaign. When the City of Birmingham declared the protests illegal, the protestors, including Martin Luther King, Jr., persisted and were arrested and jailed.

PIECES OF LEGISLATION PASSED AS A RESULT OF THE CIVIL RIGHTS MOVEMENT

Three major pieces of legislation passed as a result of the Civil Rights movement are:

- **Brown v. Board of Education** (1954)—the Supreme Court declared that "separate but equal" accommodations and services were unconstitutional.
- **Civil Rights Act of 1964**—this declared discrimination illegal in employment, education, or public accommodation.
- **Voting Rights Act of 1965**—this act ended various activities practiced, mostly in the South, to bar blacks from exercising their voting rights. These included poll taxes and literacy tests.

US Perspective on the Progression of the Vietnam War

After World War II, the US pledged, as part of its foreign policy, to come to the assistance of any country threatened by **communism**. When Vietnam was divided into a communist North and democratic South, much like Korea before it, the eventual attempts by the North to unify the country under Communist rule led to intervention by the US. On the home front, the **Vietnam War** became more and more unpopular politically, with Americans growing increasingly discontent with the inability of the US to achieve the goals it had set for the Asian country. When President **Richard Nixon** took office in 1969, his escalation of the war led to protests at Kent State in Ohio, during which several students were killed by National Guard troops. Protests continued, eventually resulting in the end of the compulsory draft in 1973. In that same year, the US departed Vietnam. In 1975, the South surrendered, and Vietnam became a unified country under communist rule.

Effects of US Cold War Foreign Policy Acts on the International Relationships

The following are US Cold War foreign policy acts and how they affected international relationships, especially between the US and the Soviet Union:

- **Marshall Plan**—this sent aid to war-torn Europe after WWII, largely focusing on preventing the spread of communism.
- **Containment Policy**—proposed by George F. Kennan, the containment policy focused on containing the spread of Soviet communism.
- **Truman Doctrine**—Harry S. Truman stated that the US would provide both economic and military support to any country threatened by Soviet takeover.
- **National Security Act**—passed in 1947, this act reorganized the government's military departments into the Department of Defense and created the Central Intelligence Agency and the National Security Council.

The combination of these acts led to the **Cold War**, with Soviet communists attempting to spread their influence and the US and other countries trying to contain or stop this spread.

NATO, Warsaw Pact, and the Berlin Wall

NATO, the **North Atlantic Treaty Organization**, came into being in 1949. It essentially amounted to an agreement among the US and Western European countries that an attack on any one of these countries was to be considered an attack against the entire group. Under the influence of the Soviet Union, the Eastern European countries of the USSR, Bulgaria, East Germany, Poland, Romania, Albania, Hungary, and Czechoslovakia responded with the **Warsaw Pact**, which created a similar agreement among those nations. In 1961, a wall was built to separate communist East Berlin from democratic West Berlin. This was a literal representation of the "**Iron Curtain**" that separated the democratic and communist countries throughout the world.

Effect of the Arms Race on Post WWII International Relations

After World War II, major nations, particularly the US and USSR, rushed to develop highly advanced weapons systems such as the **atomic bomb** and later the **hydrogen bomb**. These countries seemed determined to outpace each other with the development of numerous, deadly weapons. These weapons were expensive and extremely dangerous, and it is possible that the war between US and Soviet interests remained "cold" due to the fear that one side or the other would use these powerful weapons.

End of the Cold War and the Dissolution of the Soviet Union

In the late 1980s, **Mikhail Gorbachev** led the Soviet Union. He introduced a series of reform programs. **Ronald Reagan** famously urged Gorbachev to tear down the **Berlin Wall** as a gesture of growing freedom in the Eastern Bloc, and in 1989 it was demolished, ending the separation of East and West Germany. The Soviet Union relinquished its power over the various republics in Eastern Europe, and they became independent nations with their own individual governments. In 1991, the **USSR** was dissolved and the Cold War also came to an end.

Review Video: How Did the Cold War End?
Visit mometrix.com/academy and enter code: 278032

TECHNOLOGICAL ADVANCES THAT OCCURRED THROUGHOUT THE 1900S

Numerous technological advances throughout the 1900s led to more effective treatment of diseases, more efficient communication and transportation, and new means of generating power. Advances in **medicine** increased the human lifespan in developed countries, and near-instantaneous **communication** opened up a myriad of possibilities. Some of these advances include:

- Discovery of penicillin (1928)
- Supersonic air travel (1947)
- Nuclear power plants (1951)
- Orbital satellite leading to manned space flight (Sputnik, 1957)
- First man on the moon (1969)

US POLICY TOWARD IMMIGRANTS AFTER WORLD WAR II

Prior to WWII, the US had been limiting **immigration** for several decades. After WWII, policy shifted slightly to accommodate political refugees from Europe and elsewhere. So many people were displaced by the war that in 1946, the UN formed the **International Refugee Organization** to deal with the problem. In 1948, the US Congress passed the **Displaced Persons Act**, which allowed over 400,000 European refugees to enter the US, most of them concentration camp survivors and refugees from Eastern Europe.

In 1952, the **United States Escapee Program (USEP)** increased the quotas, allowing refugees from communist Europe to enter the US, as did the **Refugee Relief Act**, passed in 1953. At the same time, however, the **Internal Security Act of 1950** allowed deportation of declared communists, and Asians were subjected to a quota based on race, rather than country of origin. Later changes included:

- **Migration and Refugee Assistance Act** (1962)—provided aid for refugees in need
- **Immigration and Nationality Act** (1965)—ended quotas based on nation of origin
- **Immigration Reform and Control Act** (1986)—prohibited the hiring of illegal immigrants but also granted amnesty to about three million illegals already in the country

POLICIES AND LEGISLATION ENACTED EXPANDING MINORITY RIGHTS

Several major acts have been passed, particularly since WWII, to protect the rights of minorities in America. These include:

- Civil Rights Act (1964)
- Voting Rights Act (1965)
- Age Discrimination Act (1967)
- Americans with Disabilities Act (1990)

Other important movements for civil rights included a prisoner's rights movement, movements for immigrant rights, and the women's rights movement. The National Organization for Women (NOW) was established in 1966 and worked to pass the Equal Rights Amendment. The amendment was passed, but not enough states ratified it for it to become part of the US Constitution.

INTERVENTIONIST AND ISOLATIONIST APPROACHES IN WORLD WAR II

When war broke out in Europe in 1939, President Roosevelt stated that the US would remain **neutral**. However, his overall approach was considered "**interventionist**," as he was willing to provide aid to the Allies without actually entering the conflict. Thus, the US supplied a wide variety of war materials to the Allied nations in the early years of the war.

Isolationists believed the US should not provide any aid to the Allies, including supplies. They felt Roosevelt, by assisting the Allies, was leading the US into a war for which it was not prepared. Led by Charles Lindbergh, the Isolationists believed that any involvement in the European conflict endangered the US by weakening its national defense.

SEQUENCE OF EVENTS THAT LED THE US TO DECLARE WAR AND ENTER WORLD WAR II

In 1937, Japan invaded China, prompting the US to eventually halt exports to Japan. Roosevelt also did not allow Japanese interests to withdraw money held in US banks. In 1941, **General Tojo** rose to power as the Japanese prime minister. Recognizing America's ability to bring a halt to Japan's expansion, he authorized the bombing of **Pearl Harbor** on December 7. The US responded by declaring war on Japan. Partially because of the **Tripartite Pact** among the Axis Powers, Germany and Italy then declared war on the US, later followed by Bulgaria, Hungary, and other Axis nations.

> **Review Video: World War II Overview**
> Visit mometrix.com/academy and enter code: 759402

OCCURRENCES OF WORLD WAR II THAT LED TO THE SURRENDER OF GERMANY

In 1941, **Hitler** violated the non-aggression pact he had signed with Stalin two years earlier by invading the USSR. **Stalin** then joined the **Allies**. Stalin, Roosevelt, and Winston Churchill planned to defeat Germany first, then Japan, bringing the war to an end.

In 1942-1943, the Allies drove **Axis** forces out of Africa. In addition, the Germans were soundly defeated at Stalingrad.

The **Italian Campaign** involved Allied operations in Italy between July 1943 and May 1945, including Italy's liberation. On June 6, 1944, known as **D-Day**, the Allies invaded France at Normandy. Soviet troops moved on the eastern front at the same time, driving German forces back. By April 25, 1945, Berlin was surrounded by Soviet troops. On May 7, Germany surrendered.

MAJOR EVENTS OF WORLD WAR II THAT LED TO THE SURRENDER OF JAPAN

War continued with **Japan** after Germany's surrender. Japanese forces had taken a large portion of Southeast Asia and the Western Pacific, all the way to the Aleutian Islands in Alaska. **General Doolittle** bombed several Japanese cities while American troops scored a victory at Midway. Additional fighting in the Battle of the Coral Sea further weakened Japan's position. As a final blow, the US dropped two **atomic bombs** on Japan, one on Hiroshima and the other on Nagasaki. This was the first time atomic bombs had been used in warfare, and the devastation was horrific and demoralizing. Japan surrendered on September 2, 1945, which became **V-J Day** in the US.

SIGNIFICANCE OF THE 442ND REGIMENTAL COMBAT TEAM, THE TUSKEGEE AIRMEN, AND THE NAVAJO CODE TALKERS DURING WORLD WAR II

The 442nd Regimental Combat Team consisted of Japanese-Americans fighting in Europe for the US. The most highly decorated unit per member in US history, they suffered a 93% casualty rate during the war. The **Tuskegee Airmen** were African American aviators, the first black Americans allowed to fly for the military. In spite of being ineligible to become official navy pilots, they flew over 15,000 missions and were highly decorated. The **Navajo Code Talkers** were native Navajo who used their traditional language to transmit information among Allied forces. Because Navajo is a language and not simply a code, the Axis powers were never able to translate it. The use of Navajo Code Talkers to transmit information was instrumental in the taking of Iwo Jima and other major victories of the war.

CIRCUMSTANCES AND OPPORTUNITIES FOR WOMEN DURING WORLD WAR II

Women served widely in the military during WWII, working in numerous positions, including the **Flight Nurses Corps**. Women also moved into the workforce while men were overseas, leading to over 19 million women in the US workforce by 1944. **Rosie the Riveter** stood as a symbol of these women and a means of recruiting others to take needed positions. Women, as well as their families left behind during wartime, also grew **Victory Gardens** to help provide food.

IMPORTANCE OF THE ATOMIC BOMB DURING WORLD WAR II

The atomic bomb, developed during WWII, was the most powerful bomb ever invented. A single bomb, carried by a single plane, held enough power to destroy an entire city. This devastating effect was demonstrated with the bombing of **Hiroshima** and **Nagasaki** in 1945 in what later became a controversial move, but ended the war. The bombings resulted in as many as 150,000 immediate deaths and many more as time passed after the bombings, mostly due to **radiation poisoning**.

Whatever the arguments against the use of "The Bomb," the post-WWII era saw many countries develop similar weapons to match the newly expanded military power of the US. The impact of those developments and use of nuclear weapons continues to haunt international relations today.

IMPORTANCE OF THE YALTA CONFERENCE AND THE POTSDAM CONFERENCE

In February 1945, Joseph Stalin, Franklin D. Roosevelt, and Winston Churchill met in Yalta to discuss the post-war treatment of the **Axis nations**, particularly Germany. Though Germany had not yet surrendered, its defeat was imminent. After Germany's official surrender, Joseph Stalin, Harry Truman (Roosevelt's successor), and Clement Attlee (replacing Churchill partway through the conference) met to formalize those plans. This meeting was called the **Potsdam Conference**. Basic provisions of these agreements included:

- Dividing Germany and Berlin into four zones of occupation
- Demilitarization of Germany
- Poland remaining under Soviet control
- Outlawing the Nazi Party
- Trials for Nazi leaders
- Relocation of numerous German citizens
- The USSR joining the United Nations, established in 1945
- Establishment of the United Nations Security Council, consisting of the US, the UK, the USSR, China, and France

AGREEMENTS MADE WITH POST-WAR JAPAN

General Douglas MacArthur led the American **military occupation of Japan** after the country surrendered. The goals of the US occupation included removing Japan's military and making the country a democracy. A 1947 constitution removed power from the emperor and gave it to the people, as well as granting voting rights to women. Japan was no longer allowed to declare war, and a group of 28 government officials were tried for war crimes. In 1951, the US finally signed a peace treaty with Japan. This treaty allowed Japan to rearm itself for purposes of self-defense but stripped the country of the empire it had built overseas.

US TREATMENT OF IMMIGRANTS DURING AND AFTER WORLD WAR II

In 1940, the US passed the **Alien Registration Act**, which required all aliens older than fourteen to be fingerprinted and registered. They were also required to report changes of address within five days.

Tension between whites and Japanese immigrants in **California**, which had been building since the beginning of the century, came to a head with the bombing of **Pearl Harbor** in 1941. Believing that even those Japanese living in the US were likely to be loyal to their native country, the president ordered numerous Japanese to be arrested on suspicion of subversive action and isolated in exclusion zones known as **War Relocation Camps**. Approximately 120,000 Japanese-Americans, two-thirds of them US citizens, were sent to these camps during the war.

GENERAL STATE OF THE US AFTER WORLD WAR II

Following WWII, the US became the strongest political power in the world, becoming a major player in world affairs and foreign policies. The US determined to stop the spread of **communism**, having named itself the "**arsenal of democracy**" during the war. In addition, America emerged with a greater sense of itself as a single, integrated nation, with many regional and economic differences diminished. The government worked for greater equality, and the growth of communications increased contact among different areas of the country. Both the aftermath of the Great Depression and the necessities of WWII had given the government greater **control** over various institutions as well as the economy. This also meant that the American government took on greater responsibility for the well-being of its citizens, both in the domestic arena, such as providing basic needs, and in protecting them from foreign threats. This increased role of providing basic necessities for all Americans has been criticized by some as "**the welfare state**."

ACCOMPLISHMENTS OF HARRY S. TRUMAN

Harry S. Truman took over the presidency from Franklin D. Roosevelt near the end of WWII. He made the final decision to drop atomic bombs on Japan and played a major role in the final decisions regarding the treatment of post-war Germany. On the domestic front, Truman initiated a 21-point plan known as the **Fair Deal**. This plan expanded Social Security, provided public housing, and made the Fair Employment Practice Committee permanent. Truman helped support Greece and Turkey (which were under threat from the USSR), supported South Korea against communist North Korea, and helped with recovery in Western Europe. He also participated in the formation of **NATO**, the North Atlantic Treaty Organization.

EVENTS AND IMPORTANCE OF THE KOREAN WAR

The Korean War began in 1950 and ended in 1953. For the first time in history, a world organization—the **United Nations**—played a military role in a war. North Korea sent communist troops into South Korea, seeking to bring the entire country under communist control. The UN sent out a call to member nations, asking them to support South Korea. Truman sent troops, as did many other UN member nations. The war ended three years later with a **truce** rather than a peace treaty,

51

and Korea remains divided at the **38th parallel north**, with communist rule remaining in the North and a democratic government ruling the South.

ACCOMPLISHMENTS OF DWIGHT D. EISENHOWER

Eisenhower carried out a middle-of-the-road foreign policy and brought the US several steps forward in equal rights. He worked to minimize tensions during the Cold War and negotiated a peace treaty with Russia after the death of Stalin. He enforced desegregation by sending troops to Little Rock Central High School in Arkansas, as well as ordering the desegregation of the military. Organizations formed during his administration included the Department of Health, Education, and Welfare, and the National Aeronautics and Space Administration (NASA).

PRESIDENCY OF JOHN F. KENNEDY

Although his term was cut short by his assassination, **JFK** instituted economic programs that led to a period of continuous expansion in the US unmatched since before WWII. He formed the Alliance for Progress and the Peace Corps, organizations intended to help developing nations. He also oversaw the passage of new civil rights legislation and drafted plans to attack poverty and its causes, along with support of the arts. Kennedy's presidency ended when he was assassinated by **Lee Harvey Oswald** in 1963.

EVENTS OF THE CUBAN MISSILE CRISIS

The Cuban Missile Crisis occurred in 1962, during John F. Kennedy's presidency. Russian Premier **Nikita Khrushchev** decided to place nuclear missiles in **Cuba** to protect the island from invasion by the US. An American U-2 plane flying over the island photographed the missile bases as they were being built. Tensions rose, with the US concerned about nuclear missiles so close to its shores, and the USSR concerned about American missiles that had been placed in **Turkey**. Eventually, the missile sites were removed, and a US naval blockade turned back Soviet ships carrying missiles to Cuba. During negotiations, the US agreed to remove their missiles from Turkey and agreed to sell surplus wheat to the USSR. A telephone hotline between Moscow and Washington was set up to allow instant communication between the two heads of state to prevent similar incidents in the future.

EVENTS OF THE RICHARD NIXON PRESIDENCY

Richard Nixon is best known for the **Watergate scandal** during his presidency, but other important events marked his tenure as president, including:

- End of the Vietnam War
- Improved diplomatic relations between the US and China, and the US and the USSR
- National Environmental Policy Act passed, providing for environmental protection
- Compulsory draft ended
- Supreme Court legalized abortion in Roe v. Wade
- Watergate

The Watergate scandal of 1972 ended Nixon's presidency. Rather than face impeachment and removal from office, he **resigned** in 1974.

EVENTS OF THE GERALD FORD PRESIDENCY

Gerald Ford was appointed to the vice presidency after Nixon's vice president **Spiro Agnew** resigned in 1973 under charges of tax evasion. With Nixon's resignation, Ford became president.

Ford's presidency saw negotiations with Russia to limit nuclear arms, as well as struggles to deal with inflation, economic downturn, and energy shortages. Ford's policies sought to reduce governmental control of various businesses and reduce the role of government overall. He also worked to prevent escalation of conflicts in the Middle East.

EVENTS OF THE JIMMY CARTER PRESIDENCY

Jimmy Carter was elected as president in 1976. Faced with a budget deficit, high unemployment, and continued inflation, Carter also dealt with numerous matters of international diplomacy, including:

- **Torrijos-Carter Treaties**—the US gave control of the Panama Canal to Panama.
- **Camp David Accords**—negotiations between Anwar el-Sadat, the president of Egypt, and Menachem Begin, the Israeli Prime Minister, led to a peace treaty between Egypt and Israel.
- **Strategic Arms Limitation Talks (SALT)**—these led to agreements and treaties between the US and the Soviet Union.
- **Iran Hostage Crisis**—after the Shah of Iran was deposed, an Islamic cleric, Ayatollah Khomeini, came to power. The shah came to the US for medical treatment, and Iran demanded his return so he could stand trial. In retaliation, a group of Iranian students stormed the US Embassy in Iran. Fifty-two American hostages were held for 444 days.

Jimmy Carter was awarded the **Nobel Peace Prize** in 2002.

EVENTS OF THE RONALD REAGAN PRESIDENCY

Ronald Reagan, at 69, became the oldest American president. The two terms of his administration included notable events such as:

- Reaganomics, also known as supply-side, trickle-down, or free-market economics, involving major tax cuts
- Economic Recovery Tax Act of 1981
- First female justice appointed to the Supreme Court—Sandra Day O'Connor
- Massive increase in the national debt—from $1 trillion to $3 trillion
- Reduction of nuclear weapons via negotiations with Mikhail Gorbachev
- Iran-Contra scandal—cover-up of US involvement in revolutions in El Salvador and Nicaragua
- Deregulation of savings and loan industry
- Loss of the space shuttle *Challenger*

EVENTS OF THE GEORGE H. W. BUSH PRESIDENCY

Reagan's presidency was followed by a term under his former vice president, **George H. W. Bush**. Bush's run for president included the famous "**thousand points of light**" speech, which was instrumental in increasing his standing in the election polls. During Bush's presidency, numerous international events took place, including:

- Fall of the Berlin wall and Germany's unification
- Panamanian dictator Manuel Noriega captured and tried on drug and racketeering charges
- Dissolution of the Soviet Union
- Gulf War, or Operation Desert Storm, triggered by Iraq's invasion of Kuwait
- Tiananmen Square Massacre in Beijing, China
- Ruby Ridge
- The arrival of the World Wide Web

53

EVENTS OF THE WILLIAM CLINTON PRESIDENCY

William Jefferson "Bill" Clinton was the second president in US history to be impeached, but he was not convicted, and maintained high approval ratings in spite of the impeachment. Major events during his presidency included:

- Family and Medical Leave Act
- "Don't Ask, Don't Tell," a compromise position regarding homosexuals serving in the military
- North American Free Trade Agreement, or NAFTA
- Defense of Marriage Act
- Oslo Accords
- Siege at Waco, Texas, involving the Branch Davidians led by David Koresh
- Bombing of the Murrah Federal Building in Oklahoma City, Oklahoma
- Troops sent to Haiti, Bosnia, and Somalia to assist with domestic problems in those areas

EVENTS OF THE GEORGE W. BUSH PRESIDENCY

George W. Bush, son of George H. W. Bush, became president after Clinton. Major events during his presidency included:

- September 11, 2001, al-Qaeda terrorists hijack commercial airliners and fly into the World Trade Center towers and the Pentagon, killing nearly 3,000 Americans
- US troops sent to Afghanistan to hunt down al-Qaeda leaders, including the head of the organization, Osama Bin Laden; beginning of the War on Terror
- US troops sent to Iraq, along with a multinational coalition, to depose Saddam Hussein and prevent his deployment of suspected weapons of mass destruction
- Subprime mortgage crisis and near collapse of the financial industry, leading to the Great Recession; first of multiple government bailouts of the financial industry

BARACK OBAMA

In 2008, Barack Obama, a senator from Illinois, became the first African American US president. His administration focused on improving the lot of a country suffering from a major recession. His major initiatives included:

- Economic bailout packages
- Improvements in women's rights
- Moves to broaden LGBT rights
- Health care reform legislation
- Reinforcement of the war in Afghanistan

DONALD TRUMP

In 2016, Donald Trump, previously a real estate developer and television personality, was elected 45th president after a tumultuous election in which he won the electoral college but lost the popular vote. Marked by tension between the administration and domestic media, Trump's initiatives included:

- Appointing three Supreme Court Justices: Neil Gorsuch, Brett Kavanaugh, and Amy Coney Barrett
- Passing a major tax reform bill

- Enacting travel and emigration restrictions on eight nations: Iran, Libya, Syria, Yemen, Somalia, Chad, North Korea, and Venezuela
- Recognizing Jerusalem, rather than Tel Aviv, as the capital of Israel
- Responding to the novel coronavirus (SARS-CoV-2) outbreak

Almost completely along party lines, Donald Trump was impeached by the House on charges of abuse of power and obstruction of Congress; he was acquitted by the Senate.

Georgia History

GEORGIA CONSTITUTION OF 1777

The Georgia Constitution of 1777 was written to install a constitutional government after large meetings were held throughout the colony in 1776. The constitution was enacted without being ratified by voters, but it set up a large number of procedures that are now considered standard. It put most governmental authority in the state assembly and established a separation of powers. It also ensured the right to freedom of religion, freedom of press, and trial by jury. The 1777 constitution's description of the governmental setup and the separation of powers was not specific. It also did not provide detailed information about the judicial review system. It did not include a long bill of rights and only spelled out a handful of personal liberties. Slavery and universal suffrage were also not clearly addressed in this constitution. Subsequent constitutions would address all of these issues.

GEORGIA'S INVOLVEMENT IN FRAMING AND ADOPTION OF U.S. CONSTITUTION

After the United States declared independence from Britain on July 4, 1776, the states worked on a **confederation agreement** until 1777. The **Articles of Confederation** were initially signed in 1778 by the first of thirteen states, but it took until 1781 for all states to sign. The Articles of Confederation created a weak national government, and some states objected to the lack of provisions for potential growth. Georgia expected major growth, both in territory and population, and was one of several states that felt the one-state, one-vote philosophy in the Articles was unsatisfying. Georgian signers of the Articles of Confederation were John Walton, Edward Telfair, and Edward Langworthy. After vigorous debate, the Articles of Confederation were revised into the **U.S. Constitution** during the summer of 1787. The Constitution set up a strong central government, with distinct responsibilities. Georgia was the fourth state to **ratify** the U.S. Constitution, signing on January 2, 1788.

POLITICAL CAREERS OF ELLIS ARNALL, JIMMY CARTER, AND ANDREW YOUNG

Ellis Arnall finished UGA Law School in 1931, was elected to the Georgia House of Representatives in 1932, and became state attorney general in 1938. He became the youngest U.S. governor when he defeated Talmadge for governor in 1942. During his term, **Arnall** reformed the state constitution, lowered the voting age, paid off state debt, established teachers' retirement and repealed the poll tax. Arnall became an attorney and businessman after Talmadge defeated him in 1946. **Jimmy Carter** was elected to the Georgia Senate in 1962 and 1964 after working in the U.S. Navy and on his family's peanut farm. He ran for governor in 1970. He opposed racial segregation and improved state bureaucracies, education, and social programs while governor. He ran for President in 1976. His term occurred during economic stagnation and an energy crisis, but he worked towards social and economic reforms. He also was renowned for conducting significant international diplomacy. Carter now works on international relief programs. **Andrew Young** was a minister and a civil rights activist elected as a Democratic Congressman in 1972 and re-elected in 1974 and 1976. In 1977 he was appointed Ambassador to the United Nations. He conducted diplomacy with Africa but resigned in 1979 after meeting with Palestinian Liberation Organization leaders. In 1981 Young was elected Atlanta's mayor, and was re-elected in 1985. He ran for governor in 1990 and lost.

EFFECTS OF END OF COUNTY-UNIT SYSTEM AND RISE OF TWO-PARTY SYSTEM ON GEORGIA

The county-unit system was a method of elections used in Georgia from 1917 to 1963, when it was declared unconstitutional. Each county received a set number of votes, and the candidate who won the most votes in that county would win the county unit. 410 county units were divided by population. The eight urban regions would have six-unit votes each, the 30 town regions would have four votes apiece, and the 121 rural counties got two votes apiece. This approach skewed the voting power towards rural, low-population areas. Georgia was dominated by the Democratic Party beginning shortly after Reconstruction, which gave rise to the **county-unit system**. During the county-unit system, primaries were more important than the final election, and candidates spent a great deal of time seeking county support instead of the popular vote. After the county-unit system was eliminated, candidates needed to spend campaigning time divided by population density. During President Ronald Reagan's term, large numbers of Southerners began to join the Republican Party, which once again created party-based competition during elections. Currently, the balance has changed so much that two-party politics in Georgia are again endangered, only now by the large numbers of Republicans in the state instead of Democrats.

CIVIL RIGHTS MOVEMENT IN GEORGIA

The civil rights movement in Georgia began with the **abolition of slavery**. Black communities formed strong schools and churches despite white oppression. They supported national campaigns like Marcus Garvey's Back to Africa movement and the National Association for the Advancement of Colored People (NAACP). During the New Deal, black Georgians had greater access to public assistance and economic opportunity. Racial tension during World War II caused race riots on Georgia's military bases. In 1946, the courts ruled that blacks could vote in Democratic primaries, and black voter registration rose. Officials who would appoint black police and fund black schools were elected in cities. After Eugene Talmadge's 1946 re-election, white supremacy strengthened, and civil rights was associated with Communism through the 1950s. In the early 1960s, the Georgia cities of Albany, Savannah, Atlanta, Brunswick, Macon, and Rome saw significant unrest and protests. Protests in Augusta often generated violence. In rural areas, the civil rights movement stalled because of black poverty and traditional race-based violence. National civil rights legislation in 1964 and 1965 helped, but it did not end the economic problems that contributed to black suppression. Race riots followed in 1965-1970, but large-scale inequality continued through the 1980s, and economic repercussions endure to this day.

GEORGIA CONSTITUTION

The Georgia Constitution begins with a preamble, stating its purpose. The constitution provides for legislative, executive and judicial branches. The **legislative branch** consists of a General Assembly with two chambers, the Senate and the House of Representatives. The **executive branch** is controlled by the governor. The **judicial branch** is controlled by the state Supreme Court. The constitution clearly states the responsibilities of each of these branches. It also contains a Bill of Rights, rules for how voting will be organized, descriptions of counties and municipalities, and sections dealing with constitutional boards and commissions, taxation and finance, and education.

GEORGIA ASSEMBLY

The assembly consists of a Senate and a House of Representatives. At least 56 senators and 180 representatives are mandated by the constitution. Representatives are elected from districts apportioned by the assembly after each census. Members of the assembly serve for two years. Presiding officers are called president and president pro tempore and are elected by the members of each legislative body. The responsibility of the assembly is the **enactment of laws** for the state. Representatives must be at least 21 years of age, have lived in the state for at least two years, and also lived for at least one year in the district they represent. Senators must be at least 25, with two years of residence in Georgia and one year in their district.

EXECUTIVE BRANCH OF GEORGIA STATE GOVERNMENT

The executive branch of Georgia state government consists of the governor and lieutenant governor. The **governor** holds office for four years and may succeed himself once for second four-year term. The **lieutenant governor** is also elected to a four-year term, and is the presiding officer of the senate. The governor must be at least 30 years in age at the time of assuming office, and have been a U. S. citizen for 15 years and have resided in the state for six years. The same qualifications apply to the lieutenant governor. The lieutenant governor will assume the duties of governor if the governor is disabled. The governor will have executive power, will see that laws are enforced, will be commander in chief of the state's military forces, and may veto, approve, or take no action on each bill passed by the assembly. At the beginning of each assembly session, the governor will report on the state of the state. The governor may convene special sessions of the assembly.

COURT SYSTEM AND SELECTION OF JUDGES IN GEORGIA

The Georgia constitution establishes the following types of **courts**: magistrate courts, probate courts, juvenile courts, state courts, superior courts, court of appeals, and supreme court. In addition, the general assembly may authorize municipal courts. All courts in the state constitute a **unified judicial system** and have **unified jurisdiction**. Courts are divided into judicial circuits which must include at least one county. Each county will have a superior court, magistrate court, and probate court. Superior and state judges are elected on a nonpartisan basis for four-year terms. Supreme court justices and justices of the court of appeals have a six-year term. Appellate and superior court judges must have practiced law for seven years. The term is five years for state and juvenile court judges. All judges must reside in the area which they serve.

COUNTY GOVERNMENTS IN GEORGIA

Georgia's 159 counties are the primary political subdivisions of the state. **Counties** are responsible for administering elections and issuing marriage licenses and drivers' licenses. They can also provide local government services, especially in rural areas. Counties were first organized in 1741 when the trustees divided Georgia into two counties: Savannah and Frederica. When Georgia became a royal colony, eight "parishes" or counties were established. After the War for Independence, the number of counties began to grow as Native American tribes of Creeks and Cherokees were forced from their land and immigrants took it over. The state constitution of 1945 set an absolute limit of 159 counties, a limit that is still in force today.

CITY GOVERNMENTS IN GEORGIA

Georgia has 535 **cities** and **towns**. Each has been granted a **charter of municipal incorporation** by the general assembly. Charters establish the city or town's form of government, authority and boundaries. Among a city's functions are planning and zoning, environmental protection, police and fire services, public transportation, waste disposal and water and sewer services. Larger cities may have a municipal court to deal with traffic offenses and local ordinances. Many city governments are organized with a mayor or city manager and a city council as *governing bodies*. Another form of city government is called the *commission form*. In this type of organization, elected commissioners act as a city council and select a chairperson from among their group. Each commissioner is responsible for a different city function such as police or water/sewer. This form of government is rare for Georgia's cities but common for counties.

RELATIONSHIP BETWEEN STATE AND LOCAL GOVERNMENTS IN GEORGIA

In Georgia's legal systems, **trials** are held in one of 49 circuit courts and state courts throughout the state, and **appeals** are made at the state level to the state appeals court or supreme court. **Local governments** in Georgia are responsible for issues relating to their local situations, and for passing and enforcing local ordinances. Local ordinances may deal with such matters as speed limits on local roads, trash collection, recycling practices etc. **State government** deals with matters that affect everyone in the state, such as state taxes, the election process and speed limits on state highways.

ELECTORAL PROCESS IN GEORGIA

The state of Georgia does not have a voter residency requirement. However, voters must **register to vote** at least 30 days before an election, and first-time voters must provide photo identification. Georgia voters may vote by absentee ballot. Employees may be granted time off to vote if necessary. A simple majority of the votes is required to win an election at the state and local level. In order to vote in a federal election, a person must be a citizen of the U.S., at least 18 years old, and must register to vote. First-time voters must provide identification. Voters cast their votes in their local communities, or by absentee ballot. When voting for president and vice president of the U.S, the total of statewide ballots determines how electors sent to the Electoral College should vote for president and vice president. The group of state electors votes as a block for the candidate who received the most votes in the state. These are the primary differences between state and federal electoral systems.

INITIATIVE, REFERENDUM, AND RECALL PROCESSES IN GEORGIA

The **initiative process** allows citizens to place an issue on the ballot or propose a law to the legislature. The **referendum process** is the referral of a law, passed by the legislature, to citizens who vote for or against the law's approval. Georgia does not have initiatives or referendums at the state level. Constitutional amendments proposed by the legislature are referred for popular vote. Cities allow citizens to use the initiative process to propose ordinances and city charter amendments. The **recall process** allows the removal of elected officials from office for cause. In Georgia, citizens may propose a recall election if the elected official has committed an act of malfeasance or misconduct or violated the oath of office, failed to perform duties of the office, or misappropriated public property or funds. A recall petition must be signed by at least 15 percent of the total number of voters who voted in the election that elected the official in question. Recall petitions must be circulated within 90 days of registration.

NATIVE AMERICAN TRIBES IN GEORGIA WHEN EUROPEANS ARRIVED

At the time of the arrival of European explorers, Native Americans in Georgia were organized into **chiefdoms**. Historians have named this culture the **Mississippians**. Mississippians were probably descendants of the Moundbuilders and Woodland Indians, whose cultures were in decline by 1500. Mississippian culture is divided into early, middle and late. The Spanish came to Georgia during the late Mississippian period, an era when the large chiefdoms of the early and middle period had disintegrated into smaller entities throughout the state. In the late Mississippian period, chiefdoms were organized around villages situated along the rivers of Georgia, and the land surrounding those villages. At the time of Hernan De Soto's exploration from 1540--1543, the largest chiefdom was that of the **Coosa** in northern Georgia. The Coosa chief ruled over not only his own village but a group of about seven smaller chiefdoms as well.

IMPACT ON NATIVE AMERICANS BY SPANISH EXPLORATIONS OF GEORGIA BETWEEN 1539—1543

The most positive effect of the **De Soto expedition** of 1540—1543 was the gathering of **information**. Spanish chroniclers of De Soto's expedition described in detail each Native American chiefdom they visited. Since most of these chiefdoms subsequently disappeared due to illness or subjugation, these accounts provide all that is known about them. The most negative effect of this expedition was the spread of **diseases** by the Europeans such as smallpox. Native Americans, having no previous exposure to these diseases, suffered losses of life in large numbers. It is likely that information brought back to Spain by members of the De Soto expedition prompted the ultimate settlement of the **De Luna colony** near the chiefdom of Coosa in northern Georgia. While there, the colonists assisted the Native American tribe of Coosa in a raid against another tribe, the

Napochin, in what is now Tennessee. The De Luna colony failed after several months and the colonists returned to Mexico.

FORMATION OF CREEK, CHEROKEE, AND SEMINOLE NATIVE AMERICAN TRIBES

Many of the original chiefdoms in Georgia were **depopulated** due to epidemics of European diseases such as smallpox. Populations were also diminished by the capture of tribal members by European slave traders. A European interest in deerskins prompted some native groups to move from their original locations along rivers to areas where deer could be found and hunted in large numbers and their skins sold or bartered to Europeans. Chiefdoms disintegrated due to all of these reasons, and former chiefdom members were scattered and basically leaderless. The Native Americans who survived eventually organized themselves into **new tribes**, the largest of which were the Creek, Cherokee, and Seminole tribes.

PURPOSE FOR INITIAL SETTLEMENT OF GEORGIA BY SPANIARDS

Although the Spanish exploration of Georgia and other southern areas was motivated by a search for gold, actual settlement came from different goals. **The initial settlement** of Georgia was probably motivated by the desire of the Spaniards to **convert** the natives to Christianity. Several colonies were unsuccessfully attempted in the 1500s, including the Ayllon colony of 600 members, called San Miguel de Gualdape. This settlement lasted only six weeks due to a slave uprising and disagreements among the colonists. The De Luna colony of 140 soldiers and 2 priests settled in the Coosa chiefdom for several months but ultimately returned to Mexico. These colonists may have been motivated by a desire for land as well as an effort to spread their Catholic faith. In the 1600s several missions were established in various parts of Georgia by Spanish Franciscan priests in order to convert the Indians.

FRENCH IMMIGRATION TO GEORGIA

In the 1700s and 1800s large groups of **French immigrants** settled in Georgia. Groups of **Huguenots** came in search of freedom from religious persecution which they had endured in France. During the French and Indian War, 1754—1763, **Acadian settlers**, distrusted by the English, were sent from Canada to Georgia. After the war ended, the Acadian settlers left Georgia, but many did not return to Canada and instead settled in Haiti. Between 1790 and 1793, French immigrants to Georgia came, fleeing the **French Revolution**. In 1791, groups of French-speaking immigrants arrived in Georgia from **Haiti** because of a slave rebellion there.

ENGLISH IMMIGRATION TO GEORGIA

The main reason English settlers came to Georgia was the availability of **land**, which they could obtain cheaply by bartering with the Native Americans, or take without payment by simply settling someplace, building a cabin and farming the surrounding land. Land was one of the enticements offered groups of immigrants by the trusteeship that governed the area from 1732-1752. To establish the Georgia colony, the trustees offered colonists free land, provisions for one year, and tools.

MAJOR EVENTS OF THE TRUSTEE PERIOD IN GEORGIA'S HISTORY

For the first twenty years of its existence as a British colony, from 1732 to 1752, Georgia was governed from England by a board of unpaid **trustees** who were prohibited from owning land in Georgia. The Georgia colony's charter did not provide for local government. The colonists, having no way to complain about decisions made from across the Atlantic, eventually sent a representative with a list of grievances that was presented to the British parliament, which sided with the trustees. Three important laws were passed by the trustees during their 20-year tenure. The first required that traders west of the Savannah River have a **Georgia license**. The second prohibited **rum** in Georgia. The third outlawed **slavery**. All three laws were eventually revised. In 1750 the trustees authorized an elected assembly in Georgia, but it was to be only an advisory body. The trustee period ended in 1752 when the charter expired and Georgia became a royal colony.

DEVELOPMENT OF GEORGIA AS ROYAL COLONY

Georgia became a **royal colony** in 1752. Its first appointed governor, **John Reynolds**, arrived from England in 1754. Reynolds lacked the political skills to govern effectively. He alienated many of the colonists. He also did not get along with the Native Americans. Reynolds was recalled in 1756 and replaced by **Henry Ellis**, from 1757 to 1760. Ellis had the skills Reynolds had lacked. He persuaded Georgians of the need for taxes. He regulated trade with Native Americans, established forts to protect the provinces, and established eight electoral districts. He maintained good relations with the Native American Creeks. His only failure was his effort to abolish slavery. He left office due to poor health in 1760 and was replaced by **James Wright**, who continued the progress begun by Ellis. As criticism of the British colonial government increased in Georgia in 1775-76, Wright was basically stripped of his authority by locally formed government. He left Georgia on board a British ship in 1776.

GEORGIA'S ROLE IN AMERICAN REVOLUTION

Georgia joined the move for **American independence** in May, 1775, when Georgians heard of the battles at Lexington and Concord in Massachusetts. In July, 1775, Georgians gathered in a **Provincial Congress** at Savannah, elected delegates to the Continental Congress and formed a Council of Safety to govern the colony, supplanting Governor Wright's authority. Trade with England was banned. Three delegates from Georgia signed the **Declaration of Independence** in Philadelphia on July 4, 1776. On May 23, 1776, British ships sailed into Savannah harbor and seized merchant ships loaded with rice. There was little other direct conflict until December 28, 1778, when British Lieutenant Colonel Archibald Campbell captured Savannah with 3,000 soldiers. A month later, he seized Augusta, but withdrew when he learned that 1,400 South Carolinian soldiers were coming to the defense of Augusta. Two important battles had opposite results. The **Battle of Kettle Creek** was a victory for Georgian patriots, but the defeat at the **Battle of Briar Creek** resulted in southern Georgia remaining a British colony.

STRENGTHS AND WEAKNESSES OF GEORGIA CONSTITUTION OF 1777

The Georgia constitution of 1777 was created at a constitutional convention attended by delegates from 12 future counties and from the towns of Savannah and Sudbury. The constitution they adopted was considered somewhat radical because it allowed all men to **vote** who held property valued at ten pounds, and also gave the vote to artisans. The constitution created **counties** within the state. It also provided for an **assembly** which would pass laws for the state and also select the governor, judges and other state officers. Foreseeing that changes in this constitution might be needed, the constitution provided for future **conventions** where delegates could revise the constitution. Although the constitution provided for three branches, (legislative, executive, judicial) in actual practice the government was run by the **assembly**, which could hire and fire governors and judges. This was the main weakness of the constitution.

GEORGIA'S ROLE IN FRAMING AND ADOPTION OF U.S. CONSTITUTION

Georgia sent four **delegates** to the convention in Philadelphia that created the U.S. Constitution. An issue important to Georgia was how **slaves** would be counted when population determined the number of representatives. The decision to count a slave as three-fifths of a person was a compromise that Georgia and other slaveholding states accepted. Another issue was the prohibition of slave trade. Georgia's delegates threatened to withdraw if prohibition of slave trade became part of the constitution. A compromise was finally enacted providing that congress would acquire that authority in twenty years. The final version of the constitution was signed by Georgia delegates **Abraham Baldwin** and **William Few**. The other two delegates did not sign. Georgia was the fourth state to **ratify** the U. S. Constitution. A convention was held in Augusta, consisting of three delegates from each county. The sole purpose of the convention was to examine the proposed U.S Constitution and either ratify or reject it. The convention's letter of ratification was signed by every delegate.

UNIVERSITY OF GEORGIA

The Georgia state assembly authorized the incorporation of a **state-supported university** in 1785, the first state university in the United States. Forty thousand acres of land were set aside for the university. Joshua Meigs was named the first university president, and the first class graduated in 1804. In 1843 the traditional classical curriculum was expanded to include classes in law. In 1872 the university received federal funds to establish classes in agriculture and mechanical arts. It grew from a liberal arts college to a major research university. Today the university system of Georgia is governed statewide by a board of regents.

SPREAD OF BAPTIST AND METHODIST CHURCHES IN GEORGIA BETWEEN 1789 AND 1840

During the period of slavery in Georgia, several religious groups attempted to serve the spiritual needs of slaves. The **First African Baptist Church of Savannah** was founded in 1777 under the leadership of **George Leile**, a slave who held services for slaves on plantations. Leile traveled along the Savannah River preaching and converting slaves. Around this time, **Baptist churches** were founded in Savannah and Augusta, and more Baptist congregations were planted throughout the state. During the period from 1790 to 1830, known as the **Second Great Awakening**, Protestant values were spread among both black and white populations of Georgia. Methodist preachers known as "**circuit riders**" traveled on horseback throughout rural Georgia. By 1790, Methodist Georgians numbered 2,294 members. New converts were also acquired through outdoor revival services called **camp meetings**. Methodist evangelists preached to congregations of slaves on the plantations. By 1861, more than 11,000 slaves worshiped in these missions, and even more in established Methodist churches. Methodists were interested in education and founded several colleges, including some for blacks.

YAZOO LAND FRAUD

The Yazoo land fraud occurred when several Georgia governors and state officials, serving between 1794 and 1803, sold large amounts of public land to speculators for very low prices, actually selling more land than was available. Ownership of some of the land was still claimed by Native American tribes such as the Creeks. The first land sale in 1789 fell through when the speculative groups attempted to pay for the land with old, worthless currency. In 1794 four land speculation companies purchased from the state of Georgia 40 million acres of land for $500,000. They were soon exposed for having used bribery to obtain this land. Public outcries forced the next governor to nullify the deal and publicly burn all copies of the bill. Georgia then developed a lottery system as a fairer means of distributing public land. The effect of this scandal was a loss of faith in state government, and a decline of immigration to Georgia because of the uncertainty of obtaining land.

EFFECTS OF RAILROADS ON GEORGIA

In the 1830s, **railroads** were constructed linking Athens, Augusta, Macon, Savannah and the new city of Atlanta which became a **rail hub** for the entire South. Railroads made it possible to ship and receive goods quickly and for people to travel easily within and beyond the state. The coming of the railroads added greatly to Georgia's economy. Railroads linked Georgia to other states like Tennessee and opened up trade with those states, leading to greater production of goods, mostly cotton, within the state and greater prosperity due to the sale of those goods.

EFFECTS OF COTTON GIN ON GEORGIA'S ECONOMY

Before the invention of the cotton gin, production of cotton was highly labor-intensive. Slaves picked the cotton and more slaves pulled out the seeds one at a time, a slow process. With the **cotton gin**, cotton could be prepared for market much more quickly and easily, and cotton production increased. Cotton production became the single most profitable industry in Georgia. Unfortunately, plantation owners still needed slaves to pick the cotton and run it through the gin so they continued to oppose any action to abolish slavery. With cotton as its major industry, Georgia was more agricultural than the industrial states in the North. Another effect of continuously growing cotton was the depletion of nutrients in the soil. The production of cotton per acre decreased over time, which led to a desire to acquire more land.

REMOVAL OF CREEKS AND CHEROKEES FROM GEORGIA

The reasons for the removal of the Creeks and Cherokees from Georgia lay in the desire of white settlers for more **cotton** producing land, and the discovery of **gold** on Cherokee land. The Creeks were the first to go. Governor Troup, elected in 1825, forced the removal of all the Creeks from their land by 1827. The Cherokees met a similar fate. The **Treaty of Hopewell** in 1785 granted Cherokees independent nation status. However, in the **Compact of 1802** the U. S. government agreed to remove the Cherokees from Georgia. Georgia politicians pressured the federal government to act on this compact. Cherokees appealed to the U.S. Supreme Court which found in their favor, but the decision was not enforced. In 1827 and 1831 the Georgia legislature seized Cherokee land and abolished the Cherokees' government. In 1838 the U.S army marched all Georgia Cherokees over the "**Trail of Tears**" to new land in Oklahoma. Now immigrants and land speculators were able to purchase former Indian lands from the Georgia government.

GEORGIA'S PROPOSED SECESSION

The main reason southern states, including Georgia, considered **secession** was slavery. The economy of the South depended on slave labor and Southerners were sure that abolitionists in Congress wanted to abolish it. Another controversy existed over admitting territories and states to the union as slave or free. When **Lincoln**, representing the anti-slavery Republican Party, became president, southern states panicked, fearing Congress under his leadership would abolish slavery. Each state held conventions to discuss seceding. Secessionists argued that the Northern states were determined to abolish slavery, upon which the economy of the South depended. The opposing group, called **cooperationists**, suggested that southern states could join together to obtain cooperation from congress by threatening secession unless congress promised not to abolish slavery. This argument was weakened at Georgia's convention by the fact that several southern states had already seceded. At the convention, delegates voted 166 to 130 in favor of immediate secession. Georgia later participated in the convention held in Montgomery, Alabama to draw up a constitution for the newly created **Confederate States**.

GEORGIA'S MILITARY ROLE IN CIVIL WAR

The first Union action of the war was to blockade southern ports so goods could be neither exported nor imported. The first battle in Georgia was the successful attack by Union soldiers on **Fort Pulaski**, above Savannah harbor, on April 11, 1862. Union control of the fort enforced the blockade of Savannah harbor. Next, the Union attacked Georgia's transportation systems, the Mississippi River and the railroads, to cut off all supply routes to the South. Georgian troops won an important battle at **Chicamauga** in September, but it was their last victory. On May 8, 1864, Union **General Sherman** led 98,000 troops toward Georgia. Battles were fought all over the state. Confederate troops led by a skillful **General Johnson** were forced to retreat again and again. Atlanta turned itself into a fortress with palisades around the city, but Union troops surrounded the city. When Sherman arrived, Atlanta surrendered. The Confederate army was subsequently overcome in other locations, and the war ended with **General Lee's surrender** at Appomattox courthouse on April 26, 1865.

Georgia's Situation Immediately After End of Civil War

In the immediate aftermath of the war, Georgia was in chaos. Food was scarce, drought affected crop production, there was no government, and bands of Confederate soldiers looted everything they found. In January, after a meeting between General Sherman, War Secretary Stanton and 20 educated black leaders, an order was issued giving any black freedman who asked for it **forty acres of land** along the coast. The Confederate government of Georgia was abolished, and President Johnson appointed an attorney from Columbus, **Charles Johnson**, to govern the state until Georgia could draw up a constitution acceptable to the federal government. That constitution was required to repeal the secession declaration, end slavery, abandon an $18 million debt to the Confederacy, and express loyalty to the United States government. The state complied in December 1865, but its troubles were not over. Newly freed slaves presented an enormous challenge.

Effects of War and Reconstruction on Georgia's Economy

Georgia's economy had been essentially **agricultural**, and during the war the means of shipping products to market had been damaged or destroyed. Georgia's railroad system was in ruins. Conflict arose between the newly freed slaves and their former masters, who now sought to hire them and pay them for the work they had been doing as slaves. The former slaves did not want to work the long hours they had formerly been forced to work, and they did not want to accept the small wages offered by plantation owners. A **Freedman's Bureau** was established to deal with problems like these, but it was not very effective and those freedmen who had received the land grants from Sherman and Stanton were driven from their newly acquired land.

Political Effects of Reconstruction on Georgia

Although Georgia had complied in 1865 with the federal government's requirements for a new state constitution, in 1867 radical Republicans who controlled Congress made three new demands. Georgia must ratify the **14th amendment** (which gave voting rights to all male citizens including blacks), allow blacks to vote, and draw up a new **constitution** once blacks had the right to vote on it. Delegates to this new Georgia constitutional convention represented a different group from the traditional plantation holders and wealthy businessmen. The new delegates included farmers and former slaves. The constitution they created included the federal demands but also gave **women** the right to own land, and protected farmers from debt collectors. However, when the new state government convened in 1868, Democrats refused to seat black delegates because although they had been given the right to vote they had not specifically been granted the right to hold office. Democrats also opposed ratification of the 14th amendment, and only under threat of federal military reoccupation did this occur.

New South

The New South was a term applied to the South after Reconstruction by wealthy white southerners who visualized a future South in which southern states, including Georgia, would move away from their mostly agricultural economic base (mainly the growth of cotton) and become industrialized and prosperous like the North, with equal opportunity afforded blacks and whites. The federal government assisted Georgia's industrialization by funding the rebuilding of the **railroads**. Civil leaders like Henry Grady, editor of The Atlantic Constitution newspaper, encouraged northern investment in southern industries. Three major industries emerged in the South: **cotton mills**, **iron and steel factories**, and **tobacco processing**. The southern economy was improving, but racial relations were not. Southerners continued to **segregate** blacks and treat them as second-class citizens. Few blacks managed to vote because of intimidation and the introduction of "poll taxes" paid in order to vote, taxes which the majority of blacks could not afford. The **New South** represented a renewed economy but racial relations remained essentially unchanged.

POPULIST MOVEMENT IN GEORGIA

The Populist movement arose in the late 1880s as a reaction to falling cotton prices and the rising cost of railroad freight. A group called the **Farmers Alliance** pressured the government to remedy these problems by printing more money. The Alliance also favored direct election of senators and government takeover of the railroads. When the Republican and Democratic parties refused to press for these reforms, some members of the Alliance formed the **People's Party** which became known as the **Populist Party**. Populism gained wide support in Georgia. After the Panic of 1893, a severe depression, the Populist Party gained strength with its proposals for financial and economic reform. The Populist candidate for Georgia governor lost a close election as did the Georgia Populist candidate for Congress. Populists charged election fraud in both these cases, but the issue was not investigated. In the election for president in 1894, Populists joined with Democrats to support William Jennings Bryan. After Bryan's defeat, the party slowly disintegrated.

SIGNIFICANCE OF JIM CROW AND EFFECTS ON GEORGIAN SOCIETY

Jim Crow laws were laws passed in the southern states during the 1880s through the 1920s to restrict the rights of **African Americans**. These laws provided for supposedly separate but equal schools, public restrooms, restaurants, public transportation and other facilities for African Americans and whites. Jim Crow laws regulated voting, and some required literacy and/or residency tests as well as poll taxes, with the result that most African Americans and some poor whites were unable to vote. The **Jim Crow laws** solidified the stratification of Georgia's population into two groups: black and white citizens with highly unequal opportunities.

DISENFRANCHISEMENT AND RACIAL VIOLENCE IN GEORGIA

African Americans lived within the constrictions of **segregation** as well as they could. Black schools made extreme efforts to educate their students, and the result was a large growth in **literacy**. At the end of the Civil war, less than 7 percent of the newly freed African Americans could read and write. By 1880 this number had risen to 45% and by 1930 70% of African Americans were literate. African Americans also formed lodges and social groups, volunteer fire departments, and life insurance companies. Because of segregation, African Americans in the South had to adopt postures of submission. They were not addressed as Mr. or Mrs., but instead called "boy," "girl," "uncle," or "auntie." They expected to be waited on last in stores, eat only in certain all-black restaurants, and to sit in the back of a city bus. They endured these indignities because they had no choice. Powerful societies such as the **Ku Klux Klan** dealt violently with any African Americans suspected of defiance or even disrespect.

EFFECTS OF WORLD WAR I ON GEORGIA

The first effect of World War I on Georgia was **economic**. The British blockaded ports in Germany and Austria where Georgia normally shipped cotton, tobacco, and timber. The creation of war-related industries encouraged the "**Great Migration**" of African Americans from Georgia to northern states where factories needed workers. The Great Migration was also encouraged by the rebirth of the Ku Klux Klan and increased racial violence in Georgia. By 1930, ten percent of Georgia's African American population had moved from the state. When the U.S. entered the war in 1917, Georgia enthusiastically supported the war. However, many were less supportive of the **draft**. Many white landowners did not want to give up their black sharecroppers. The worst disaster of the war for Georgia was the sinking of the troop ship **Otranto** off the coast of Scotland in a bad storm. About 130 soldiers from Georgia were among the total of 370 who lost their lives.

EFFECTS OF WORLD WAR II ON GEORGIA

The war provided new **jobs** in Georgia and promoted **industrialization**. The economy of the state recovered from the Great Depression due to an influx of federal dollars that were used for military installations and production of items needed for the war. In the coastal region, **shipbuilding** became a major industry. As in other states, **women** became an important part of the working population. **African Americans** also prospered from new employment opportunities, although there were some clashes over blacks working in the same workspace with whites. After the war, industries easily converted their production to **civilian manufacturing**, and the prosperity of wartime continued after the war ended. About 320,000 Georgians served in the armed forces during the war.

EFFECTS OF BOLL WEEVIL AND DROUGHT ON GEORGIA'S ECONOMY DURING INTERWAR PERIOD

The boll weevil is a small beetle. Adult **boll weevils** puncture cotton buds and lay eggs there. When the larvae hatch, they feed on the cotton bolls, thereby destroying them. The boll weevil ravaged **cotton production** in Georgia and other southern states in the period between World War I and World War II, and beyond. Production of cotton dropped dramatically from 2.8 million bales in 1914 to 600,000 bales in 1923. In the 1920s, spraying cotton crops with calcium arsenate dust had some effect, but the industry never completely recovered. An additional blow to cotton farmers was brought about by a series of **droughts**, the first in 1924—27 and another in 1930—1935. These droughts had a serious affect on agriculture and industry in Georgia.

POLITICAL CAREER OF EUGENE TALMADGE

Eugene Talmadge's political career began when he was elected **agriculture commissioner** of the State of Georgia in 1926 and re-elected several times. He claimed to be an advocate of farmers. Some members of the state legislature accused him of violations of state law, including use of state funds for his personal advantage. Despite these accusations, **Talmadge** ran for and was elected **governor** in 1932 and re-elected in 1934. He was a strong leader. When the Georgia legislature refused to pass his recommended reduction in automobile license fees, he reduced them by executive order. When a committee elected by voters refused to lower utility rates, he dissolved the committee and appointed a new one favorable to his viewpoint. He removed the state attorney general and comptroller from their offices when they proved uncooperative. He ran for U.S. Senator unsuccessfully in 1936 and 1938 and was elected governor for a third time in 1940. He was a strong supporter of segregation and the Jim Crow laws. He died in 1946.

IMPACT OF MAJOR NEW DEAL PROGRAMS ON GEORGIA BEFORE WORLD WAR II

New Deal programs brought **electricity** to rural areas, paid for the construction of new **highways**, and brought about improved **housing and health care** in Georgia. President Franklin Roosevelt spent a great deal of time in Warm Springs, and became sympathetic to Georgia's needs. Opponents of the **New Deal** opposed it because they believed it constituted government interference with state independence. At the time of the beginning of New Deal assistance, farmers in Georgia desperately needed government help. A series of federal laws attempted to control the price and production of cotton with the goal of making cotton farming more profitable. Cotton prices rose and fell like a roller coaster during the 1930s, but with the aid of government programs, prices stabilized in the late 1930s. Another New Deal program, the **NYA (National Youth Authority) program** in Georgia helped hundreds of African American and white students obtain an education.

Transformation of Agriculture After World War II

After World War II, Georgia shifted from a mainly **agricultural** state to a more **industrialized** state. The percentage of rural population decreased from 85% in 1900 to 25% in 1990, due in part to the movement of people to cities. Georgia moved from single crop agriculture (cotton) to more diverse agricultural production. Most of the farms in Georgia are still family farms and average only about $10,000 annual income each. Along with cotton, the major production is in poultry, eggs, peanuts and pecans.

Effects of Hartsfield International Airport on Georgia's Economy

Hartsfield International Airport was constructed on the grounds of **Candler Airport** in Atlanta, which was founded in 1926. During World War II, Candler was a military airport. In 1946 it was renamed **Atlanta Municipal Airport**, and became a hub for the aircraft industry. In 1957 work was begun on a new terminal for the busy airport. In that year, more than two million people flew into and out of this airport. In 1961 the new $2 million airport was opened, named **Hartsfield International Airport**, and quickly became the largest and busiest in the country. The airport is considered the largest employer in the state, with more than 53,000 employees. It has contributed greatly to Georgia's economy because of its two-billion-dollar payroll.

Growth of Atlanta After World War II

Atlanta began in the 1800s as a small town named **Terminus** because of its location at the terminus of the Western and Atlantic railroad. It grew into a major city during the early 1900s. During World War II, Atlanta's economy boomed. Thousands of military troops were stationed there, and 100 Atlanta businesses including **Bell Aircraft** and **Coca-Cola** converted their total output to wartime production. After the war these businesses continued to flourish with production now geared toward civilian consumers. New businesses were added, such as **Ford** and **General Motors** factories. Bell Aircraft was reincarnated as **Lockheed Georgia**. These businesses attracted thousands of workers and Atlanta's population grew rapidly. The city enlarged its borders and built a network of freeways. Some of this construction required land that had previously been used for housing, and the result was a housing shortage, particularly among the African American population.

Herman Talmadge, Ellis Arnall, Lester Maddox, and Jimmy Carter

Herman Talmadge was Georgia's governor from 1947 through 1954. He brought about a **sales tax** to fund education, attracted new industry, and promoted the timber industry. He also favored **segregation**. Talmadge served four terms in the U.S senate, beginning in 1956. He was an advocate for rural citizens and farmers and worked for balanced budgets.

Elliss Arnall was governor from 1943 to 1947. He successfully accomplished ten **reforms**, including repeal of the poll tax and revision of the state constitution. He also paid off the state's **debt**.

Lester Maddox became governor in 1966 during the controversial period of **desegregation** in Georgia. Despite his segregationist leanings, Maddox appointed more **African Americans** to public offices than any other governor.

Jimmy Carter is the only Georgian elected U.S. President. Prior to this, he served in the Georgia assembly, and was governor for one term. Carter championed **equal rights** for women and minorities, and financial stability. He was given the **Nobel Peace Prize** in 2000.

COUNTY-UNIT SYSTEM

The county-unit system in Georgia was a voting method in which votes were cast by counties rather than individuals. Counties were divided into three types: rural, town and urban. **Rural counties** had 2 unit votes, **town counties** had 4 unit votes and **urban counties** had 6. Although counties were categorized according to population, rural counties actually had a disproportionate control over voting. Rural voters tended to be more pro-segregation than residents of town and urban counties, and the result was that civil rights actions in Georgia were impeded. The **county-unit system** ended when the Supreme Court ruled that the system was contrary to the concept of one-man, one-vote. When the total popular vote determined results of an election, Georgia became more liberal in its laws.

EFFECTS OF TWO-PARTY SYSTEM ON GEORGIA

After the Civil War, Georgia, composed essentially of white voters, had a **one-party system**, the **Democratic Party**. This system began to change in 1948 when the national Democratic Party adopted a position in favor of the civil rights movement at their national convention. A number of southern Democrats left the party and formed a party called "**The States Rights Party**" also known as the **Dixiecrats**. The party didn't last long, but its existence marked the beginning of a movement in the state away from a single-party structure. In 1962 four **Republicans** were elected to the Georgia state senate. In 1964, the state voted for Republican Barry Goldwater for president. After that, the Republican Party in Georgia continued to grow.

MARTIN LUTHER KING, JR., MAYNARD JACKSON, AND ANDREW YOUNG

Dr. Martin Luther King, Jr. was a Baptist minister in Alabama at the beginning of the civil rights movement. He became a **civil rights activist**, led the bus boycott in Montgomery in 1955, and was a founding member of the Southern Christian Leadership Conference. He advocated nonviolent methods of protest and had a profound influence on the progress of the civil rights movement. In 1964 he received the **Nobel Peace Prize**. He was assassinated in 1968.

Maynard Jackson was the first African American **mayor** of a southern city, elected Mayor of Atlanta in 1973. During his tenure, he began **affirmative action programs** that resulted in more city business being awarded to African American companies.

Andrew Young, born in 1932, has served as a pastor, mayor, congressman and United Nations representative. As a young man, Andrew Young became interested in the writings of Mohandas K. Gandhi, who advocated **nonviolent resistance**. Young encouraged African Americans during the 1960s to follow this ideal as they pushed for their civil rights. Today he is regarded as a wise senior spokesman for African Americans.

NEW IMMIGRANT COMMUNITIES IN GEORGIA

Immigrant communities in Georgia include documented and undocumented **Hispanic** immigrants, and immigrants from **Asia** and the **Middle East**. A study published in 2006 concluded that immigrants, even undocumented immigrants to Georgia, pay more in taxes than they use in state services, making their presence profitable for the state. The influx of new cultural influences has enriched the traditions in the state and expanded religious variety. While it is still mostly Protestant, Georgia now includes Buddhists, Muslims, Catholics, and members of other faiths.

MAJOR NATIVE AMERICAN GROUPS LIVING IN GEORGIA IN THE PAST

Early Native Americans living in Georgia were part of the **Mississippian** culture. These groups built mounds, on which sat temples that overlooked central town areas. These groups had sophisticated religious, trading, and craft traditions. The later **Creek Nation** is believed to be the descendants of these "**Moundbuilders**." The Creek Nation (Muskogee) was a large collection of Native American groups living throughout Georgia before the mid-16th century. These groups were agriculturalists. Contact with white settlers and Cherokee Indians from elsewhere in the southeast forced the Creeks westward, away from the coasts. Creek populations suffered from these land battles and from sickness brought by the whites. Their lands were all taken by 1827. **Cherokee** Indians were a large population of Native Americans in the Southeast U.S. They survived somewhat better than the Creeks because they assimilated white culture and had large numbers of people. They were also affected by illnesses of white settlers. Conflict between the white settlers over land eventually drove Cherokees west along the "**Trail of Tears**," where thousands of Native Americans died.

HISTORY OF EUROPEAN CONTACT WITH NATIVE AMERICAN GROUPS IN GEORGIA

Georgia was first settled by Europeans in **1733**, even though white settlers had been in North America for nearly 200 years by then. Europeans displaced Native Americans and brought diseases that Native Americans had no immunity to, so illnesses as simple as a common cold could kill scores of Indians. At first, Georgia settlers negotiated and traded with Native Americans. As the population grew, Indians began to be displaced westward by the colonists, who continually sought more land. Once the United States became independent, it enacted a series of **treaties** with Indian nations that gradually took away more rights and territory. Georgia passed a law in 1828 that made all Cherokee Indian laws void in 1830. Gold was discovered on Cherokee lands in North Georgia in 1829, which spurred white settlers to remove Native Americans from their lands completely. After a series of legal battles, Georgia lobbied for the creation of the **Treaty of New Echota**, which was signed in 1835. This Treaty ordered the removal of all Native Americans beyond the Mississippi River within two years.

TRAIL OF TEARS

The **Treaty of New Echota** was implemented in 1838. To begin, United States Army troops rounded up all Native American groups in the Eastern states and held them in forts throughout North Carolina, Alabama, Georgia, and Tennessee. Native Americans were treated cruelly during their movement into these internment camps. Eventually, Indian leaders received permission from the U.S. government to remove themselves beyond the Mississippi River. 16 groups of 1,000 Native Americans each went west on the "**Trail of Tears**." About 3,000 of them traveled west by water, moving up the Tennessee River to the Ohio River, and on to the Arkansas River. The rest traveled west by a number of different land routes. Food was scarce and traveling was difficult. Drought was a constant problem during the removal. 3,000-4,000 people died during the land-route removal. The remaining Cherokees settled along the Illinois River and developed a system of self-governance similar to the U.S. Government. After the Civil War, the Cherokees again lost their land claims and were further marginalized.

CURRENT POPULATIONS OF NATIVE AMERICANS LIVING IN GEORGIA TODAY

Very few Native Americans live in Georgia today. Only 0.3% of the state's population claims a **Native American** identity. When Cherokees were being rounded up for internment prior to their trip westward during the "Trail of Tears" period, many who escaped joined a group in North Carolina. This particular group had signed a treaty with the U.S. Government in 1819 that had granted them lands separate from the Cherokee Nation (which was taken away during the Treaty of New Echota) and granted them American citizenship. This group, along with the Oconaluftee Indians and escaping Cherokees, formed the **Eastern Band of Cherokee Indians**. They still live in North Carolina today.

MAJOR EVENTS DURING COLONIAL PERIOD OF GEORGIA'S HISTORY

Early settlement began around **1670**, when an English settlement was placed near present-day South Carolina. Spanish missions had already been located for 100 years on the Sea Islands of Georgia. Fighting finally drove the Spanish settlers to what is now Florida. In the early 1700s, interest peaked in establishing an English settlement in Georgia. Georgia was first settled by **poor English citizens** with permission from King George II in 1733. The colony was a buffer between Florida and South Carolina, and also a place to put English debtors. The citizens were not permitted to govern themselves and were overseen by royally-appointed trustees. Early settlements were organized into townships that were relatively isolated from each other. Georgia became a **royal colony** in 1752 when the trustees ceded power over the colony to the King after England stopped providing important subsidies. In 1776, the colony joined 12 others in signing the **Declaration of Independence**, even though there were many English loyalists in Georgia.

GEORGIA'S INVOLVEMENT IN AMERICAN REVOLUTION

Although Georgia sent three delegates to sign the Declaration of Independence in 1776, the colony was not greatly affected by the start of the **Revolutionary War**. Most of the early fighting took place in the northern colonies or in naval battles. In 1778, Britain captured **Savannah** and drove the patriot government to Augusta. Fighting at the **Battle of Kettle Creek** in Wilkes County prevented the entire colony from being occupied. After that battle, Loyalist forces in Georgia were essentially dispersed into the Carolinas. In 1779, American and French forces unsuccessfully laid siege to Savannah, still occupied by the British. Until the end of the Revolutionary War, some loyalists remained along the coast in the only other stronghold than New York. Georgia signed the **U.S. Constitution** in 1788. The state had eight counties at the time.

FOUNDING AND HISTORY OF UNIVERSITY OF GEORGIA

The University of Georgia was founded by the Georgia General Assembly in 1785. It was the first university established by a state government. The General Assembly designated 40,000 acres of land to a **Senatus Academicus** for a college or seminary, and the Senatus began the university in 1799. The college was situated on the banks of the Oconee River. The first classes were held in 1801, and the first class graduated in 1804. The Senatus Academicus was replaced by a **Board of Trustees** in 1859. The university closed during the Civil War for three years, after which many veterans enrolled. The university added an **Agricultural school** in 1872 to take advantage of the recent land-grant legislation in the United States government which granted additional land to academic institutions so that they could teach agriculture and mechanics. **Females** were admitted in 1903 and the first **black** students were admitted in 1961.

SPREAD OF PROTESTANT RELIGION AND EFFECTS ON GEORGIA'S CULTURE

During the late 1700s and early 1800s, great religious fervor spread through American Protestant communities. After about 1730, the **First Great Awakening** significantly altered Protestant philosophies such as Congregational and Presbyterian, and strengthened Baptist and Methodist followings. Methodists believed in personal piety, morality, abolition, and evangelism. Baptists believed in conservative philosophies, individual baptism, and evangelism. **Abolition** caused Northern and Southern Methodist churches to split; this split was mended after slavery became illegal. Anti-slavery Methodist teachings may have provided a foothold to the Baptists, whose churches have dominated the southern U.S. ever since. The **Second Great Awakening** occurred around 1800, and reached out to people who had not previously been believers. The Baptist and Methodist faiths gained many followers during this time. In the state of Georgia today, these religions are predominant: 39% of residents are Baptist, and 12% of the residents are Methodist.

Technologies That Revolutionized Georgia's Economy and Social System During Late 1700s and Early 1800s

Eli Whitney patented the **cotton gin**, which efficiently removed seeds from large quantities of cotton, in 1794. The Georgia climate was well-suited for growing cotton, and large slave-owning plantations could now produce a very lucrative crop. Even though cotton could be seeded easily, slaves were still needed to harvest it by hand. Because of this, the southern economy depended heavily on both slavery and cotton and, by about 1860, cotton provided about 60% of U.S. exports.

After the invention of the **spinning jenny** in 1770 and the **rotary motion steam engine** in 1781, large-scale textile factories were built in Britain and the United States. At the same time, railroads were being built throughout the United States from 1785 to 1830. The **McCormick reaper** was patented in 1830, which allowed even more efficient ways to harvest crops. Cotton and other crops could get to market on the railroads more easily than before, making large-scale agriculture practical even though it was far removed from urban centers. During the **American Industrial Revolution** from 1810 to 1860, textiles became a large part of the U.S. economy.

Events of the Yazoo Land Fraud

The Yazoo Land Fraud was land speculation that occurred from 1785 to 1803. In 1785, the **Combined Society** was secretly formed at the same time Bourbon County, GA was founded on the Mississippi River. The Combined Society's purpose was to leverage politicians for land grants, which would then be sold at inflated prices for the Society's gain. Bourbon County was the first parcel of land granted for sale this way. The United States Government pressured Georgia to disband the county in 1788, ending the Combined Society. In 1789, the South Carolina Yazoo Company, the Virginia Yazoo Company, and the Tennessee Company were formed to buy land from the Georgia legislature. They attempted to buy 20 million acres of land from Georgia for $200,000, but did not succeed because they paid with **worthless currency**. In 1795, the Georgia Company, the Georgia-Mississippi Company, the Upper Mississippi Company, and the new Tennessee Company bought 40 million acres from Georgia for $500,000. It was later revealed that Georgia officials and legislators held stock in these companies. The sale was nullified in 1796 after public outcry. Money was returned to some buyers, yet others contested the refunds. In 1803 Georgia gave up all lands beyond its current western border, but the Supreme Court ruled in 1810 that sales of these lands had been binding.

Georgia's Role Leading Up to Civil War

After the invention of the cotton gin in 1789, **slavery** was revitalized as the need for field workers increased in Georgia's cotton-producing agricultural lands. The Georgia economy became heavily dependent on the institution of slavery to continue to prosper. At the same time, an economic **depression** affected the U.S., increasing the importance of Southern cotton production in the nation's economy. Trade conflicts, such as tariffs designed to promote national commerce and purchase of Northern manufactured products even when international purchases were cheaper, inflamed the agricultural South. **States' rights versus federal control** became an important issue, and Constitutional interpretation philosophy divided the country into political factions. The rapid growth of Northern populations also threatened to turn areas adhering to Southern philosophies into minority areas. The threat of Northern governments taking away Southerners' personal property (the potential abolition of slavery and the Dred Scott decision) was the last straw that divided the nation.

Major Civil War Events in Georgia

Georgia **seceded** from the Union on January 18, 1861. Throughout the war, Georgia's **ports** were blockaded by Northern fleets, but smugglers brought supplies through the blockade into Georgia's tidal creeks. The war did not come to Georgia until 1863, when the **Battle of Chickamauga** was fought in northwestern Georgia and southeastern Tennessee. Confederate troops won, but this battle was followed by General Sherman's **Atlanta campaign**, which captured and burned Atlanta in 1864. Sherman then began the "**March to the Sea**" campaign, designed to destroy as much of Georgia as possible. Union troops marched from Atlanta to Macon, Milledgeville, and on to Savannah, destroying land and burning homes. After Sherman reached Savannah, he was resupplied by Northern ships and took Savannah in December, 1864. After this, smaller battles and skirmishes occurred in Georgia but the major campaign continued in the Carolinas.

RECONSTRUCTION IN GEORGIA

PLAN

Just after the Civil war in 1865, Georgia's **economy** was depressed due to the social upheaval of Emancipation, physical destruction of agricultural lands, and bad weather. Freed slaves moved to towns where jobs were scarce and disease was common. The **Freedmen's Bureau**, a new government-formed organization originally designed to aid newly freed slaves in claiming land, helped them develop sharecropping labor agreements with white landowners. These agreements often put former slaves back to work for their previous owners. From 1866 to 1867, the South was under military occupation. At the same time, laws were passed preventing ex-Confederates from holding office, so officeholders included **Freedmen** (ex-slaves), **carpetbaggers** (Northerners who moved South to hold office or help reconstruct the south), and **Scalawags** (Southern Republicans who had opposed secession). The **Ku Klux Klan** was formed around this time to promote white supremacy and prevent black education and voting rights. Unrest from 1868 to 1870 over states' rights and the right of blacks to hold public office led to military rule again in 1869, after which black legislators were readmitted to the state government, making the majority Republican. In 1870, the state was readmitted to the Union. Voting restrictions against ex-Confederates were removed and, by 1872, legislators were largely conservative Democrats.

CONSEQUENCES

Reconstruction's overall purpose was to bring Georgia back into the Union, which succeeded by 1872. Other social and economic changes during Reconstruction had lasting effects on the state. Without slave labor, Southern production was limited. **Prisoners** in Milledgeville whose labor could be hired cheaply were leased to private companies, like mining operations. In 1908 convict leasing was outlawed, but chain gangs continued to work on public road projects. Convicts still clean roadsides even though they are no longer chained together. In the agricultural regions of Georgia, black citizens and whites who had previously owned small land parcels before the war sharecropped the fields of wealthy landowners until World War II. **Black** voters were disenfranchised in the 1890s. The Georgia assembly had no black members from 1907 to 1963. However, public education spread across the state to both black and white citizens. Railroad construction was subsidized to encourage transport of economic products, but the subsidy system was subject to corruption.

GEORGIA'S ROLE IN EMERGENCE OF THE NEW SOUTH

The American South has been called the **New South** since the Civil War; the term was originally intended to invoke a new reliance on industry instead of slave labor-driven agriculture. Part of the New South philosophy was to encourage **railroad construction** to promote industry and commerce. **Henry Grady**, a Georgia journalist, wrote stirringly of the contributions Georgia could make in the New South. As a result of his writing, he was given part ownership of the **Atlanta Constitution newspaper**. While there, Grady editorialized about his views on temperance laws, veteran healthcare, and library construction. He became heavily involved in Atlanta politics, and leveraged election of pro-industry, pro-urbanization candidates. He campaigned in the North for alliances between Northern and Southern business, which increased investment in Atlanta businesses. Grady's efforts also spurred the founding of the Georgia Institute of Technology and encouraged several cotton expositions in Atlanta that attracted investment and created jobs. Largely as a result of Grady's campaigning, Georgia became an important part of the "New South."

EFFECT OF POPULIST MOVEMENT ON LIFE IN GEORGIA

The **Populist Movement** began in about 1892 with the rise of the Populist Party. Poor white farmers in the 1880s and 1890s suffered from low cotton prices, high railroad fees, and debt. They organized the **Farmers' Alliance**, which demanded that the government print more money to combat economic control by the wealthy. The group campaigned for direct election of congressmen, federal control of the railroads, and banking reform. They also lobbied for the sub-treasury plan, which would allow farmers to borrow against the value of stored crop products while waiting for agricultural prices to improve. Neither the Republican Party nor the Democratic Party supported these ideas, so the Populist Party was formed.

The **Populist Party** tried to attract Republican blacks and called to end the convict lease system. In the 1896 presidential election, a conservative Republican was elected because the Populist Party split the Democratic vote, after which most Populists returned to the Democratic Party. Black Populists moved back to the Republican Party, having realized that Populist overtures were more about increasing voter numbers rather than addressing black concerns. After 1896, the Populist Party was gone, but its members later successfully disenfranchised Georgia's black voters.

JIM CROW LAWS AND CUSTOMS AND EFFECTS ON LIFE IN GEORGIA

Jim Crow laws and customs were developed and applied between 1876 and 1965 to oppress free blacks and prevent them from interacting with whites or reaching equal footing. Each state passed specific **laws** focusing on black/white interactions. Georgia's major laws were increasingly specific iterations of the following ideas: no intermarriage between races, separate public transportation, separate education, separate prisons and hospitals, and identification of a person with black heritage. **Voter registration** became increasingly difficult, with the additional requirement that the registrant must correctly answer 10 of 30 very difficult questions designed to confuse the applicant. Laws and customs required alcohol and food sales to be completely separated, and in some states, burials and recreation must be conducted separately. Even though laws provided for "separate but equal" facilities, those for blacks were usually of much lower quality.

EFFECTS OF DISENFRANCHISEMENT ON AFRICAN AMERICAN RESIDENTS OF GEORGIA

During Reconstruction, the **Ku Klux Klan** began physically intimidating black voters throughout the South to prevent them from voting. This was outlawed in 1871 with the **Force Act of 1870**, which authorized the President to use armed forces against people attempting to deny other citizens' Fourteenth Amendment rights. Georgia followed with **poll taxes**, which were requirements that in order to vote, citizens must have paid taxes or a special poll tax, and must bring the receipt to the polls. Georgia was one southern state that did not use an educational qualification to judge whether a citizen was permitted to vote or not. Other southern states also used grandfather clauses, educational requirements, literacy requirements, or labyrinthine registration procedures to prevent black voters from reaching the polls. Intimidation and economic strategies (like eviction or job loss) were used to prevent blacks from voting in all Southern states until the passage of the **Voting Rights Act of 1965**.

EFFECTS OF WORLD WAR I ON GEORGIA

World War I's initial impact on Georgia occurred during the British **blockade** of European ports that followed the Lusitania sinking and Archduke Ferdinand's assassination. Due to the blockade,

Georgia cotton, timber, and naval stores could no longer reach German and Austrian markets, which injured the state's economy and turned citizens against the war. As soon as the United States declared war, Georgia fervently supported the conflict to show that it was committed to American unity and goals. When the **draft** was instituted, white planters sought to prevent black workers from being drafted. Ultimately the draft was applied statewide and 500,000 men registered from Georgia. Five federal military installations and ten training camps were located in the state. Several of these camps provided specialty training. Many camps were significantly impacted by the 1918 Spanish influenza outbreak. In addition, 130 Georgia soldiers were killed when the **HMS Otranto**, a troop transport ship, accidentally sank near Scotland in 1918. After the war, residents of Nashville, Georgia, a town which had lost many soldiers, erected a monument designed by a resident of Americus, Georgia named **E.M. Viquesney**. He later created more than 150 memorial statues across the nation.

EFFECTS OF BOLL WEEVIL AND DROUGHT ON GEORGIA'S ECONOMY BETWEEN TWO WORLD WARS

During World War I, intensive American agriculture efforts to recover maximum wartime profits pushed the land beyond its capacity. Marginal land was cultivated, and this **overproduction** continued after the war. Surplus production destabilized the economy. During the 1920s, the United States experienced a period of great prosperity, but the stock market crash of 1929 completely depressed the economy. At the same time, the **boll weevil**, a cotton-destroying insect, spread through Georgia beginning in 1915. This drastically reduced cotton production from 5.2 million acres in 1914 to 2.6 million acres by 1923. Insecticides were used, but they were expensive and led to ecological imbalances in insect-predator food webs. Nationwide **drought** and record heat struck the country from 1933 to 1936, further reducing agricultural production. Georgia's economy between the world wars heavily depended on cotton, and lack of diversification caused the economy to suffer as cotton production declined. The American economy also suffered because agricultural production in the Great Plains essentially ceased when most of the topsoil of this land dried up and blew away in massive **dust storms**. In the mid to late 1930s, the **New Deal** attempted to aid the high unemployment rates in Georgia and elsewhere.

EUGENE TALMADGE

Eugene Talmadge was a Georgia native elected four times as **Governor**. After law school at UGA and public office in Telfair County, he unsuccessfully ran for state legislature twice and then was elected state agriculture commissioner in 1926. He was re-elected twice. **Talmadge** successfully ran for governor in 1932 and was re-elected in 1934. He was popular with rural farmers, whom he attracted with his agricultural knowledge and anti-corporate, evangelical, and white-supremacist philosophies. He condemned the New Deal and warned against its "Communist" tendencies. While governor, Talmadge opposed federal New Deal relief programs. State law prevented him from running a third time in 1936. By the late 1930s, popular opinion in Georgia had turned away from federal relief programs and favored conservative fiscal philosophies. Talmadge again won the 1940 gubernatorial election and spent most of the period dealing with the Cocking affair, in which he leveraged Dean Walter Cocking's firing from the University of Georgia for political reasons. As a result, the University lost accreditation for a year and Georgia public higher education suffered greatly. Talmadge was defeated in 1942, but was re-elected yet again after a change in election law in 1946 with rural support for his Jim Crow platform. He died in December 1946 before taking office.

EFFECTS OF NEW DEAL ON GEORGIA

Franklin Roosevelt spent a great deal of time in Warm Springs, Georgia for hydrotherapy. While there, he closely examined the relationships between Georgia's social, economic, and educational problems. From 1933 to 1940, **New Deal federal aid** provided $250 million to Georgia citizens and created programs to address the linkage of these three issues. Roosevelt wanted to enable sharecroppers to become independent, land-owning farmers, and his programs sought to stabilize the agricultural economy with quotas and price adjustments. Unfortunately, these citizens received less economic benefit in reality than was planned. Rural poor citizens received work relief through the **Works Progress Administration (WPA)**, the **Civilian Conservation Corps**, and the **National Youth Administration (NYA)**. These measures were opposed by more wealthy Georgia citizens, who feared that workers would rather receive higher wages from the government rather than working in the traditional sharecropper structure. Urban housing projects also met resistance from wealthier city dwellers. Eleanor Roosevelt was heavily involved in the Georgia NYA, which encouraged young women and black youths to pursue their educations and provided work at colleges and universities. The egalitarian programs of the New Deal helped black citizens work towards achieving equal employment and equal citizenship.

Georgia Geography

MAJOR GEOLOGICAL REGIONS OF GEORGIA

Georgia can be divided into four distinct geologic regions. The northwest corner is the **"Valley and Ridge" region**, which was formed during the middle Ordovician period when two continental plates collided and formed the Appalachian Mountains. Rippled rock layers in this region alternate between hard and soft layers. The north and northeast part of the state is the **"Blue Ridge" region**. This area contains the North Georgia Mountains, which are made of rocks formed metamorphically. The region contains many mineral resources, including talc and marble, and once contained gold which has since been mined. The upper half of the state, south of these two regions, is the hilly **"Piedmont" region**. This region has intermediate elevations that are lower than the northern mountains, but still higher than the coastal plains to the south. The Piedmont terrain was formed by metamorphosis of coastal ocean sediments between 300 and 600 million years ago. The southern portion of the state is the **"Coastal Plain" region**. This area was more recently coastal ocean sediments, during the Late Cretaceous through Holocene periods 100 million years ago or less. Marine life and dinosaur fossils can be found in the region, and kaolinite minerals are commonly produced there.

SWAMPLANDS OF GEORGIA

The **Okefenokee Swamp** is the primary swamp in Georgia. It is one of the four largest swamps in the United States. It straddles the Georgia-Florida border. Over the past 6500 years, the swamp has been formed as peat (decaying vegetation) accumulated in a shallow depression on the coastal plain which used to be the mouth of an estuary. High ground around the swamp was likely beach dunes or similar features that have worn down. Most of the swamp is low, jelly-like ground with numerous ponds and waterways through it. Prairies and forests are also found in the swamp. The Okefenokee's water is a dark tea color due to its organic material from rotting vegetation. Native Americans lived in the Okefenokee Swamp as early as 2500 BC, but European exploitation of the swamp only began in the late 1800s. Agriculture of sugar, rice, and cotton was attempted in the 1890s, but after it failed, the swamp was logged for cypress trees. By 1937, the Okefenokee Swamp was named a national wildlife refuge.

WATERWAYS IN GEORGIA

Georgia has more than 71,000 miles of **rivers and streams**. Most lakes in the state of Georgia are man-made, because the natural landscape does not favor collections of water. The southern part of the state is an exception due to many low areas that accumulate water in and around the Okefenokee Swamp. The Altamaha River watershed includes the Oconee and Ocmulgee Rivers, and is the third largest river on the East Coast of the United States. It flows into the Atlantic Ocean from central and Northeast Georgia. The Ogeechee and Savannah River watersheds flow along the southeast border of the state into the Atlantic. The Satilla and St. Mary's Rivers flow from southeastern Georgia to the Atlantic. The Suwannee and Ochlocknee River Watersheds flow from the southern portion of the state into Florida. The Flint and Chattahoochee Rivers flow southwest from central and Northern Georgia into the Florida Panhandle. The Tallapoosa and Coosa Rivers flow from the northwestern portion of the state into Alabama.

INFLUENCE OF CLIMATE AND GEOGRAPHY ON GEORGIA'S DEVELOPMENT

Georgia's climate is consistent with that of the southeastern United States; summer weather is hot and humid while winter weather is mild. Average winter temperatures do not dip below freezing. The Piedmont and coastal plain regions tend to be much warmer on the whole than the mountain areas. As a result, the growing season in south Georgia is 300 days long, while in north Georgia it is only 185 days. Georgia's economy has historically depended on **agricultural products**, made possible by its geography and climate. In the 1700s and early 1800s, livestock and subsistence farms were common in the Piedmont and coastal regions. After the cotton gin's invention in 1793, large-scale agricultural efforts focused on **cotton**. The labor demands of cotton farming led Georgia's economy to depend heavily on slavery, which affected its politics and economic policies. Cotton is still raised in Georgia, along with other products. Large central forested areas provide lumber, wood pulp, and timber products like turpentine. Chickens, pigs, and cattle are raised throughout the state. Agricultural products also include nuts (pecans and peanuts), peaches, vegetables, and grains like rye.

Effects of Agriculture on Georgia's Economy Today

Agriculture has always been a key component of Georgia's economy. When the colony was first settled, one of its planned economic activities was **exporting agricultural goods** to England. Early exports began with corn, and later expanded to include indigo, silk, and wine. Rice also became an important export. After the cotton gin was invented, **cotton** became a major agricultural commodity. Today's agriculture in Georgia is more diversified. The state is the number-one producer of young chickens, peanuts, and pecans. It is the second-largest producer of cotton and rye, and is the third-largest producer of peaches and tomatoes. It is the fifth-largest producer of tobacco. Additional crops today include fruits and vegetables, grains, soybeans, and turf grass. Agriculture produces $57 billion of Georgia's $350 billion annual production.

Effects of Development of Atlanta, the Hartsfield-Jackson International Airport, and the Interstate Highway System on the Southeast

After World War II, Atlanta continued to grow. Companies such as Ford and Bell Aircraft (the early Lockheed Georgia) opened **plants** in the city. The interstate system increased access. The civil rights movement began to integrate politics and provide increased opportunities to black citizens. Today, Atlanta has become the business hub of the Southeast United States, and is the home base of many corporations including Coca-Cola, Delta Air Lines, CNN, Home Depot, and Georgia-Pacific. It also hosts the Centers for Disease Control. The **Atlanta Municipal Airport**, now known as the Hartsfield-Jackson International Airport, was expanded in 1961 and again in 1971. After airline deregulation in 1970, Atlanta became a hub in the new hub-and-spoke system. The airport now provides flights to most continents. It was expanded again in the 1990s, when Atlanta hosted the 1996 Summer Olympic Games. The **Interstate Highway System** connects all parts of Georgia with the Southeast, permitting workers to reach their jobs and products to reach their markets. The system was implemented in the 1950s, and was overseen by General Lucius Clay, a Marietta native. One disadvantage of the system is that it has promoted urban sprawl, or uncontrolled spreading, around Atlanta.

Georgia Government

GEORGIA STATE CONSTITUTION

The current Georgia State Constitution is organized into eleven **Articles**. Each Article is divided into a number of sections. Each paragraph of the section is numbered, and divided into clauses designated with a lower-case letter. Before the first Article, there is a short preamble. In order, the Articles are: Bill of Rights, Voting and Elections, Legislative Branch, Constitutional Boards and Commissions, Executive Branch, Judicial Branch, Taxation and Finance, Education, Counties and Municipal Corporations, Amendments to the Constitution, and Miscellaneous Provisions. At the end, the Constitution includes a table showing the number of amendments proposed, ratified by the General Assembly, and rejected by the General Assembly by year.

PRINCIPLES

The **Georgia State Constitution** is intended "to perpetuate the principles of free government, insure justice to all, preserve peace, promote the interest and happiness of the citizen and of the family, and transmit to posterity the enjoyment of liberty" (Constitution, Preamble). To meet these goals, the document lays out **regulations** governing all aspects of life in Georgia. Previous versions used difficult language that has been eliminated in the current version, which has been revised for clarity and brevity. The Bill of Rights ensures the basic rights of Georgia citizens. The Voting Article covers who may vote, election rules, and laws governing public officials. The Legislative Branch section describes the composition of the General Assembly and its duties. Constitutional Boards and Commissions describes the setup of state boards and organizations. The Executive Branch section discusses the structure of the Governor's office, the Governor's duties, and the installation and removal procedures for Executive officers. The Judicial Branch Article describes the structure of the courts, rules governing judgeships, and other legal procedures. The Taxation and Finance, Education, and Counties sections discuss specific rules regarding taxation, tax collection, education, and the way the state is divided into counties.

RIGHTS AND RESPONSIBILITIES OF GEORGIA CITIZENS IN STATE GOVERNMENT

The rights of Georgia citizens are spelled out in the state's **Bill of Rights**. Citizens are free to pursue life, liberty, and property, and these rights are equally protected for all citizens. Religious discrimination is not permitted, and free speech and free press are protected. Citizens may bear arms and have the right to a trial by jury and legal counsel. Penalties in jail and bail amounts must be reasonable, and people may not be tried twice for the same crime unless an appeal is granted or a mistrial is declared. Involuntary servitude is outlawed. The state government is set up for the benefit of Georgia citizens, and it is their right and responsibility to regulate it and change it. Citizens have the right to vote, so that they may regulate their government and be involved in improving it.

VOTING REQUIREMENTS AND ELECTORAL PROCESS IN GEORGIA

U.S. citizens who are at least 18 years old and reside in Georgia may **vote**, as long as they have not been convicted of a felony that they have not yet made restitution for. Citizens who are mentally incompetent may not vote. **Voter registration** can be done by mail at a number of public facilities, but must be completed by 30 days before an election. Elections must be conducted by **secret ballot**. Elections are conducted annually, and fifteen state-level offices may be elected: governor, lieutenant governor, two senators, secretary of state, attorney general, school superintendent, agriculture commissioner, labor commissioner, insurance commissioner, and five public service commissioners. The Georgia Supreme Court and the Georgia Court of Appeals are also elected. Local offices filled by election also include General Assembly representatives, county, and city officers. Other public authorities may also be elected. Current election procedure uses a touch-screen computer with three backup devices to minimize election problems.

ROLE OF POLITICAL PARTIES IN GEORGIA GOVERNMENT

Having at least two political parties moderates Georgia's government and provides room for philosophical debate. The first system in the state was the **Federalist Party**, opposed by the **Democratic-Republican Party**. By the 1830s, the two parties were the **States' Rights Party** and the **Union Party**. These parties merged with the **Democratic Party** and the **Whigs**, respectively. The Whig party later collapsed, and **Republicans** came to Georgia during Reconstruction. Between 1870 and 1960, Georgia was consistently Democratic. After that, Republicans gained a foothold and the two-party system was refreshed. Throughout Georgia's history, third parties have also been key in the outcome of some elections by splitting the vote of one of the main parties, which usually allows the other party to win the election. In Georgia, a **political party** is defined by law as a group that received at least 20% of the votes for governor or president in a general election. A **political body** is a group that can collect 1% of Georgia voters' signatures on a petition or in a statewide election vote. Political bodies may only place candidates on the ballot for local and statewide offices. Third parties must collect signatures equal to 5% of the number of registered voters in order to place a candidate on the ballot for district-office elections.

CITY GOVERNMENTS IN GEORGIA

In Georgia, cities and towns operate under a **charter of municipal incorporation** approved by the state assembly, which controls their existence and boundaries. The charter describes the basic governmental structure of the city. The city government oversees anything pertaining to **public life**. This includes protecting the citizens in emergencies with fire and police responders, protecting the environment and overseeing solid and sewer sanitation, levying taxes, spending money on public works, managing public transportation and roads, and planning laws for city growth and zoning. City governments in Georgia are one of three types: the strong mayor-council, the weak mayor-council, or the council-manager. In the **strong mayor-council form**, the mayor represents the executive branch and the council represents the legislative branch. The mayor oversees the running of the government and the council adopts legislation and ordinances that dictate government policies. The **weak mayor-council form** shares the duties between the mayor and the city council. The mayor is the primary executive body, but his or her duties may also be primarily ceremonial. In the **council-manager format**, the city council decides policy and hires a manager to carry them out.

COUNTY GOVERNMENTS IN GEORGIA

Currently, there are 159 **counties** in Georgia. The large number of counties reflects Georgia's rural history; nearly each town was a county seat, which gave rural residents a cultural, judicial, and political center and also enhanced their representation in state government. Counties' duties are numerous. They issue license plates and taxes, hold court, register voters, maintain roads, administer public assistance, probate wills, maintain police and fire forces, oversee garbage collection and hospitals, manage parks and recreation, govern sewage and water management, build libraries, and preserve building codes. These numerous roles provide all of Georgia's citizens with services similar to those available in cities, even if they live in rural areas.

GEORGIA GENERAL ASSEMBLY MEMBERS, GOVERNOR, AND LIEUTENANT GOVERNOR

Georgia General Assembly House members must be 21 years old, have lived in their districts for a year, and in the state for at least two years. **Senate members** must be 25 years old and meet the same residency requirements. **House members** serve on committees focused on state business. The committees develop legislation that then passes to the House. The Senate has similar committees. Terms are two years. The **governor** must be at least 30 years old, a U.S. Citizen for at least 15 years, and a Georgia resident for at least 6 years. The governor may be elected for two consecutive four-year terms, but must relinquish the position for four years before running again. The governor is the top executive and law enforcement officer, making him the commander in chief of the state's military. He can veto legislation and appoint officials to fill in gaps until the next election. He also oversees the state budget and can award discretionary money to specific projects. The **lieutenant governor** must meet the same qualifications as the governor. He may be re-elected an unlimited number of times. This office is voted separately from the governor. The lieutenant governor fills the governor's office until the next general election if the governor cannot hold office and presides over the state senate. Informal duties of this office are to appoint members to statewide committees.

ORGANIZATION OF GEORGIA GENERAL ASSEMBLY

The Georgia General Assembly is divided into two chambers, the **House of Representatives** (180 members; lower house) and the **Senate** (56 members; upper house). Each chamber is divided into committees whose party composition is the same as that of the chamber. These committees discuss and debate issues that affect the state. The leader of the House of Representatives is the **Speaker of the House**, who is a member of the majority political party and who is elected by the entire chamber. This person schedules debates, votes, and can assign representatives to committees. The majority and minority parties are also presided over by the majority and minority leader, whose functions are to advance their parties' interests. If a bill is approved by the House, it passes to the Senate. The Senate is also divided into committees which debate and introduce legislation. The **lieutenant governor** presides over the Senate instead of a Speaker. The **president pro tempore** of the Senate is the leader of the majority party. Duties of the Georgia Assembly include introducing new legislation, amending the Georgia State Constitution, passing the state budget every year, and re-drawing legislative districts every decade.

MAJOR POLICY AREAS COVERED BY GEORGIA STATE PROGRAMS

Georgia state programs fall mainly into executive, legislative, and judicial categories. **Executive programs** include the Department of Agriculture; the Department of Labor; Insurance and Fire Safety; Public Services; and the offices of Executive members which includes the governor, lieutenant governor, attorney general, secretary of state, and the state school superintendent. These programs are all designed to protect and improve the lives of Georgia citizens. **Legislative programs** include the General Assembly, voting, lawmaking, and districting. These programs are intended to permit Georgia citizens to participate in their government. **Judicial programs** include all the courts of the state, which are in place to protect the liberties of citizens and to address any wrongdoing.

STEPS FOLLOWED BY A BILL THAT BECOMES GEORGIA LAW

Issues raised in the **Georgia House of Representatives** begin when a legislator drafts a bill or resolution. He usually relies on the **Office of Legal Counsel** to write the actual text to make sure it is in the correct format. The bill summary, or title, is read aloud on the floor of the house on three separate days. The bill is assigned to a committee for consideration. Bills that are favorably considered by their committees are forwarded to consideration by the entire House. Debates and questions follow, amendments may be suggested, and the bill is voted on. If it passes the House, it moves on to the Senate. The same process occurs, and the bill is sent back and forth between House and Senate until it is either rejected or approved upon by both bodies. If approved, the bill is then sent on to the governor for consideration. He may sign the bill within 40 days or he may veto it. His veto can be overridden by a two-thirds majority of the Senate.

GEORGIA COURT SYSTEM AND SELECTION OF JUDGES

The Georgia court system has limited, general, and appellate courts. **Limited-jurisdiction courts** include magistrate courts, probate courts, county courts, and juvenile courts. These courts oversee smaller legal issues, such as small civil suits, violation of county ordinances, misdemeanors, traffic violations, juvenile violations and issuing search warrants. **General-jurisdiction courts** are the superior courts of the state, and they oversee any felony and any civil or criminal case. **Appellate-jurisdiction courts** are the Court of Appeals and the Supreme Court. These courts rule on cases generated in the other two levels of the judicial system. Except for juvenile courts, judges of limited-jurisdiction courts are elected every four years in general or partisan elections by the geographic unit over which they would preside. Juvenile court judges are appointed by superior court judges in four-year terms. Part-time judges may continue to work as lawyers separately from their judicial work. General-jurisdiction, or superior court judges, are also elected for four-year terms by the public. Appellate court judges are elected for six-year terms by the public.

JUVENILE AND ADULT JUSTICE SYSTEMS IN GEORGIA

The **juvenile justice system** of Georgia is applied to delinquent children under the age of 17 and deprived children under 18. In situations concerning capital felonies, custody, and parental rights, the juvenile justice system works with the superior courts. Juvenile courts oversee issues of traffic violations as well as violent felonies such as murder, rape, and armed robbery. Trials are not conducted in front of a jury, and issues go directly to the Court of Appeals or the Supreme Court if there is a problem. Designated detention centers are used for juvenile offenders, and rehabilitation is an important goal. The **adult justice system** applies to everyone over the age of 17. Trials are typically conducted in front of a jury unless the issue is addressed in magistrate court. Probate and magistrate issues may be addressed in Superior Court before they are sent to the Court of Appeals or Supreme Court. Sentencing tends to be harsher than in the juvenile system.

Government and Economics

US Government and Citizenship

POLITICAL SCIENCE AND ITS TIES TO OTHER MAJOR DISCIPLINES

Political science focuses on studying different governments and how they compare to each other, general political theory, ways political theory is put into action, how nations and governments interact with each other, and a general study of governmental structure and function. Other elements of **political science** include the study of elections, governmental administration at various levels, development and action of political parties, and how values such as freedom, power, justice, and equality are expressed in different political cultures. Political science also encompasses elements of other disciplines, including:

- **History**—how historical events have shaped political thought and process
- **Sociology**—the effects of various stages of social development on the growth and development of government and politics
- **Anthropology**—the effects of governmental process on the culture of an individual group and its relationships with other groups
- **Economics**—how government policies regulate the distribution of products and how they can control and/or influence the economy in general

GENERAL POLITICAL THEORY

Based on general political theory, the four major purposes of any given government are:

- **Ensuring national security**—the government protects against international, domestic, and terrorist attacks and also ensures ongoing security through negotiating and establishing relationships with other governments.
- **Providing public services**—the government should "promote the general welfare," as stated in the Preamble to the US Constitution, by providing whatever is needed to its citizens.
- **Ensuring social order**—the government supplies means of settling conflicts among citizens as well as making laws to govern the nation, state, or city.
- **Making decisions regarding the economy**—laws help form the economic policy of the country, regarding both domestic and international trade and related issues. The government also has the ability to distribute goods and wealth to some extent among its citizens.

MAIN THEORIES REGARDING THE ORIGIN OF THE STATE

There are four main theories regarding the origin of the state:

- **Evolutionary**—the state evolved from the family, with the head of state the equivalent of the family's patriarch or matriarch.
- **Force**—one person or group of people brought everyone in an area under their control, forming the first government.
- **Divine Right**—certain people were chosen by the prevailing deity to be the rulers of the nation, which is itself created by the deity or deities.

82

- **Social Contract**—there is no natural order. The people allow themselves to be governed to maintain social order, while the state, in turn, promises to protect the people they govern. If the government fails to protect its people, the people have the right to seek new leaders.

INFLUENCES OF PHILOSOPHERS ON POLITICAL STUDY

Ancient Greek philosophers **Aristotle** and **Plato** believed political science would lead to order in political matters and that this scientifically organized order would create stable, just societies.

Thomas Aquinas adapted the ideas of Aristotle to a Christian perspective. His ideas stated that individuals should have certain rights but also certain duties, and that these rights and duties should determine the type and extent of government rule. In stating that laws should limit the role of government, he laid the groundwork for ideas that would eventually become modern constitutionalism.

Niccolò Machiavelli, author of *The Prince*, was a proponent of politics based on power. He is often considered the founder of modern political science.

Thomas Hobbes, author of *Leviathan* (1651), believed that individuals' lives were focused solely on a quest for power and that the state must work to control this urge. Hobbes felt that people were completely unable to live harmoniously without the intervention of a powerful, undivided government.

CONTRIBUTIONS OF JOHN LOCKE, MONTESQUIEU, AND ROUSSEAU TO POLITICAL SCIENCE

John Locke published *Two Treatises of Government* in 1689. This work argued against the ideas of Thomas Hobbes. He put forth the theory of *tabula rasa*—that people are born with minds like blank slates. Individual minds are molded by experience, not innate knowledge or intuition. He also believed that all men should be independent and equal. Many of Locke's ideas found their way into the Constitution of the United States.

The two French philosophers, **Montesquieu** and **Rousseau**, heavily influenced the French Revolution (1789-1799). They believed government policies and ideas should change to alleviate existing problems, an idea referred to as "liberalism." Rousseau, in particular, directly influenced the Revolution with writings such as *The Social Contract* (1762) and *Declaration of the Rights of Man and of the Citizen* (1789). Other ideas Rousseau and Montesquieu espoused included:

- Individual freedom and community welfare are of equal importance
- Man's innate goodness leads to natural harmony
- Reason develops with the rise of civilized society
- Individual citizens carry certain obligations to the existing government

POLITICAL IDEOLOGIES OF DAVID HUME, JEREMY BENTHAM, JOHN STUART MILL, JOHANN GOTTLIEB FICHTE, AND FRIEDRICH HEGEL

David Hume and **Jeremy Bentham** believed politics should have as its main goal maintaining "the greatest happiness for the greatest number." Hume also believed in empiricism, or that ideas should not be believed until the proof has been observed. He was a natural skeptic and always sought out the truth of matters rather than believing what he was told.

John Stuart Mill, a British philosopher as well as an economist, believed in progressive policies such as women's suffrage, emancipation, and the development of labor unions and farming cooperatives.

Johann Fichte and **Georg Hegel**, German philosophers in the late 18th and early 19th centuries, supported a form of liberalism grounded largely in socialism and a sense of nationalism.

MAIN POLITICAL ORIENTATIONS

The four main political orientations are:

- **Liberal**—liberals believe that government should work to increase equality, even at the expense of some freedoms. Government should assist those in need, focusing on enforced social justice and free basic services for everyone.
- **Conservative**—a conservative believes that government should be limited in most cases. The government should allow its citizens to help one another and solve their own problems rather than enforcing solutions. Business should not be overregulated, allowing a free market.
- **Moderate**—this ideology incorporates some liberal and some conservative values, generally falling somewhere between in overall belief.
- **Libertarian**—libertarians believe that the government's role should be limited to protecting the life and liberty of citizens. Government should not be involved in any citizen's life unless that citizen is encroaching upon the rights of another.

MAJOR PRINCIPLES OF GOVERNMENT AS OUTLINED IN THE UNITED STATES CONSTITUTION

The six major principles of government as outlined in the United States Constitution are:

- **Federalism**—the power of the government does not belong entirely to the national government but is divided between federal and state governments.
- **Popular sovereignty**—the government is determined by the people and gains its authority and power from the people.
- **Separation of powers**—the government is divided into three branches (executive, legislative, and judicial) with each having its own set of powers.
- **Judicial review**—courts at all levels of government can declare laws invalid if they contradict the constitutions of individual states, or the US Constitution, with the Supreme Court serving as the final judicial authority on decisions of this kind.
- **Checks and balances**—no single branch can act without input from another, and each branch has the power to "check" any other, as well as balance other branches' powers.
- **Limited government**—governmental powers are limited, and certain individual rights are defined as inviolable by the government.

> **Review Video: Supreme Court**
> Visit mometrix.com/academy and enter code: 270434

TYPES OF POWERS DELEGATED TO THE NATIONAL GOVERNMENT BY THE US CONSTITUTION

The structure of the US government divides power between national and state governments. Powers delegated to the federal government by the Constitution are:

- **Expressed powers**—powers directly defined in the Constitution, including power to declare war, regulate commerce, make money, and collect taxes
- **Implied powers**—powers the national government must have in order to carry out the expressed powers
- **Inherent powers**—powers inherent to any government, not expressly defined in the Constitution

Some of these powers, such as collection and levying of taxes, are also granted to the individual state governments.

PRIMARY POSITIONS OF FEDERALISM AND DEVELOPMENT THROUGH THE YEARS IN THE US

The way federalism should be practiced has been the subject of debate since the writing of the Constitution. There were—and still are—two main factions regarding this issue:

- **States' rights**—those favoring the states' rights position feel that the state governments should take the lead in performing local actions to manage various problems.
- **Nationalist**—those favoring a nationalist position feel the national government should take the lead to deal with those same matters.

The flexibility of the Constitution has allowed the US government to shift and adapt as the needs of the country have changed. Power has often shifted from the state governments to the national government and back again, and both levels of government have developed various ways to influence each other.

EFFECTS OF FEDERALISM ON POLICY-MAKING AND THE BALANCE OF POLITICS IN THE US

Federalism has three major effects on **public policy** in the US:

- Determining whether the local, state, or national government originates policy
- Affecting how policies are made
- Ensuring policy-making functions under a set of limitations

Federalism also influences the **political balance of power** in the US by:

- Making it difficult, if not impossible, for a single political party to seize total power
- Ensuring that individuals can participate in the political system at various levels
- Making it possible for individuals working within the system to be able to affect policy at some level, whether local or more widespread

THREE BRANCHES OF THE US FEDERAL GOVERNMENT

The following are the three branches of the US Federal government and the individuals that belong to each branch:

- **Legislative Branch**—this consists of the two houses of Congress: the House of Representatives and the Senate. All members of the Legislative Branch are elected officials.
- **Executive Branch**—this branch is made up of the president, vice president, presidential advisors, and other various cabinet members. Advisors and cabinet members are appointed by the president, but they must be approved by Congress.
- **Judicial Branch**—the federal court system, headed by the Supreme Court.

> **Review Video: Three Branches of Government**
> Visit mometrix.com/academy and enter code: 718704

MAJOR RESPONSIBILITIES OF THE THREE BRANCHES OF THE FEDERAL GOVERNMENT

The three branches of the federal government each have specific roles and responsibilities:

- The **Legislative Branch** is largely concerned with lawmaking. All laws must be approved by Congress before they go into effect. They are also responsible for regulating money and trade, approving presidential appointments, and establishing organizations like the postal service and federal courts. Congress can also propose amendments to the Constitution, and can impeach, or bring charges against, the president. Only Congress can declare war.
- The **Executive Branch** carries out laws, treaties, and war declarations enacted by Congress. The president can also veto bills approved by Congress, and serves as commander in chief of the US military. The president appoints cabinet members, ambassadors to foreign countries, and federal judges.
- The **Judicial Branch** makes decisions on challenges as to whether laws passed by Congress meet the requirements of the US Constitution. The Supreme Court may also choose to review decisions made by lower courts to determine their constitutionality.

US CITIZENSHIP

QUALIFICATIONS OF A US CITIZEN/HOW CITIZENSHIP MAY BE LOST

Anyone born in the US, born abroad to a US citizen, or who has gone through a process of naturalization is considered a **citizen** of the United States. It is possible to lose US citizenship as a result of conviction of certain crimes such as treason. Citizenship may also be lost if a citizen pledges an oath to another country or serves in the military of a country engaged in hostilities with the US. A US citizen can also choose to hold dual citizenship, work as an expatriate in another country without losing US citizenship, or even to renounce citizenship if he or she so chooses.

RIGHTS, DUTIES, AND RESPONSIBILITIES GRANTED TO OR EXPECTED FROM CITIZENS

Citizens are granted certain rights under the US government. The most important of these are defined in the **Bill of Rights**, and include freedom of speech, religion, assembly, and a variety of other rights the government is not allowed to remove. A US citizen also has a number of **duties**:

- Paying taxes
- Loyalty to the government (though the US does not prosecute those who criticize or seek to change the government)
- Support and defense of the Constitution
- Serving in the Armed Forces when required by law
- Obeying laws as set forth by the various levels of government.

Responsibilities of a US citizen include:

- Voting in elections
- Respecting one another's rights and not infringing on them
- Staying informed about various political and national issues
- Respecting one another's beliefs

BILL OF RIGHTS
IMPORTANCE OF THE BILL OF RIGHTS

The first ten amendments of the US Constitution are known as the **Bill of Rights**. These amendments prevent the government from infringing upon certain freedoms that the Founding Fathers felt were natural rights that already belonged to all people. These rights included freedom of speech, freedom of religion, freedom of assembly, and the right to bear arms. Many of the rights were formulated in direct response to the way the colonists felt they had been mistreated by the British government.

RIGHTS GRANTED IN THE BILL OF RIGHTS

The first ten amendments were passed by Congress in 1789. Three-fourths of the existing thirteen states had ratified them by December of 1791, making them official additions to the Constitution. The rights granted in the Bill of Rights are:

- **First Amendment**—freedom of religion, speech, freedom of the press, and the right to assemble and to petition the government
- **Second Amendment**—the right to bear arms
- **Third Amendment**—Congress cannot force individuals to house troops
- **Fourth Amendment**—protection from unreasonable search and seizure
- **Fifth Amendment**—no individual is required to testify against himself, and no individual may be tried twice for the same crime
- **Sixth Amendment**—the right to criminal trial by jury and the right to legal counsel
- **Seventh Amendment**—the right to civil trial by jury
- **Eighth Amendment**—protection from excessive bail or cruel and unusual punishment

- **Ninth Amendment**—prevents rights not explicitly named in the Constitution from being taken away because they are not named
- **Tenth Amendment**—any rights not directly delegated to the national government, or not directly prohibited by the government from the states, belong to the states or to the people

> **Review Video: Bill of Rights**
> Visit mometrix.com/academy and enter code: 585149

SITUATIONS WHERE THE GOVERNMENT RESTRICTS OR REGULATES FIRST AMENDMENT FREEDOMS

In some cases, the government restricts certain elements of First Amendment rights. Some examples include:

- **Freedom of religion**—when a religion espouses illegal activities, the government often restricts these forms of religious expression. Examples include polygamy, animal sacrifice, and use of illicit drugs or illegal substances.
- **Freedom of speech**—this can be restricted if exercise of free speech endangers other people.
- **Freedom of the press**—laws prevent the press from publishing falsehoods.

In **emergency situations** such as wartime, stricter restrictions are sometimes placed on these rights, especially rights to free speech and assembly, and freedom of the press, in order to protect national security.

CONSTITUTION'S ADDRESS OF THE RIGHTS OF THOSE ACCUSED OF CRIMES

The US Constitution makes allowances for the **rights of criminals**, or anyone who has transgressed established laws. There must be laws to protect citizens from criminals, but those accused of crimes must also be protected and their basic rights as individuals preserved. In addition, the Constitution protects individuals from the power of authorities to prevent police forces and other enforcement organizations from becoming oppressive. The fourth, fifth, sixth, and eighth amendments specifically address these rights.

SUPREME COURT'S PROVISION OF EQUAL PROTECTION UNDER THE LAW FOR ALL INDIVIDUALS

When the Founding Fathers wrote in the Declaration of Independence that "all men are created equal," they actually were referring to men, and, in fact, defined citizens as white men who owned land. However, as the country has developed and changed, the definition has expanded to more wholly include all people.

"**Equality**" does not mean all people are inherently the same, but it does mean they all should be granted the same rights and should be treated the same by the government. Amendments to the Constitution have granted citizenship and voting rights to all Americans regardless of race or gender. The Supreme Court evaluates various laws and court decisions to determine if they properly represent the idea of **equal protection**. One sample case was Brown v. Board of Education in 1954, which declared separate-but-equal treatment to be unconstitutional.

CIVIL LIBERTY CHALLENGES ADDRESSED IN CURRENT POLITICAL DISCUSSIONS

The **civil rights movements** of the 1960s and the ongoing struggle for the rights of women and other minorities have sparked **challenges to existing law**. In addition, debate has raged over how much information the government should be required to divulge to the public. Major issues in the 21st century political climate include:

- Continued debate over women's rights, especially regarding equal pay for equal work
- Debate over affirmative action to encourage hiring of minorities
- Debate over civil rights of homosexuals, including marriage and military service
- Decisions as to whether minorities should be compensated for past discriminatory practices
- Balance between the public's right to know and the government's need to maintain national security
- Balance between the public's right to privacy and national security

CIVIL LIBERTIES VS. CIVIL RIGHTS

While the terms *civil liberties* and *civil rights* are often used interchangeably, in actuality, their definitions are slightly different. The two concepts work together, however, to define the basics of a free state:

- **"Civil liberties"** define the constitutional freedoms guaranteed to citizens. Examples include freedoms such as free speech, privacy, or free thought.
- **"Civil rights"** are guarantees of or protections of civil liberties. One comparison can be found in the case of freedom of religion. The civil liberty is that one has the freedom to practice the religion of his or her choice, whereas the civil right would protect that individual from being denied a job on the basis of their religion.

SUFFRAGE, FRANCHISE, AND THE CHANGE OF VOTING RIGHTS OVER THE COURSE OF AMERICAN HISTORY

Suffrage and franchise both refer to the right to **vote**. As the US developed as a nation, there was much debate over which individuals should hold this right. In the early years, only white male landowners were granted suffrage. By the 19th century, most states had franchised, or granted the right to vote, to all adult white males. The **Fifteenth Amendment** of 1870 granted suffrage to formerly enslaved men. The **Nineteenth Amendment** gave women the right to vote in 1920, and in 1971 the **Twenty-sixth Amendment** expanded voting rights to include any US citizen over the age of eighteen. However, those who have not been granted full citizenship and citizens who have committed certain crimes do not have voting rights.

WAYS IN WHICH THE VOTING PROCESS HAS CHANGED OVER THE YEARS

The first elections in the US were held by **public ballot**. However, election abuses soon became common, since public ballot made it easy to intimidate, threaten, or otherwise influence the votes of individuals or groups of individuals. New practices were put into play, including **registering voters** before elections took place and using a **secret or Australian ballot**. In 1892, the introduction of the **voting machine** further privatized the voting process, since it allowed complete privacy for voting. Today, debate continues about the accuracy of various voting methods, including high-tech voting machines and even low-tech punch cards.

EFFECT OF POLITICAL PARTIES ON THE FUNCTIONING OF AN INDIVIDUAL GOVERNMENT

Different types and numbers of political parties can have a significant effect on how a government is run. If there is a **single party**, or a one-party system, the government is defined by that one party, and all policy is based on that party's beliefs. In a **two-party system**, two parties with different viewpoints compete for power and influence. The US is basically a two-party system, with checks and balances to make it difficult for one party to gain complete power over the other. There are also

multiparty systems, with three or more parties. In multiparty systems, various parties will often come to agreements in order to form a majority and shift the balance of power.

DEVELOPMENT OF POLITICAL PARTIES IN THE US.

George Washington was adamantly against the establishment of **political parties**, based on the abuses perpetrated by such parties in Britain. However, political parties developed in US politics almost from the beginning. Major parties throughout US history have included:

- **Federalists and Democratic-Republicans**—these parties formed in the late 1700s and disagreed on the balance of power between national and state government.
- **Democrats and Whigs**—these developed in the 1830s, and many political topics of the time centered on national economic issues.
- **Democrats and Republicans**—the Republican Party developed before the Civil War, after the collapse of the Whig party, and the two parties debated issues centering on slavery and economic issues, such as taxation.

While third parties sometimes enter the picture in US politics, the government is basically a two-party system, dominated by the Democrats and Republicans.

FUNCTIONS OF POLITICAL PARTIES

Political parties form organizations at all levels of government. Activities of individual parties include:

- Recruiting and backing candidates for offices
- Discussing various issues with the public, increasing public awareness
- Working toward compromise on difficult issues
- Staffing government offices and providing administrative support

At the administrative level, parties work to ensure that viable candidates are available for elections and that offices and staff are in place to support candidates as they run for office and afterward, when they are elected.

PROCESSES OF SELECTING POLITICAL CANDIDATES

Historically, in the quest for political office, a potential candidate has followed one of the following four processes:

- **Nominating convention**—an official meeting of the members of a party for the express purpose of nominating candidates for upcoming elections. The Democratic National Convention and the Republican National Convention, convened to announce candidates for the presidency, are examples of this kind of gathering.
- **Caucus**—a meeting, usually attended by a party's leaders. Some states still use caucuses, but not all.
- **Primary election**—the most common method of choosing candidates today, the primary is a publicly held election to choose candidates.
- **Petition**—signatures gathered to place a candidate on the ballot. Petitions can also be used to place legislation on a ballot.

WAYS THE AVERAGE CITIZEN PARTICIPATES IN THE POLITICAL PROCESS

In addition to voting for elected officials, American citizens are able to participate in the political process through several other avenues. These include:

- Participating in local government
- Participating in caucuses for large elections
- Volunteering to help political parties
- Running for election to local, state, or national offices

Individuals can also donate money to political causes or support political groups that focus on specific causes such as abortion, wildlife conservation, or women's rights. These groups often make use of **representatives** who lobby legislators to act in support of their efforts.

WAYS IN WHICH POLITICAL CAMPAIGN GAINS FUNDING

Political campaigns are very expensive. In addition to the basic necessities of a campaign office, including office supplies, office space, etc., a large quantity of the money that funds a political campaign goes toward **advertising**. Money to fund a political campaign can come from several sources, including:

- The candidate's personal funds
- Donations by individuals
- Special interest groups

The most significant source of campaign funding is **special interest groups**. Groups in favor of certain policies will donate money to candidates they believe will support those policies. Special interest groups also do their own advertising in support of candidates they endorse.

> **Review Video: Political Campaigns**
> Visit mometrix.com/academy and enter code: 838608

IMPORTANCE OF FREE PRESS AND THE MEDIA

The right to free speech guaranteed in the first amendment to the Constitution allows the media to report on **government and political activities** without fear of retribution. Because the media has access to information about the government, the government's policies and actions, and debates and discussions that occur in Congress, it can keep the public informed about the inner workings of the government. The media can also draw attention to injustices, imbalances of power, and other transgressions the government or government officials might commit. However, media outlets may, like special interest groups, align themselves with certain political viewpoints and skew their reports to fit that viewpoint. The rise of the **internet** has made media reporting even more complex, as news can be found from an infinite variety of sources, both reliable and unreliable.

FORMS OF GOVERNMENT

ANARCHISM, COMMUNISM, AND DICTATORSHIP

Anarchists believe that all government should be eliminated and that individuals should rule themselves. Historically, anarchists have used violence and assassination to further their beliefs.

Communism is based on class conflict, revolution, and a one-party state. Ideally, a communist government would involve a single government for the entire world. Communist government controls the production and flow of goods and services rather than leaving this to companies or individuals.

91

Dictatorship involves rule by a single individual. If rule is enforced by a small group, this is referred to as an oligarchy. Dictators tend to rule with a violent hand, using a highly repressive police force to ensure control over the populace.

FASCISM AND MONARCHY

Fascism centers on a single leader and is, ideologically, an oppositional belief to communism. **Fascism** includes a single-party state and centralized control. The power of the fascist leader lies in the "cult of personality," and the fascist state often focuses on expansion and conquering of other nations. **Monarchy** was the major form of government for Europe through most of its history.

A monarchy is led by a king or a queen. This position is hereditary, and the rulers are not elected. In modern times, constitutional monarchy has developed, where the king and queen still exist, but most of the governmental decisions are made by democratic institutions such as a parliament.

PRESIDENTIAL SYSTEM AND SOCIALISM

A presidential system, like a parliamentary system, has a legislature and political parties, but there is no difference between the head of state and the head of government. Instead of separating these functions, an elected president performs both. Election of the president can be direct or indirect, and the president may not necessarily belong to the largest political party. In **socialism**, the state controls the production of goods, though it does not necessarily own all means of production. The state also provides a variety of social services to citizens and helps guide the economy. A democratic form of government often exists in socialist countries.

> **Review Video: Socialism**
> Visit mometrix.com/academy and enter code: 917677

TOTALITARIAN AND AUTHORITARIAN SYSTEMS

A totalitarian system believes everything should be under the control of the government—from resource production, to the press, to religion, and other social institutions. All aspects of life under a totalitarian system must conform to the ideals of the government. **Authoritarian** governments practice widespread state authority but do not necessarily dismantle all public institutions. If a church, for example, exists as an organization but poses no threat to the authority of the state, an authoritarian government might leave it as it is. While all totalitarian governments are by definition authoritarian, a government can be authoritarian without becoming totalitarian.

> **Review Video: Totalitarianism vs. Authoritarianism**
> Visit mometrix.com/academy and enter code: 104046

PARLIAMENTARY AND DEMOCRATIC SYSTEMS

In a parliamentary system, government involves a legislature and a variety of political parties. The head of government, usually a prime minister, is typically the head of the dominant party. A head of state can be elected, or this position can be taken by a monarch, as in Great Britain's constitutional monarchy system.

In a **democratic system** of government, the people elect their government representatives. The word *democracy* is a Greek term that means "rule of the people." There are two forms of democracy: direct and indirect. In a direct democracy, each issue or election is decided by a vote where each individual is counted separately. An indirect democracy employs a legislature that votes on issues that affect large numbers of people whom the legislative members represent. Democracy can exist as a parliamentary system or a presidential system. The US is a presidential, indirect democracy.

REALISM, LIBERALISM, INSTITUTIONALISM, AND CONSTRUCTIVISM IN INTERNATIONAL RELATIONS

The theory of realism states that nations are by nature aggressive and work in their own self-interest. Relations between nations are determined by military and economic strength. The nation is seen as the highest authority. **Liberalism** believes states can cooperate and that they act based on capability rather than power. This term was originally coined to describe Woodrow Wilson's theories on international cooperation. In **institutionalism**, institutions provide structure and incentive for cooperation among nations. Institutions are defined as a set of rules used to make international decisions. These institutions also help distribute power and determine how nations will interact. **Constructivism**, like liberalism, is based on international cooperation but recognizes that perceptions countries have of each other can affect their relations.

> **Review Video: Social Liberalism**
> Visit mometrix.com/academy and enter code: 624507

EFFECTS OF FOREIGN POLICY ON A COUNTRY'S POSITION IN WORLD AFFAIRS

Foreign policy is a set of goals, policies, and strategies that determine how an individual nation will interact with other countries. These strategies shift, sometimes quickly and drastically, according to actions or changes occurring in the other countries. However, a nation's **foreign policy** is often based on a certain set of ideals and national needs. Examples of US foreign policy include isolationism versus internationalism. In the 1800s, the US leaned more toward isolationism, exhibiting a reluctance to become involved in foreign affairs. The World Wars led to a period of internationalism, as the US entered these wars in support of other countries and joined the United Nations. Today's foreign policy tends more toward **interdependence**, or **globalism**, recognizing the widespread effects of issues like economic health.

MAJOR FIGURES INVOLVED IN DETERMINING AND ENACTING US FOREIGN POLICY

US foreign policy is largely determined by Congress and the president, influenced by the secretary of state, secretary of defense, and the national security adviser. Executive officials carry out policies. The main departments in charge of these day-to-day issues are the **US Department of State**, also referred to as the State Department. The Department of State carries out policy, negotiates treaties, maintains diplomatic relations, assists citizens traveling in foreign countries, and ensures that the president is properly informed of any international issues. The **Department of Defense**, the largest executive department in the US, supervises the armed forces and provides assistance to the president in his role as commander-in-chief.

MAJOR TYPES OF INTERNATIONAL ORGANIZATIONS

Two types of international organizations are:

- **Intergovernmental organizations (IGOs)**. These organizations are made up of members from various national governments. The UN is an example of an intergovernmental organization. Treaties among the member nations determine the functions and powers of these groups.
- **Nongovernmental organizations (NGOs)**. An NGO lies outside the scope of any government and is usually supported through private donations. An example of an NGO is the International Red Cross, which works with governments all over the world when their countries are in crisis but is formally affiliated with no particular country or government.

ROLE OF DIPLOMATS IN INTERNATIONAL RELATIONS

Diplomats are individuals who reside in foreign countries in order to maintain communications between that country and their home country. They help negotiate trade agreements and environmental policies, as well as conveying official information to foreign governments. They also help to resolve conflicts between the countries, often working to sort out issues without making the conflicts official in any way. **Diplomats**, or **ambassadors**, are appointed in the US by the president. Appointments must be approved by Congress.

ROLE OF THE UNITED NATIONS IN INTERNATIONAL RELATIONS AND DIPLOMACY

The United Nations (**UN**) helps form international policies by hosting representatives of various countries who then provide input into policy decisions. Countries that are members of the UN must agree to abide by all final UN resolutions, but this is not always the case in practice, as dissent is not uncommon. If countries do not follow UN resolutions, the UN can decide on sanctions against those countries, often economic sanctions, such as trade restriction. The UN can also send military forces to problem areas, with "peacekeeping" troops brought in from member nations. An example of this function is the Korean War, the first war in which an international organization played a major role.

Economics

ECONOMICS

Economics is the study of the ways specific societies **allocate** resources to individuals and groups within that society. Also important are the choices society makes regarding what efforts or initiatives are funded and which are not. Since resources in any society are finite, allocation becomes a vivid reflection of that society's values. In general, the economic system that drives an individual society is based on:

- What goods are produced
- How those goods are produced
- Who acquires the goods or benefits from them

Economics consists of two main categories: **macroeconomics**, which studies larger systems, and **microeconomics**, which studies smaller systems.

MARKET ECONOMY

A market economy is based on supply and demand. **Demand** has to do with what customers want and need, as well as what quantity those consumers are able to purchase based on other economic factors. **Supply** refers to how much can be produced to meet demand, or how much suppliers are willing and able to sell. Where the needs of consumers meet the needs of suppliers is referred to as a market equilibrium price. This price varies depending on many factors, including the overall health of a society's economy and the overall beliefs and considerations of individuals in society. The following is a list of terms defined in the context of a market economy:

- **Elasticity**—this is based on how the quantity of a particular product responds to the price demanded for that product. If quantity responds quickly to changes in price, the supply/demand for that product is said to be elastic. If it does not respond quickly, then the supply/demand is inelastic.
- **Market efficiency**—this occurs when a market is capable of producing output high enough to meet consumer demand.
- **Comparative advantage**—in the field of international trade, this refers to a country focusing on a specific product that it can produce more efficiently and more cheaply, or at a lower opportunity cost, than another country, thus giving it a comparative advantage in production.

> **Review Video: Basics of Market Economy**
> Visit mometrix.com/academy and enter code: 791556

PLANNED ECONOMY VS. MARKET ECONOMY

In a **market economy**, supply and demand are determined by consumers. In a **planned economy**, a public entity or planning authority makes the decisions about what resources will be produced, how they will be produced, and who will be able to benefit from them. The means of production, such as factories, are also owned by a public entity rather than by private interests. In **market socialism**, the economic structure falls somewhere between the market economy and the planned economy. Planning authorities determine the allocation of resources at higher economic levels, while consumer goods are driven by a market economy.

MICROECONOMICS

While economics generally studies how resources are allocated, **microeconomics** focuses on economic factors such as the way consumers behave, how income is distributed, and output and input markets. Studies are limited to the industry or firm level rather than an entire country or society. Among the elements studied in microeconomics are factors of production, costs of production, and factor income. These factors determine production decisions of individual firms, based on resources and costs.

> **Review Video: Microeconomics**
> Visit mometrix.com/academy and enter code: 779207

CLASSIFICATION OF VARIOUS MARKETS BY ECONOMISTS

The conditions prevailing in a given market are used to **classify** markets. Conditions considered include:

- Existence of competition
- Number and size of suppliers
- Influence of suppliers over price
- Variety of available products
- Ease of entering the market

Once these questions are answered, an economist can classify a certain market according to its structure and the nature of competition within the market.

> **Review Video: Classification of Markets**
> Visit mometrix.com/academy and enter code: 904798

MARKET FAILURE

When any of the elements for a successfully competitive market are missing, this can lead to a **market failure**. Certain elements are necessary to create what economists call "**perfect competition**." If one of these factors is weak or lacking, the market is classified as having "**imperfect competition**." Worse than imperfect competition, though, is a market failure. There are five major types of market failure:

- Inadequate competition
- Inadequate information
- Immobile resources
- Negative externalities, or side effects
- Failure to provide public goods

Externalities are side effects of a market that affect third parties. These effects can be either negative or positive.

> **Review Video: Market Failure**
> Visit mometrix.com/academy and enter code: 889023

FACTORS OF PRODUCTION AND COSTS OF PRODUCTION

Every good and service requires certain resources, or **inputs**. These inputs are referred to as **factors of production**. Every good and service requires four factors of production:

- Labor
- Capital
- Land
- Entrepreneurship

These factors can be fixed or variable and can produce fixed or variable costs. Examples of **fixed costs** include land and equipment. **Variable costs** include labor. The total of fixed and variable costs makes up the cost of production.

FACTOR INCOME

Factors of production each have an associated **factor income**. Factors that earn income include:

- **Labor**—earns wages
- **Capital**—earns interest
- **Land**—earns rent
- **Entrepreneurship**—earns profit

Each factor's income is determined by its **contribution**. In a market economy, this income is not guaranteed to be equal. How scarce the factor is and the weight of its contribution to the overall production process determines the final factor income.

KINDS OF MARKET STRUCTURES IN AN OUTPUT MARKET.

The four kinds of market structures in an output market are:

- **Perfect competition**—all existing firms sell an identical product. The firms are not able to control the final price. In addition, there is nothing that makes it difficult to become involved in or leave the industry. Anything that would prevent entering or leaving an industry is called a barrier to entry. An example of this market structure is agriculture.
- **Monopoly**—a single seller controls the product and its price. Barriers to entry, such as prohibitively high fixed cost structures, prevent other sellers from entering the market.
- **Monopolistic competition**—a number of firms sell similar products, but they are not identical, such as different brands of clothes or food. Barriers to entry are low.
- **Oligopoly**—only a few firms control the production and distribution of products, such as automobiles. Barriers to entry are high, preventing large numbers of firms from entering the market.

TYPES OF MONOPOLIES

Four types of monopolies are:

- **Natural monopoly**—a single supplier has a distinct advantage over the others.
- **Geographic monopoly**—only one business offers the product in a certain area.
- **Technological monopoly**—a single company controls the technology necessary to supply the product.
- **Government monopoly**—a government agency is the only provider of a specific good or service.

ACTIONS TAKEN BY THE US GOVERNMENT TO CONTROL MONOPOLIES

The US government has passed several acts to regulate businesses, including:

- **Sherman Antitrust Act (1890)**—this prohibited trusts, monopolies, and any other situations that eliminated competition.
- **Clayton Antitrust Act (1914)**—this prohibited price discrimination.
- **Robinson-Patman Act (1936)**—this strengthened provisions of the Clayton Antitrust Act, requiring businesses to offer the same pricing on products to any customer.

The government has also taken other actions to ensure competition, including requirements for public disclosure. The **Securities and Exchange Commission (SEC)** requires companies that provide public stock to provide financial reports on a regular basis. Because of the nature of their business, banks are further regulated and required to provide various information to the government.

MARKETING AND UTILITY

Marketing consists of all of the activity necessary to convince consumers to acquire goods. One major way to move products into the hands of consumers is to convince them that any single product will satisfy a need. The ability of a product or service to satisfy the need of a consumer is called **utility**. There are four types of utility:

- **Form utility**—a product's desirability lies in its physical characteristics.
- **Place utility**—a product's desirability is connected to its location and convenience.
- **Time utility**—a product's desirability is determined by its availability at a certain time.
- **Ownership utility**—a product's desirability is increased because ownership of the product passes to the consumer.

Marketing behavior will stress any or all of these types of utility when marketing to the consumer.

PRODUCERS DETERMINING WHAT CUSTOMERS DESIRE FOR THEIR PRODUCTS

Successful marketing depends not only on convincing customers they need the product but also on focusing the marketing towards those who already have a need or desire for the product. Before releasing a product into the general marketplace, many producers will **test** markets to determine which will be the most receptive to the product. There are three steps usually taken to evaluate a product's market:

- **Market research**—this involves researching a market to determine if it will be receptive to the product.
- **Market surveys**—a part of market research, market surveys ask consumers specific questions to help determine the marketability of a product to a specific group.
- **Test marketing**—this includes releasing the product into a small geographical area to see how it sells. Often test marketing is followed by wider marketing if the product does well.

MAJOR ELEMENTS OF A MARKETING PLAN

The four major elements of a marketing plan are:

- **Product**—this includes any elements pertaining directly to the product, such as packaging, presentation, or services to include along with it.
- **Price**—this calculates the cost of production, distribution, advertising, etc., as well as the desired profit to determine the final price.

- **Place**—this determines which outlets will be used to sell the product, whether traditional outlets such as brick and mortar stores or through direct mail or internet marketing.
- **Promotion**—this involves ways to let consumers know the product is available, through advertising and other means.

Once these elements have all been determined, the producer can proceed with production and distribution of his product.

DISTRIBUTION CHANNELS

Distribution channels determine the route a product takes on its journey from producer to consumer, and can also influence the final price and availability of the product. There are two major forms of distributions: wholesale and retail. A **wholesale distributor** buys in large quantities and then resells smaller amounts to other businesses. **Retailers** sell directly to the consumers rather than to businesses. In the modern marketplace, additional distribution channels have grown up with the rise of markets such as club warehouse stores as well as purchasing through catalogs or over the internet. Most of these newer distribution channels bring products more directly to the consumer, eliminating the need for middlemen.

DISTRIBUTION OF INCOME IN A SOCIETY

Distribution of income in any society ranges from poorest to richest. In most societies, income is not distributed evenly. To determine **income distribution**, family incomes are ranked from lowest to highest. These rankings are divided into five sections called **quintiles**, which are compared to each other. The uneven distribution of income is often linked to higher levels of education and ability in the upper classes but can also be due to other factors such as discrimination and existing monopolies. The **income gap** in America continues to grow, largely due to growth in the service industry, changes in the American family unit, and reduced influence of labor unions. **Poverty** is defined by comparing incomes to poverty guidelines. Poverty guidelines determine the level of income necessary for a family to function. Those below the poverty line are often eligible for assistance from government agencies.

MACROECONOMICS

Macroeconomics examines economies on a much larger level than microeconomics. While **microeconomics** studies economics on a firm or industry level, **macroeconomics** looks at economic trends and structures on a national level. Variables studied in macroeconomics include:

- Output
- Consumption
- Investment
- Government spending
- Net exports

The overall economic condition of a nation is defined as the **Gross Domestic Product**, or GDP. GDP measures a nation's economic output over a limited time period, such as a year.

> **Review Video: Microeconomics and Macroeconomics**
> Visit mometrix.com/academy and enter code: 538837
>
> **Review Video: Gross Domestic Product**
> Visit mometrix.com/academy and enter code: 409020

TYPES OF CONSUMER BEHAVIOR

The two major types of consumer behavior as defined in macroeconomics are:

- **Marginal propensity to consume (MPC)** defines the tendency of consumers to increase spending in conjunction with increases in income. In general, individuals with greater income will buy more. As individuals increase their income through job changes or growth of experience, they will also increase spending.
- **Utility** is a term that describes the satisfaction experienced by a consumer in relation to acquiring and using a good or service. Providers of goods and services will stress utility to convince consumers they want the products being presented.

WAYS TO MEASURE THE GROSS DOMESTIC PRODUCT OF A COUNTRY

The two major ways to measure the Gross Domestic Product of a country are:

- The **expenditures approach** calculates the GDP based on how much money is spent in each individual sector.
- The **income approach** calculates the GDP based on how much money is earned in each sector.

Both methods yield the same results, and both of these calculation methods are based on four **economic sectors** that make up a country's macro-economy:

- Consumers
- Business
- Government
- Foreign sector

TYPES OF EARNINGS GENERATED BY AN ECONOMY CONSIDERED TO CALCULATE GDP

Several factors must be considered in order to accurately calculate the GDP using the incomes approach. **Income factors** are:

- Wages paid to laborers, or compensation of employees (CE)
- Rental income derived from land
- Interest income derived from invested capital
- Entrepreneurial income

Entrepreneurial income consists of two forms. **Proprietor's income** is income that comes back to the entrepreneur himself. **Corporate profit** is income that goes back into the corporation as a whole. Corporate profit is divided by the corporation into corporate profits taxes, dividends, and retained earnings. Two other figures must be subtracted in the incomes approach. These are **indirect business taxes**, including property and sales taxes, and **depreciation**.

EFFECTS OF POPULATION OF A COUNTRY ON THE GROSS DOMESTIC PRODUCT

Changes in population can affect the calculation of a nation's **GDP**, particularly since GDP and GNP (Gross National Product) are generally measured per capita. If a country's economic production is low but the population is high, the income per individual will be lower than if the income is high and the population is lower. Also, if the population grows quickly and the income grows slowly, individual income will remain low or even drop drastically.

Population growth can also affect overall **economic growth**. Economic growth requires both that consumers purchase goods and workers produce them. A population that does not grow quickly enough will not supply enough workers to support rapid economic growth.

IDEAL BALANCE TO BE OBTAINED IN AN ECONOMY

Ideally, an economy functions efficiently, with the **aggregate supply**, or the amount of national output, equal to the **aggregate demand**, or the amount of the output that is purchased. In these cases, the economy is stable and prosperous. However, economies more typically go through **phases**. These phases are:

- **Boom**—GDP is high and the economy prospers
- **Recession**—GDP falls and unemployment rises
- **Trough**—the recession reaches its lowest point
- **Recovery**—unemployment lessens, prices rise, and the economy begins to stabilize again

These phases tend to repeat in cycles that are not necessarily predictable or regular.

UNEMPLOYMENT AND INFLATION

When demand outstrips supply, prices are driven artificially high, or are **inflated**. This occurs when too much spending causes an imbalance in the economy. In general, inflation occurs because an economy is growing too quickly. When there is too little spending, and supply has moved far beyond demand, a **surplus** of product results. Companies cut back on production and reduce the number of employees, and **unemployment** rises as people lose their jobs. This imbalance occurs when an economy becomes sluggish. In general, both these economic instability situations are caused by an imbalance between supply and demand. Government intervention may be necessary to stabilize an economy when either inflation or unemployment becomes too serious.

DIFFERENT FORMS OF UNEMPLOYMENT

- **Frictional**—when workers change jobs and are unemployed while waiting for new jobs
- **Structural**—when economic shifts reduce the need for workers
- **Cyclical**—when natural business cycles bring about loss of jobs
- **Seasonal**—when seasonal cycles reduce the need for certain jobs
- **Technological**—when advances in technology result in the elimination of certain jobs

Any of these factors can increase unemployment in certain sectors.

Inflation is classified by the overall rate at which it occurs:

- **Creeping inflation**—this is an inflation rate of about 1%-3% annually.
- **Walking inflation**—this is an inflation rate of 3%-10% annually.
- **Galloping inflation**—this is a high inflation rate of more than 10% but less than 1,000% annually.
- **Hyperinflation**—this is an inflation rate of over 1,000% per year. Hyperinflation usually leads to complete monetary collapse in a society, as individuals cannot generate sufficient income to purchase necessary goods.

> **Review Video: Forms of Unemployment**
> Visit mometrix.com/academy and enter code: 774028

GOVERNMENT INTERVENTION POLICIES THAT CAN HELP MITIGATE INFLATION AND UNEMPLOYMENT

When an economy becomes too imbalanced, either due to excessive spending or not enough spending, **government intervention** often becomes necessary to put the economy back on track. Government fiscal policy can take several forms, including:

- Contractionary policy
- Expansionary policy
- Monetary policy

Contractionary policies help counteract inflation. These include increasing taxes and decreasing government spending to slow spending in the overall economy. **Expansionary policies** increase government spending and lower taxes in order to reduce unemployment and increase the level of spending in the economy overall. **Monetary policy** can take several forms and affects the amount of funds available to banks for making loans.

STUDY AND QUANTIFICATION OF POPULATIONS AND POPULATION GROWTH

Populations are studied by **size**, rates of **growth** due to immigration, the overall **fertility rate**, and **life expectancy**. For example, though the population of the United States is considerably larger than it was two hundred years ago, the rate of population growth has decreased greatly, from about three percent per year to less than one percent per year.

In the US, the fertility rate is fairly low, with most choosing not to have large families, and life expectancy is high, creating a projected imbalance between older and younger people in the near future. In addition, immigration and the mixing of racially diverse cultures are projected to increase the percentages of Asians, Hispanics, and African Americans.

FUNCTIONS AND TYPES OF MONEY

Money is used in three major ways:

- As an accounting unit
- As a store of value
- As an exchange medium

In general, money must be acceptable throughout a society in exchange for debts or to purchase goods and services. Money should be relatively scarce, its value should remain stable, and it should be easily carried, durable, and easy to divide up. There are three basic types of money: commodity, representative, and fiat. **Commodity money** includes gems or precious metals. **Representative money** can be exchanged for items such as gold or silver that have inherent value. **Fiat money**, or legal tender, has no inherent value but has been declared to function as money by the government. It is often backed by gold or silver but not necessarily on a one-to-one ratio.

TYPES OF MONEY AVAILABLE IN THE US AND ECONOMISTS' MEASURE OF IT

Money in the US is not just currency. When economists calculate the amount of money available, they must take into account other factors, such as deposits that have been placed in checking accounts, debit cards, and "near moneys," such as savings accounts, that can be quickly converted into cash. Currency, checkable deposits and traveler's checks, referred to as **M1**, are added up, and then **M2** is calculated by adding savings deposits, CDs, and various other monetary deposits. The final result is the total quantity of available money.

ASPECTS OF MONETARY POLICY AND THE ROLE OF THE FEDERAL RESERVE SYSTEM

The Federal Reserve System, also known as the **Fed**, implements all monetary policy in the US. Monetary policy regulates the amount of money available in the American banking system. The Fed can decrease or increase the amount of available money for loans, thus helping regulate the national economy. Monetary policies implemented by the Fed are part of expansionary or contractionary monetary policies that help counteract inflation or unemployment. The **discount rate** is an interest rate charged by the Fed when banks borrow money from them. A lower discount rate leads banks to borrow more money, leading to increased spending. A higher discount rate has the opposite effect.

> **Review Video: Monetary Policy**
> Visit mometrix.com/academy and enter code: 662298

HOW BANKS FUNCTION

Banks earn their income by **loaning** out money and charging **interest** on those loans. If less money is available, fewer loans can be made, which affects the amount of spending in the overall economy. While banks function by making loans, they are not allowed to loan out all the money they hold in deposit. The amount of money they must maintain in reserve is known as the **reserve ratio**. If the reserve ratio is raised, less money is available for loans and spending decreases. A lower reserve ratio increases available funds and increases spending. This ratio is determined by the Federal Reserve System.

OPEN MARKET OPERATIONS

The Federal Reserve System can also expand or contract the overall money supply through **open market operations**. In this case, the Fed can buy or sell **bonds** it has purchased from banks or individuals. When the Fed buys bonds, more money is put into circulation, creating an expansionary situation to stimulate the economy. When the Fed sells bonds, money is withdrawn from the system, creating a **contractionary** situation to slow an economy suffering from inflation. Because of international financial markets, however, American banks often borrow and lend money in markets outside the US. By shifting their attention to international markets, domestic banks and other businesses can circumvent whatever contractionary policies the Fed may have put into place.

MAJOR CHARACTERISTICS OF INTERNATIONAL TRADE

International trade can take advantage of broader markets, bringing a wider variety of products within easy reach. By contrast, it can also allow individual countries to specialize in particular products that they can produce easily, such as those for which they have easy access to raw materials. Other products, more difficult to make domestically, can be acquired through trade with other nations. **International trade** requires efficient use of **native resources** as well as sufficient **disposable income** to purchase native and imported products. Many countries in the world engage extensively in international trade, but others still face major economic challenges.

MAJOR CHARACTERISTICS OF A DEVELOPING NATION

The five major characteristics of a developing nation are:

- Low GDP
- Rapid growth of population
- Economy that depends on subsistence agriculture

- Poor conditions, including high infant mortality rates, high disease rates, poor sanitation, and insufficient housing
- Low literacy rate

Developing nations often function under oppressive governments that do not provide private property rights and withhold education and other rights from women. They also often feature an extreme disparity between upper and lower classes, with little opportunity for the lower classes to improve their position.

STAGES OF ECONOMIC DEVELOPMENT

Economic development occurs in three stages that are defined by the activities that drive the economy:

- Agricultural stage
- Manufacturing stage
- Service sector stage

In developing countries, it is often difficult to acquire the necessary funding to provide equipment and training to move into the advanced stages of economic development. Some can receive help from developed countries via foreign aid and investment or international organizations such as the **International Monetary Fund** or the **World Bank**. Having developed countries provide monetary, technical, or military assistance can help developing countries move forward to the next stage in their development.

OBSTACLES DEVELOPING NATIONS FACE REGARDING ECONOMIC GROWTH

Developing nations typically struggle to overcome obstacles that prevent or slow economic development. Major **obstacles** can include:

- Rapid, uncontrolled population growth
- Trade restrictions
- Misused resources, often perpetrated by the government
- Traditional beliefs that can slow or reject change

Corrupt, oppressive governments often hamper the economic growth of developing nations, creating huge **economic disparities** and making it impossible for individuals to advance, in turn preventing overall growth. Governments sometimes export currency, called **capital flight**, which is detrimental to a country's economic development. In general, countries are more likely to experience economic growth if their governments encourage entrepreneurship and provide private property rights.

PROBLEMS WHEN INDUSTRIALIZATION OCCURS TOO QUICKLY

Rapid growth throughout the world leaves some nations behind and sometimes spurs their governments to move forward too quickly into **industrialization** and **artificially rapid economic growth**. While slow or nonexistent economic growth causes problems in a country, overly rapid industrialization carries its own issues. Four major problems encountered due to rapid industrialization are:

- Use of technology not suited to the products or services being supplied
- Poor investment of capital

- Lack of time for the population to adapt to new paradigms
- Lack of time to experience all stages of development and adjust to each stage

Economic failures in Indonesia were largely due to rapid growth that was poorly handled.

IMPORTANCE OF E-COMMERCE IN TODAY'S MARKETPLACE

The growth of the internet has brought many changes to our society, not the least of which is the modern way of business. Where supply channels used to move in certain necessary ways, many of these channels are now bypassed as **e-commerce** makes it possible for nearly any individual to set up a direct market to consumers, as well as direct interaction with suppliers. Competition is fierce. In many instances, e-commerce can provide nearly instantaneous gratification, with a wide variety of products. Whoever provides the best product most quickly often rises to the top of a marketplace. How this added element to the marketplace will affect the economy in the future remains to be seen. Many industries are still struggling with the best ways to adapt to the rapid, continuous changes.

KNOWLEDGE ECONOMY AND POSSIBLE EFFECT ON FUTURE ECONOMIC GROWTH

The knowledge economy is a growing sector in the economy of developed countries, and includes the trade and development of:

- Data
- Intellectual property
- Technology, especially in the area of communications

Knowledge as a resource is steadily becoming more and more important. What is now being called the **Information Age** may prove to bring about changes in life and culture as significant as those brought on by the Agricultural and Industrial Revolutions.

CYBERNOMICS

Related to the knowledge economy is what has been dubbed "**cybernomics**," or economics driven by e-commerce and other computer-based markets and products. Marketing has changed drastically with the growth of cyber communication, allowing suppliers to connect one-on-one with their customers. Other issues coming to the fore regarding cybernomics include:

- Secure online trade
- Intellectual property rights
- Rights to privacy
- Bringing developing nations into the fold

As these issues are debated and new laws and policies developed, the face of many industries continues to undergo drastic change. Many of the old ways of doing business no longer work, leaving industries scrambling to function profitably within the new system.

World Regions

GEOGRAPHY

Geography is the study of Earth. Geographers study **physical characteristics** of Earth as well as man-made borders and boundaries. They also study the **distribution of life** on the planet, such as where certain species of animals can be found or how different forms of life interact. Major elements of the study of geography include:

- Locations
- Regional characteristics
- Spatial relations
- Natural and man-made forces that change elements of Earth

These elements are studied from regional, topical, physical, and human perspectives. Geography also focuses on the origins of Earth, as well as the history and backgrounds of different human populations.

PHYSICAL VS. CULTURAL GEOGRAPHY

Physical geography is the study of the physical characteristics of Earth: how they relate to each other, how they were formed, and how they develop. These characteristics include climate, land, and water, and also how they affect human population in various areas. Different landforms, in combination with various climates and other conditions, determine the characteristics of various cultures.

Cultural geography is the study of how the various aspects of physical geography affect individual cultures. Cultural geography also compares various cultures: how their lifestyles and customs are affected by their geographical location, climate, and other factors, as well as how they interact with their environment.

> **Review Video: Regional Geography**
> Visit mometrix.com/academy and enter code: 350378

DIVISIONS OF GEOGRAPHICAL STUDY AND TOOLS USED

The four divisions of geographical study and tools used are:

- **Topical**—the study of a single feature of Earth or one specific human activity that occurs worldwide.
- **Physical**—the various physical features of Earth, how they are created, the forces that change them, and how they are related to each other and to various human activities.
- **Regional**—specific characteristics of individual places and regions.
- **Human**—how human activity affects the environment. This includes the study of political, historical, social, and cultural activities.

Tools used in geographical study include special research methods like mapping, field studies, statistics, interviews, mathematics, and the use of various scientific instruments.

IMPORTANT ANCIENT GEOGRAPHERS

The following are three important ancient geographers and their contributions to the study of geography:

- **Eratosthenes** lived in ancient Greek times and mathematically calculated the circumference of Earth and the tilt of Earth's axis. He also created the first map of the world.
- **Strabo** wrote a description of the ancient world called *Geographica* in seventeen volumes.
- **Ptolemy**, primarily an astronomer, was an experienced mapmaker. He wrote a treatise entitled *Geography*, which was used by Christopher Columbus in his travels.

WAYS GEOGRAPHERS ANALYZE AREAS OF HUMAN POPULATION

In cities, towns, or other areas where many people have settled, geographers focus on the **distribution** of populations, neighborhoods, industrial areas, transportation, and other elements important to the society in question. For example, they would map out the locations of hospitals, airports, factories, police stations, schools, and housing groups. They would also make note of how these facilities are distributed in relation to the areas of habitation, such as the number of schools in a certain neighborhood or how many grocery stores are located in a specific suburban area. Another area of study and discussion is the distribution of **towns** themselves, from widely spaced rural towns to large cities that merge into each other to form a megalopolis.

ROLE OF A CARTOGRAPHER

A cartographer is a mapmaker. Mapmakers produce detailed illustrations of geographic areas to record where various features are located within that area. These illustrations can be compiled into maps, charts, graphs, and even globes. When constructing maps, **cartographers** must take into account the problem of **distortion**. Because Earth is round, a flat map does not accurately represent the correct proportions, especially if a very large geographical area is being depicted. Maps must be designed in such a way as to minimize this distortion and maximize accuracy. Accurately representing Earth's features on a flat surface is achieved through **projection**.

TYPES OF PROJECTION USED IN CREATING WORLD MAPS

The three major types of projection used in creating world maps are:

- **Cylindrical projection**—this is created by wrapping the globe of Earth in a cylindrical piece of paper, then using a light to project the globe onto the paper. The largest distortion occurs at the outermost edges.
- **Conical projection**—the paper is shaped like a cone and contacts the globe only at the cone's base. This type of projection is most useful for middle latitudes.
- **Flat-Plane projections**—also known as a gnomonic projection, this type of map is projected onto a flat piece of paper that only touches the globe at a single point. Flat-plane projections make it possible to map out Great-Circle routes, or the shortest route between one point and another on the globe, as a straight line.

SPECIFIC TYPES OF MAP PROJECTIONS

Four specific types of map projections that are commonly used today are:

- **Winkel tripel projection**—this is the most common projection used for world maps since it was accepted in 1998 by the National Geographic Society as a standard. The Winkel tripel projection balances size and shape, greatly reducing distortion.
- **Robinson projection**—east and west sections of the map are less distorted, but continental shapes are somewhat inaccurate.

- **Goode homolosine projection**—sizes and shapes are accurate, but distances are not. This projection basically represents a globe that has been cut into connected sections so that it can lie flat.
- **Mercator projection**—though distortion is high, particularly in areas farther from the equator, this cylindrical projection is commonly used by seafarers.

MAJOR ELEMENTS OF ANY MAP

The five major elements of any map are:

- **Title**—this tells basic information about the map, such as the area represented.
- **Legend**—also known as the key, the legend explains what symbols used on a particular map represent, such as symbols for major landmarks.
- **Grid**—this most commonly represents the geographic grid system, or latitude and longitude marks used to precisely locate specific locations.
- **Directions**—a compass rose or other symbol is used to indicate the cardinal directions.
- **Scale**—this shows the relation between a certain distance on the map and the actual distance. For example, one inch might represent one mile, or ten miles, or even more, depending on the size of the map.

> **Review Video: 5 Elements of Any Map**
> Visit mometrix.com/academy and enter code: 437727

EQUAL-AREA MAPS VS. CONFORMAL MAPS

An equal-area map is designed such that the proportional sizes of various areas are accurate. For example, if one landmass is one-fifth the size of another, the lines on the map will be shifted to accommodate for distortion so that the proportional size is accurate. In many maps, areas farther from the equator are greatly distorted; this type of map compensates for this phenomenon. A **conformal map** focuses on representing the correct shape of geographical areas, with less concern for comparative size.

CONSISTENT SCALE MAPS AND THEMATIC MAPS

With a consistent scale map, the same scale, such as one inch being equal to ten miles, is used throughout the entire map. This is most often used for maps of smaller areas, as maps that cover larger areas, such as the full globe, must make allowances for distortion. Maps of very large areas often make use of more than one scale, with scales closer to the center representing a larger area than those at the edges.

A **thematic map** is constructed to show very specific information about a chosen theme. For example, a thematic map might represent political information, such as how votes were distributed in an election, or could show population distribution or climatic features.

RELIEF MAPS

A relief map is constructed to show details of various **elevations** across the area of the map. Higher elevations are represented by different colors than lower elevations. **Relief maps** often also show additional details, such as the overall ruggedness or smoothness of an area. Mountains would be represented as ridged and rugged, while deserts would be shown as smooth.

Elevation in relief maps can also be represented by contour lines, or lines that connect points of the same elevation. Some relief maps even feature textures, reconstructing details in a sort of miniature model.

GEOGRAPHICAL FEATURES

- **Mountains** are elevated areas that measure 2,000 feet or more above sea level. Often steep and rugged, they usually occur in groups called chains or ranges. Six of the seven continents on Earth contain at least one range.
- **Hills** are of lower elevation than mountains, at about 500-2,000 feet. Hills are usually more rounded and are found throughout every continent.
- **Plains** are large, flat areas and are usually very fertile. The majority of Earth's population is supported by crops grown on vast plains.
- **Valleys** lie between hills and mountains. Depending on their location, their specific features can vary greatly, from fertile and habitable to rugged and inhospitable.
- **Plateaus** are elevated, but flat on top. Some plateaus are extremely dry, such as the Kenya Plateau, because surrounding mountains prevent them from receiving moisture.
- **Deserts** receive less than ten inches of rain per year. They are usually large areas, such as the Sahara Desert in Africa or the Australian Outback.
- **Deltas** occur at river mouths. Because the rivers carry sediment to the deltas, these areas are often very fertile.
- **Mesas** are flat, steep-sided mountains or hills. The term is sometimes used to refer to plateaus.
- **Basins** are areas of low elevation where rivers drain.
- **Foothills** are the transitional area between plains and mountains, usually consisting of hills that gradually increase in size as they approach a mountain range.
- **Marshes** and **swamps** are also lowlands, but they are very wet and largely covered in vegetation such as reeds and rushes.

GEOGRAPHICAL TERMS REFERRING TO BODIES OF WATER

- The **ocean** refers to the salt water that covers about two-thirds of Earth's surface.
- **Ocean basins** are named portions of the ocean. The five major ocean basins are the Atlantic, Pacific, Indian, Southern, and Arctic.
- **Seas** are generally also salt water, but are smaller than ocean basins and surrounded by land. Examples include the Mediterranean Sea, the Caribbean Sea, and the Caspian Sea.
- **Lakes** are bodies of fresh water found inland. Sixty percent of all lakes are located in Canada.
- **Rivers** are moving bodies of water that flow from higher elevations to lower. They usually start as rivulets or streams and grow until they finally empty into a sea or the ocean.
- **Canals**, such as the Panama Canal and the Suez Canal, are man-made waterways connecting two large bodies of water.

HOW COMMUNITIES DEVELOP

Communities, or groups of people who settle together in a specific area, typically gather where certain conditions exist. These conditions include:

- Easy access to resources such as food, water, and raw materials
- Ability to easily transport raw materials and goods, such as access to a waterway
- Room to house a sufficient workforce

People also tend to form groups with others who are similar to them. In a typical **community**, people can be found who share values, a common language, and common or similar cultural characteristics and religious beliefs. These factors will determine the overall composition of a community as it develops.

DIFFERENCES BETWEEN CITIES IN VARIOUS AREAS OF THE WORLD

Cities develop and grow as an area develops. Modern statistics show that over half of the world's people live in **cities**. That percentage is even higher in developed areas of the globe. Cities are currently growing more quickly in developing regions, and even established cities continue to experience growth throughout the world. In developing or developed areas, cities often are surrounded by a metropolitan area made up of both urban and suburban sections. In some places, cities have merged into each other and become a **megalopolis**—a single, huge city.

Cities develop differently in different areas of the world. The area available for cities to grow, as well as cultural and economic forces, drives how cities develop. For example, North American cities tend to cover wider areas. European cities tend to have better-developed transportation systems. In Latin America, the richest inhabitants can be found in the city centers, while in North America, wealthier inhabitants tend to live in suburban areas.

In other parts of the world, transportation and communication between cities are less developed. Technological innovations such as the cell phone have increased communication even in these areas. Urban areas must also maintain communication with rural areas in order to procure food, resources, and raw materials that cannot be produced within the city limits.

WEATHER VS. CLIMATE

Weather and climate are physical systems that affect geography. Though they deal with similar information, the way this information is measured and compiled is different.

Weather involves daily conditions in the atmosphere that affect temperature, precipitation (rain, snow, hail, or sleet), wind speed, air pressure, and other factors. Weather focuses on the short-term—what the conditions will be today, tomorrow, or over the next few days.

In contrast, **climate** aggregates information about daily and seasonal weather conditions in a region over a long period of time. The climate takes into account average monthly and yearly temperatures, average precipitation over long periods of time, and the growing season of an area. Climates are classified according to latitude, or how close they lie to Earth's equator. The three major divisions are:

- **Low Latitudes**, lying from 0 to approximately 23.5 degrees
- **Middle Latitudes**, found from approximately 23.5 to 66.5 degrees
- **High Latitudes**, found from approximately 66.5 degrees to the poles

> **Review Video: Climates**
> Visit mometrix.com/academy and enter code: 991320

CLIMATES FOUND IN THE LOW LATITUDES

Rainforests, savannas, and deserts occur in low latitudes:

- **Rainforest** climates, near the equator, experience high average temperatures and humidity, as well as relatively high rainfall.
- **Savannas** are found on either side of the rainforest region. Mostly grasslands, they typically experience dry winters and wet summers.
- Beyond the savannas lie the **desert** regions, with hot, dry climates, sparse rainfall, and temperature fluctuations of up to fifty degrees from day to night.

CLIMATE REGIONS FOUND IN THE MIDDLE LATITUDES

The climate regions found in the middle latitudes are:

- **Mediterranean**—the Mediterranean climate occurs between 30- and 40-degrees latitude, both north and south, on the western coasts of continents. Characteristics include a year-long growing season; hot, dry summers followed by mild winters; and sparse rainfall that occurs mostly during the winter months.
- **Humid-subtropical**—humid-subtropical regions are located in southeastern coastal areas. Winds that blow in over warm ocean currents produce long summers, mild winters, and a long growing season. These areas are highly productive and support a larger part of Earth's population than any other climate.
- **Humid-continental**—the humid continental climate produces the familiar four seasons typical of a good portion of the US. Some of the most productive farmlands in the world lie in these climates. Winters are cold, and summers are hot and humid.

MARINE, STEPPE, AND DESERT CLIMATES

The climate regions found in the middle latitudes are:

- **Marine**—marine climates are found near water or on islands. Ocean winds help make these areas mild and rainy. Summers are cooler than humid-subtropical summers, but winters also bring milder temperatures due to the warmth of the ocean winds.
- **Steppe**—steppe climates, or prairie climates, are found far inland on large continents. Summers are hot and winters are cold, but rainfall is sparser than in continental climates.
- **Desert**—desert climates occur where steppe climates receive even less rainfall. Examples include the Gobi Desert in Asia as well as desert areas of Australia and the southwestern US.

CLIMATES FOUND IN THE HIGH LATITUDES

The high latitudes consist of two major climate areas, the tundra and taiga:

- **Tundra** means "marshy plain." The ground is frozen throughout long, cold winters, but there is little snowfall. During the short summers, it becomes wet and marshy. Tundras are not amenable to crops, but many plants and animals have adapted to the conditions.
- **Taigas** lie south of tundra regions and include the largest forest areas in the world, as well as swamps and marshes. Large mineral deposits exist here, as well as many animals valued for their fur. In the winter, taiga regions are colder than the tundra, and summers are hotter. The growing season is short.

A **vertical climate** exists in high mountain ranges. Increasing elevation leads to varying temperatures, growing conditions, types of vegetation and animals, and occurrence of human habitation, often encompassing elements of various other climate regions.

FACTORS AFFECTING CLIMATE

Because Earth is tilted, its **rotation** brings about changes in **seasons**. Regions closer to the equator, and those nearest the poles, experience very little change in seasonal temperatures. Mid-range latitudes are most likely to experience distinct seasons. Large bodies of water also affect climate. Ocean currents and wind patterns can change the climate for an area that lies in a typically cold latitude, such as England, to a much more temperate climate. Mountains can affect both short-term weather and long-term climates. Some deserts occur because precipitation is stopped by the wall of a mountain range.

Over time, established **climate patterns** can shift and change. While the issue is hotly debated, it has been theorized that human activity has also led to climate change.

EFFECT OF HUMAN SYSTEMS

HUMAN SYSTEMS THAT GEOGRAPHERS INCORPORATE INTO THE STUDY OF EARTH

Human systems affect geography in the way in which they settle, form groups that grow into large-scale habitations, and even create permanent changes in the landscape. **Geographers** study movements of people, how they distribute goods among each other and to other settlements or cultures, and how ideas grow and spread. Migrations, wars, forced relocations, and trade can all spread cultural ideas, language, goods, and other practices to widespread areas. Throughout history, cultures have been changed due to a wide range of events, including major migrations and the conquering of one people by another. In addition, **human systems** can lead to various conflicts or alliances to control access to and the use of natural resources.

HUMAN SYSTEMS THAT FORM THE BASIS OF CULTURES IN NORTH AMERICA

North America consists of 23 countries, including (in decreasing population order) the United States of America, Mexico, Canada, Guatemala, Cuba, Haiti, and the Dominican Republic. The US and Canada support similarly diverse cultures, as both were formed from groups of native races and large numbers of immigrants. Many **North American cultures** come from a mixture of indigenous and colonial European influences. Agriculture is important to North American countries, while service industries and technology also play a large part in the economy. On average, North America supports a high standard of living and a high level of development and supports trade with countries throughout the world.

HUMAN SYSTEMS THAT SHAPE SOUTH AMERICA

Home to twelve sovereign states, including Brazil (largest in area and population), Colombia, Argentina, Venezuela, and Peru; two independent territories; and one internal territory, **South America** is largely defined by its prevailing languages. The majority of countries in South America speak Spanish or Portuguese. Most of South America has experienced a similar history, having been originally dominated by Native cultures and then conquered by European nations. The countries of South America have since gained independence, but there is a wide disparity between various countries' economic and political factors. Most South American countries rely on only one or two exports, usually agricultural, with suitable lands often controlled by rich families. Most societies in South America feature major separations between classes, both economically and socially. Challenges faced by developing South American countries include geographical limitations, economic issues, and sustainable development, including the need to preserve the existing rainforests.

HUMAN SYSTEMS INFLUENCING EUROPE

Europe contains a wide variety of cultures, ethnic groups, physical geographical features, climates, and resources, all of which have influenced the distribution of its varied population. **Europe**, in general, is industrialized and developed, with cultural differences giving each individual country its own unique characteristics. Greek and Roman influences played a major role in European culture, as did Christianity. European countries spread their beliefs and cultural elements throughout the world by means of migration and colonization. They have had a significant influence on nearly every other continent in the world. While Western Europe has been largely democratic, Eastern Europe functioned under communist rule for many years. The formation of the European Union (EU) in 1993 has increased stability and positive diplomatic relations among European nations. Like other industrialized regions, Europe is now focusing on various environmental issues.

HUMAN SYSTEMS THAT HAVE SHAPED RUSSIA

After numerous conflicts, Russia became a Communist state, known as the **USSR**. With the collapse of the USSR in 1991, the country has struggled in its transition to a market-driven economy. Attempts to build a workable system have led to the destruction of natural resources as well as problems with nuclear power, including accidents such as Chernobyl. To complete the transition to a market economy, Russia would need to improve its transportation and communication systems and find a way to more efficiently use its natural resources.

The population of Russia is not distributed evenly, with three-quarters of the population living west of the Ural Mountains. The people of Russia encompass over a hundred different ethnic groups. Over eighty percent of the population is ethnically Russian, and Russian is the official language of the country.

HUMAN SYSTEMS THAT HAVE SHAPED NORTH AFRICA AND SOUTHWEST AND CENTRAL ASIA

The largely desert climate of these areas has led most population centers to rise around sources of **water**, such as the Nile River. This area is the home of the **earliest known civilizations** and the origin of Christianity, Judaism, and Islam. After serving as the site of huge, independent civilizations in ancient times, North Africa and Southwest and Central Asia were largely parceled out as **European colonies** during the 18th and 19th centuries. The beginning of the 20th century saw many of these countries gain their independence. **Islam** has served as a unifying force for large portions of these areas, and many of the inhabitants speak Arabic. In spite of the arid climate, agriculture is a large business, but the most valuable resource is **oil**. Centuries of conflict throughout this area have led to ongoing political problems. These political problems have also contributed to environmental issues.

HUMAN SYSTEMS THAT SHAPE AND INFLUENCE THE CULTURE OF SUB-SAHARAN AFRICA

South of the Sahara Desert, **Africa** is divided into a number of culturally diverse nations. The inhabitants are unevenly distributed due to geographical limitations that prevent settlement in vast areas. **AIDS** has become a major plague throughout this part of Africa, killing millions, largely due to restrictive beliefs that prevent education about the disease, as well as abject poverty and unsettled political situations that make it impossible to manage the pandemic. The population of this area of Africa is widely diverse due to extensive **migration**. Many of the people still rely on **subsistence farming** for their welfare. Starvation and poverty are rampant due to drought and political instability. Some areas are far more stable than others due to the greater availability of resources. These areas have been able to begin the process of **industrialization**.

HUMAN SYSTEMS THAT DETERMINE THE CULTURAL MAKEUP OF SOUTH ASIA

South Asia is home to one of the first human civilizations, which grew up in the **Indus River Valley**. With a great deal of disparity between rural and urban life, South Asia has much to do to improve the quality of life for its lower classes. Two major religions, **Hinduism** and **Buddhism**, have their origins in this region. Parts of South Asia, most notably India, were subject to **British rule** for several decades and are still working to improve independent governments and social systems. Overall, South Asia is very culturally diverse, with a wide mix of religions and languages throughout. Many individuals are **farmers**, but a growing number have found prosperity in the spread of **high-tech industries**. Industrialization is growing in South Asia but continues to face environmental, social, religious, and economic challenges.

HUMAN SYSTEMS SHAPING THE CULTURE OF EAST ASIA

Governments in East Asia are varied, ranging from communist to democratic governments, with some governments that mix both approaches. **Isolationism** throughout the area limited the countries' contact with other nations until the early 20th century. The unevenly distributed population of East Asia consists of over one and a half billion people with widely diverse ethnic backgrounds, religions, and languages. More residents live in **urban** areas than in **rural** areas, creating shortages of farmworkers at times. Japan, Taiwan, and South Korea are overall more urban, while China and Mongolia are more rural. Japan stands as the most industrial country in East Asia. Some areas of East Asia are suffering from major environmental issues. Japan has dealt with many of these problems and now has some of the strictest environmental laws in the world.

HUMAN SYSTEMS THAT HAVE INFLUENCED SOUTHEAST ASIA

Much of Southeast Asia was **colonized** by European countries during the 18th and 19th centuries, with the exception of Siam, now known as Thailand. All Southeast Asian countries are now independent, but the 20th century saw numerous conflicts between **communist** and **democratic** forces.

Southeast Asia has been heavily influenced by both Buddhist and Muslim religions. Industrialization is growing, with the population moving in large numbers from rural to urban areas. Some have moved to avoid conflict, oppression, and poverty.

Natural disasters, including volcanoes, typhoons, and flash flooding, are fairly common in Southeast Asia, creating extensive economic damage and societal disruption.

HUMAN SYSTEMS THAT AFFECT THE DEVELOPMENT AND CULTURE OF AUSTRALIA, OCEANA, AND ANTARCTICA

South Pacific cultures originally migrated from Southeast Asia, creating hunter-gatherer or sometimes settled agricultural communities. **European** countries moved in during later centuries, seeking the plentiful natural resources of the area. Today, some South Pacific islands remain under the control of foreign governments, and culture in these areas mixes modern, industrialized society with indigenous culture. Population is unevenly distributed, largely due to the inhabitability of many parts of the South Pacific, such as the extremely hot desert areas of Australia. **Agriculture** still drives much of the economy, with **tourism** growing. **Antarctica** remains the only continent that has not been claimed by any country. There are no permanent human habitations in Antarctica, but scientists and explorers visit the area on a temporary basis.

HUMAN-ENVIRONMENT INTERACTION

Geography also studies the ways people interact with, use, and change their **environment**. The effects, reasons, and consequences of these changes are studied, as are the ways the environment limits or influences human behavior. This kind of study can help determine the best course of action when a nation or group of people is considering making changes to the environment, such as building a dam or removing natural landscape to build or expand roads. Study of the **consequences** can help determine if these actions are manageable and how long-term, detrimental results can be mitigated.

PHYSICAL GEOGRAPHY AND CLIMATES
PHYSICAL GEOGRAPHY AND CLIMATE OF NORTH AMERICA

Together, the US and Canada make up the majority of North America and both have a similar distribution of geographical features: mountain ranges in both the east and the west, stretches of fertile plains through the center, and lakes and waterways. Both areas were shaped by **glaciers**, which also deposited highly fertile soil. Because they are so large, Canada and the US experience several varieties of **climate**, including continental climates with four seasons in median areas, tropical climates in the southern part of the US, and arctic climes in the far north. The remaining area of North America includes Mexico, Central America, the Caribbean Isles, and Greenland.

PHYSICAL GEOGRAPHY AND CLIMATE OF SOUTH AMERICA

South America contains a wide variety of geographical features, including high **mountains** such as the Andes, wide **plains**, and high-altitude **plateaus**. The region contains numerous natural resources, but many of them have remained unused due to various obstacles, including political issues, geographic barriers, and lack of sufficient economic power. Climate zones in South America are largely **tropical**, with rainforests and savannas, but vertical climate zones and grasslands also exist in some places.

PHYSICAL GEOGRAPHY AND CLIMATE OF EUROPE

Europe spans a wide area with a variety of climate zones. In the east and south are **mountain** ranges, while the north is dominated by a **plains** region. The long coastline and the island nature of some countries, such as Britain, mean the climate is often warmer than other lands at similar latitudes, as the area is warmed by **ocean currents**. Many areas of western Europe have a moderate climate, while areas of the south are dominated by the classic Mediterranean climate. Europe carries a high level of natural resources. Numerous waterways help connect the inner regions with the coastal areas. Much of Europe is **industrialized**, and **agriculture** has been developed for thousands of years.

PHYSICAL GEOGRAPHY AND CLIMATE OF RUSSIA

Russia's area encompasses part of Asia and Europe. From the standpoint of square footage alone, **Russia** is the largest country in the world. Due to its size, Russia encompasses a wide variety of climatic regions, including **plains**, **plateaus**, **mountains**, and **tundra**.

Russia's **climate** can be quite harsh, with rivers that are frozen most of the year, making transportation of the country's rich natural resources more difficult. Siberia, in northern Russia, is dominated by **permafrost**. Native peoples in this area still follow a hunting and gathering lifestyle, living in portable yurts and subsisting largely on herds of reindeer or caribou. Other areas include taiga with extensive, dense woods in north-central Russia and more temperate steppes and grasslands in the southwest.

PHYSICAL GEOGRAPHY AND CLIMATE OF NORTH AFRICA, SOUTHWEST, AND CENTRAL ASIA

This area of the world is complex in its geographical structure and climate, incorporating seas, peninsulas, rivers, mountains, and numerous other features. **Earthquakes** are common, with tectonic plates in the area remaining active. Much of the world's **oil** lies in this area. The tendency of the large rivers of North Africa, especially the Nile, to follow a set pattern of **drought** and extreme **fertility**, led people to settle there from prehistoric times. As technology has advanced, people have tamed this river, making its activity more predictable and the land around it more productive. The extremely arid nature of many other parts of this area has also led to **human intervention** such as irrigation to increase agricultural production.

PHYSICAL GEOGRAPHY AND CLIMATE OF THE SOUTHERN PORTION OF AFRICA

South of the Sahara Desert, the high elevations and other geographical characteristics have made it very difficult for human travel or settlement to occur. The geography of the area is dominated by a series of **plateaus**. There are also mountain ranges and a large rift valley in the eastern part of the country. Contrasting the wide desert areas, sub-Saharan Africa contains numerous lakes, rivers, and world-famous waterfalls. The area has **tropical** climates, including rainforests, savannas, steppes, and desert areas. The main natural resources are minerals, including gems and water.

PHYSICAL GEOGRAPHY AND CLIMATE OF SOUTH ASIA

The longest **alluvial plain**, a plain caused by shifting floodplains of major rivers and river systems over time, exists in South Asia. South Asia boasts three major **river systems** in the Ganges, Indus, and Brahmaputra. It also has large deposits of **minerals**, including iron ore that is in great demand internationally. South Asia holds mountains, plains, plateaus, and numerous islands. The climates range from tropical to highlands and desert areas. South Asia also experiences monsoon winds that cause a long rainy season. Variations in climate, elevation, and human activity influence agricultural production.

GEOGRAPHY AND CLIMATE OF EAST ASIA

East Asia includes North and South Korea, Mongolia, China, Japan, and Taiwan. Mineral resources are plentiful but not evenly distributed throughout. The coastlines are long, and while the population is large, farmlands are sparse. As a result, the surrounding ocean has become a major source of sustenance. East Asia is large enough to encompass several climate regions. **Ocean currents** provide milder climates to coastal areas, while **monsoons** provide the majority of the rainfall for the region. **Typhoons** are somewhat common, as are **earthquakes**, **volcanoes**, and **tsunamis**. The latter occur because of the tectonic plates that meet beneath the continent and remain somewhat active.

GEOGRAPHY AND CLIMATE OF SOUTHEAST ASIA

Southeast Asia lies largely on the **equator**, and roughly half of the countries of the region are island nations. These countries include Indonesia, the Philippines, Vietnam, Thailand, Myanmar, and Malaysia (which is partially on the mainland and partially an island country). The island nations of Southeast Asia feature mountains that are considered part of the **Ring of Fire**, an area where tectonic plates remain active, leading to extensive volcanic activity as well as earthquakes and tsunamis. Southeast Asia boasts many rivers and abundant natural resources, including gems, fossil fuels, and minerals. There are basically two seasons: wet and dry. The wet season arrives with the **monsoons**. In general, Southeast Asia consists of **tropical rainforest climates**, but there are some mountain areas and tropical savannas.

GEOGRAPHY AND CLIMATE OF AUSTRALIA, OCEANIA, AND ANTARCTICA

In the far southern hemisphere of the globe, Australia and Oceania present their own climatic combinations. **Australia**, the only island on Earth that is also a continent, has extensive deserts as well as mountains and lowlands. The economy is driven by agriculture, including ranches and farms, and minerals. While the steppes bordering extremely arid inland areas are suitable for livestock, only the coastal areas receive sufficient rainfall for crops without using irrigation. **Oceania** refers to over 10,000 Pacific islands created by volcanic activity. Most of these have tropical climates with wet and dry seasons. **New Zealand**, Australia's nearest neighbor, boasts rich forests, mountain ranges, and relatively moderate temperatures, including rainfall throughout the year. **Antarctica** is covered with ice. Its major resource consists of scientific information. It supports some wildlife, such as penguins, and little vegetation, primarily mosses or lichens.

THEORY OF PLATE TECTONICS

According to the geological theory of plate tectonics, Earth's crust is made up of ten major and several minor **tectonic plates**. These plates are the solid areas of the crust. They float on top of Earth's mantle, which is made up of molten rock. Because the plates float on this liquid component of Earth's crust, they move, creating major changes in Earth's surface. These changes can happen very slowly over a long time period, such as in continental drift, or rapidly, such as when earthquakes occur. **Interaction** between the different continental plates can create mountain ranges, volcanic activity, major earthquakes, and deep rifts.

TYPES OF PLATE BOUNDARIES

Plate tectonics defines three types of plate boundaries, determined by how the edges of the plates interact. These **plate boundaries** are:

- **Convergent boundaries**—the bordering plates move toward one another. When they collide directly, this is known as continental collision, which can create very large, high mountain ranges such as the Himalayas and the Andes. If one plate slides under the other, this is called subduction. Subduction can lead to intense volcanic activity. One example is the Ring of Fire that lies along the northern Pacific coastlines.
- **Divergent boundaries**—plates move away from each other. This movement leads to rifts such as the Mid-Atlantic Ridge and East Africa's Great Rift Valley.
- **Transform boundaries**—plate boundaries slide in opposite directions against each other. Intense pressure builds up along transform boundaries as the plates grind along each other's edges, leading to earthquakes. Many major fault lines, including the San Andreas Fault, lie along transform boundaries.

EROSION, WEATHERING, TRANSPORTATION, AND DEPOSITION

Erosion involves movement of any loose material on Earth's surface. This can include soil, sand, or rock fragments. These loose fragments can be displaced by natural forces such as wind, water, ice, plant cover, and human factors. **Mechanical erosion** occurs due to natural forces. **Chemical erosion** occurs as a result of human intervention and activities. **Weathering** occurs when atmospheric elements affect Earth's surface. Water, heat, ice, and pressure all lead to weathering. **Transportation** refers to loose material being moved by wind, water, or ice. Glacial movement, for example, carries everything from pebbles to boulders, sometimes over long distances. **Deposition** is the result of transportation. When material is transported, it is eventually deposited, and builds up to create formations like moraines and sand dunes.

EFFECTS OF HUMAN INTERACTION AND CONFLICT ON GEOGRAPHICAL BOUNDARIES

Human societies and their interaction have led to divisions of territories into **countries** and various other subdivisions. While these divisions are at their root artificial, they are important to geographers in discussing various populations' interactions.

Geographical divisions often occur through conflict between different human populations. The reasons behind these divisions include:

- Control of resources
- Control of important trade routes
- Control of populations

Conflict often occurs due to religious, political, language, or race differences. Natural resources are finite and so often lead to conflict over how they are distributed among populations.

STATE SOVEREIGNTY

State sovereignty recognizes the division of geographical areas into areas controlled by various governments or groups of people. These groups control not only the territory but also all its natural resources and the inhabitants of the area. The entire planet Earth is divided into **political** or **administratively sovereign areas** recognized to be controlled by a particular government, with the exception of the continent of Antarctica.

ALLIANCES

Alliances form between different countries based on similar interests, political goals, cultural values, or military issues. Six existing **international alliances** include:

- North Atlantic Treaty Organization (NATO)
- Common Market
- European Union (EU)
- United Nations (UN)
- Caribbean Community
- Council of Arab Economic Unity

In addition, very large **companies** and **multi-national corporations** can create alliances and various kinds of competition based on the need to control resources, production, and the overall marketplace.

WAYS AGRICULTURAL REVOLUTION CHANGED SOCIETY

The agricultural revolution began approximately 6,000 years ago when the **plow** was invented in **Mesopotamia**. Using a plow drawn by animals, people were able to cultivate crops in large quantities rather than gathering available seeds and grains and planting them by hand. Because large-scale agriculture was labor-intensive, this led to the development of stable communities where people gathered to make farming possible. As **stable farming communities** replaced groups of nomadic hunter-gatherers, human society underwent profound changes. Societies became dependent on limited numbers of crops as well as subject to the vagaries of weather. Trading livestock and surplus agricultural output led to the growth of large-scale **commerce** and **trade routes**.

WAYS HUMAN POPULATIONS MODIFY THEIR SURROUNDING ENVIRONMENT

The agricultural revolution led human societies to begin changing their surroundings to accommodate their needs for shelter and room to cultivate food and to provide for domestic animals. Clearing ground for crops, redirecting waterways for irrigation purposes, and building permanent settlements all create major changes in the **environment**. Large-scale agriculture can lead to loose topsoil and damaging erosion. Building large cities leads to degraded air quality, water pollution from energy consumption, and many other side effects that can severely damage the environment. Recently, many countries have taken action by passing laws to **reduce human impact** on the environment and reduce the potentially damaging side effects. This is called **environmental policy**.

ECOLOGY

Ecology is the study of the way living creatures interact with their environment. **Biogeography** explores the way physical features of Earth affect living creatures.

Ecology bases its studies on three different levels of the environment:

- **Ecosystem**—this is a specific physical environment and all the organisms that live there.
- **Biome**—this is a group of ecosystems, usually consisting of a large area with similar flora and fauna as well as similar climate and soil. Examples of biomes include deserts, tropical rain forests, taigas, and tundra.
- **Habitat**—this is an area in which a specific species usually lives. The habitat includes the necessary soil, water, and resources for that particular species, as well as predators and other species that compete for the same resources.

TYPES OF INTERACTIONS OCCURRING BETWEEN SPECIES IN AN INDIVIDUAL HABITAT

Different interactions occur among species and members of single species within a habitat. These **interactions** fall into three categories:

- **Competition** — competition occurs when different animals, either of the same species or of different species, compete for the same resources. Robins can compete with other robins for available food, but other insectivores also compete for these same resources.
- **Predation**— predation occurs when one species depends on the other species for food, such as a fox who subsists on small mammals.
- **Symbiosis** — symbiosis occurs when two different species exist in the same environment without negatively affecting each other. Some symbiotic relationships are beneficial to one or both organisms without harm occurring to either.

IMPORTANCE OF AN ORGANISM'S ABILITY TO ADAPT

If a species is relocated from one habitat to another, it must **adapt** in order to survive. Some species are more capable of adapting than others. Those that cannot adapt will not survive. There are different ways a creature can adapt, including behavior modification and structural or physiological changes. Adaptation is also vital if an organism's environment changes around it. Although the creature has not been relocated, it finds itself in a new environment that requires changes in order to survive. The more readily an organism can adapt, the more likely it is to survive. The almost infinite ability of **humans** to adapt is a major reason why they are able to survive in almost any habitat in any area of the world.

BIODIVERSITY

Biodiversity refers to the variety of habitats that exist on the planet, as well as the variety of organisms that can exist within these habitats. A greater level of **biodiversity** makes it more likely that an individual habitat will flourish along with the species that depend upon it. Changes in habitat, including climate change, human intervention, or other factors, can reduce biodiversity by causing the extinction of certain species.

GACE Practice Test

Want to take this practice test in an online interactive format?
Check out the bonus page, which includes interactive practice questions and
much more: **http://www.mometrix.com/bonus948/gacemgsocsci**

1. Some countries in the Americas still have large populations of indigenous or partly indigenous peoples. Of the following, which pair of countries does not have comparatively as large of an indigenous population as the other countries?
   a. Guatemala and Peru
   b. Ecuador and Bolivia
   c. Paraguay and Mexico
   d. Argentina and Uruguay

2. Which of the following statements is *not* true regarding English expansionism in the 16th century?
   a. England's defeat of the Spanish Armada in 1588 brought a decisive end to their war with Spain.
   b. King Henry VIII's desire to divorce Catherine of Aragon strengthened English expansionism.
   c. Queen Elizabeth's support for the Protestant Reformation strengthened English expansionism.
   d. Sir Francis Drake and other English sea captains plundered the goods that the Spaniards took from indigenous peoples.

3. Which of the following is *not* correct regarding the Virginia Companies?
   a. One of these companies, the Virginia Company of Plymouth, made its base in North America.
   b. One of these companies, the Virginia Company of London, made its base in Massachusetts.
   c. One company had a charter to colonize America between the Hudson and Cape Fear rivers.
   d. One company had a charter to colonize America from the Potomac River to north Maine.

4. Which of the following conquistadores unwittingly gave smallpox to the indigenous peoples and destroyed the Aztec empire in Mexico?
   a. Balboa
   b. Ponce de Leon
   c. Cortes
   d. De Vaca

5. Which statement best describes the significance of the Peter Zenger trial in colonial America?
   a. It was the earliest American case on the right to bear arms.
   b. It established a precedent for freedom of the press.
   c. It was the earliest American case on right of peaceable assembly.
   d. It established a precedent for freedom of religion.

120

6. Which of these factors was *not* a direct contributor to the beginning of the American Revolution?

    a. The attitudes of American colonists toward Great Britain following the French and Indian War

    b. The attitudes of leaders in Great Britain toward the American colonies and imperialism

    c. James Otis's court argument against Great Britain's Writs of Assistance as breaking natural law

    d. Lord Grenville's Proclamation of 1763, the Sugar Act, the Currency Act, and especially the Stamp Act

7. Which of the following statements is *not* true regarding the Tea Act of 1773?

    a. The British East India Company was suffering financially because Americans were buying tea smuggled from Holland.

    b. Parliament granted concessions to the British East India Company to ship tea straight to America, bypassing England.

    c. Colonists found that even with added taxes, tea directly shipped by the British East India Company cost less, and they bought it.

    d. American colonists refused to buy less expensive tea from the British East India Company on the principle of taxation.

8. Which of the following is true concerning the formation of new state governments in the new United States of America following freedom from British rule?

    a. By the end of 1777, new constitutions had been created for twelve of the American states.

    b. The states of Connecticut and Massachusetts retained their colonial charters, minus the British parts.

    c. The state of Massachusetts required a special convention for its constitution, setting a good example.

    d. The state of Massachusetts did not formally begin to use its new constitution until 1778.

9. Which of the following is *not* a true statement regarding the Louisiana Purchase?

    a. Jefferson sent a delegation to Paris to endeavor to purchase only the city of New Orleans from Napoleon.

    b. Napoleon, anticipating U.S. intrusions into Louisiana, offered to sell the U.S. the entire Louisiana territory.

    c. The American delegation accepted Napoleon's offer, though they were only authorized to buy New Orleans.

    d. The Louisiana Purchase, once it was completed, increased the territory of the U.S. by 50% overnight.

10. Which of these was *not* a factor that contributed to the duel in which Aaron Burr killed Alexander Hamilton?

    a. Some Federalists who opposed U.S. Western expansion were attempting to organize a movement to secede from the Union.

    b. Alexander Hamilton challenged Aaron Burr to a duel because he objected to U.S. expansion into the West, which Burr supported.

    c. Secessionist Federalists tried to enlist Aaron Burr's support for their cause by backing him in his run for Governor of New York.

    d. Alexander Hamilton was the leader of the group that opposed Aaron Burr's campaign to run for New York Governor.

11. Which of the following did *not* occur during the War of 1812?

a. Early in the war, the U.S. executed a three-pronged invasion of Canada and succeeded on two of three fronts.
b. Early in the war, Americans won naval battles against the British, but were soon beaten back by the British.
c. Admiral Oliver Hazard Perry's fleet defeated the British navy on Lake Erie in September, 1813.
d. William Henry Harrison invaded Canada and defeated the British and the Native Americans in the Battle of the Thames.

12. Which of the following was *not* an immediate effect of rapid urban growth in the 1800s?

a. Poor sanitation conditions in the cities
b. Epidemics of diseases in the cities
c. Inadequate police and fire protection
d. Widespread urban political corruption

13. Which of the following laws was instrumental in spurring westward migration to the Great Plains between 1860 and 1880?

a. The Homestead Act
b. The Timber Culture Act
c. The Desert Land Act
d. All of these laws were instrumental in spurring westward migration to the Great Plains during that period.

14. What did *not* contribute to ending America's neutrality in World War I?

a. Germany's telegram to Mexico that proposed they form an alliance if the US entered the war
b. Germany's declaration of a war on Russia after Archduke Ferdinand's assassination
c. Germany's sinking the British ship *Lusitania,* which killed 128 American passengers
d. Germany's declaration of unrestricted submarine warfare on all ships in the war zone

15. Of the following international diplomatic conferences, which one made US-Soviet differences apparent?

a. The Potsdam conference
b. The conference at Yalta
c. Dumbarton Oaks conference
d. The Tehran conference

16. Which statement about relations between the Middle East and the US and Europe in the 1950s is *not* correct?

a. President Nasser of Egypt refused to align with the US in the Cold War.
b. President Eisenhower removed US funding from the Aswan Dam in 1956.
c. President Nasser nationalized the Suez Canal, which was owned by England.
d. In 1956, Egypt attacked Israel, and England and France joined in the war.

17. Of the following, which person or group was *not* instrumental in postwar advancement of civil rights and desegregation during the 1940s and 1950s?

   a. The President
   b. The Supreme Court
   c. The Congress
   d. The NAACP

18. Of the programs enacted by President Lyndon B. Johnson's administration, which was most closely related to John F. Kennedy's legacy?

   a. The Economic Opportunity Act
   b. The Civil Rights Act
   c. The Great Society program
   d. Clean Air Act

19. Which statement regarding US international trade policy in the 1990s is *not* correct?

   a. In 1994, the General Agreement on Tariffs and Trade (GATT) was approved by Congress.
   b. The GATT was between 57 countries who agreed they would remove or reduce many of their tariffs.
   c. The GATT created the World Trade Organization (WTO) to settle international trade differences.
   d. The NAFTA (North American Free Trade Agreement), ratified in 1994, had originally been set up by George H.W. Bush's administration.

20. Which statement about factors related to the growth of the US economy between 1945 and 1970 is *not* correct?

   a. The Baby Boom's greatly increased birth rates contributed to economic growth during this time.
   b. The reduction in military spending after World War II contributed to the stronger US economy.
   c. Government programs and growing affluence nearly quadrupled college enrollments in 20 years.
   d. Increased mobility and bigger families caused fast suburban expansion, especially in the Sunbelt.

21. Which of the following statements regarding immigration to America during the 1980s is *not* true?

   a. Twice as many immigrants came to America during the 1980s than during the 1970s.
   b. Latin Americans comprised the largest proportion of immigrants to America in the 1980s.
   c. Most immigrants to the US in the 1980s were Latin American, Asian, and Caribbean.
   d. The 1986 Immigration Reform and Control Act reduced illegal Mexican immigration.

22. Which is *not* correct regarding black activism during the 1960s?

   a. There was a riot in the Los Angeles ghetto of Watts in 1965.
   b. There was a riot involving black activists in Newark, New Jersey, after the Watts riot.
   c. The Mississippi Freedom Democrats unseated that state's delegation at the convention.
   d. There was a riot involving black activists in Detroit, Michigan, after the riot in Watts.

23. What was the earliest written language in Mesopotamia?

a. Sumerian
b. Elamite
c. Akkadian
d. Aramaic

24. During which of these periods were pyramids *not* built in Egypt?

a. The Old Kingdom
b. The Middle Kingdom
c. The New Kingdom
d. The Third Dynasty

25. Which of the following is *not* true about the Crusades?

a. Their purpose was for European rulers to retake the Middle East from Muslims
b. The Crusades succeeded at European kings' goal of reclaiming the "holy land"
c. The Crusades accelerated the already incipient decline of the Byzantine Empire
d. Egypt saw a return as a major Middle Eastern power as a result of the Crusades

26. Which of the following is NOT true about the Italian Renaissance?

a. The Black Death killed 1/3 of the population of Europe.
b. The lower classes benefited from the need for laborers.
c. The middle classes developed from a need for services.
d. The upper class invested in banks.

27. Which of the following is *not* correct regarding assumptions of mercantilism?

a. The money and the wealth of a nation are identical properties
b. In order to prosper, a nation should try to increase its imports
c. In order to prosper, a nation should try to increase its exports
d. Economic protectionism by national governments is advisable

28. Which of the following is *not* true about the English Civil Wars between 1641 and 1651?

a. These wars all were waged between Royalists and Parliamentarians
b. The outcome of this series of civil wars was victory for Parliament
c. These wars legalized Parliament's consent as requisite to monarchy
d. Two of the wars in this time involved supporters of King Charles I

29. Which of the following choices is/are *not* considered among causes of the French Revolution?

a. Famines causing malnutrition and starvation
b. War debt, court spending, and a bad monetary system
c. Resentment against the Catholic Church's rule
d. Resentment against the Protestant Reformation

30. Which statement best describes the role played by the French economy in causing the 1789 French Revolution?

a. France's very large national debt led to heavy tax burdens on the French peasantry.
b. Nearly sixty percent of annual national expenditures financed luxuries for the French nobility.
c. Reforms in the guild system allowed many peasants to rise to the middle class.
d. The king's attempt to curtail free trade led skilled journeymen to rebel against the monarchy.

31. Which of the following statements is accurate regarding the end of the First World War?

a. The Treaty of Versailles brought peace among all countries involved in the war
b. The Treaty of Versailles contained a clause for establishing the United Nations
c. President Woodrow Wilson had proposed forming a coalition of world nations
d. President Wilson succeeded in getting the USA to ratify the League of Nations

32. How did Russia's participation in World War I influence the Russian Revolution?

a. Civilian suffering and military setbacks served as a catalyst for revolutionary forces.
b. Nicholas III capitalized on battlefield successes to temporarily silence critics.
c. The government eased laws banning collective action by factory workers to appease social discontent about the war.
d. Anti-government protesters temporarily ceased protesting to show patriotism in a difficult war.

33. During the decolonization of the Cold War years, which of the following events occurred chronologically latest?

a. The Eastern Bloc and Satellite states became independent from the Soviet Union
b. Canada became totally independent from British Parliament via the Canada Act
c. The Bahamas, in the Caribbean, became independent from the United Kingdom
d. The Algerian War ended, and Algeria became independent from France

34. Why was U.S. industrialization confined to the Northeast until after the Civil War?

a. Because the Civil War delayed the development of water-powered manufacturing
b. Because the Northeast had faster-running rivers than the rivers found in the South
c. Because Slater's first cotton mill with horse-drawn production lost so much money
d. Because the technical innovations for milling textiles had not as yet been invented

35. Which of the following statements is *not* an accurate statement about the Puritans in England?

a. The Puritans unconditionally gave all their support to the English Reformation
b. The Puritans saw the Church of England as too much like the Catholic Church
c. The Puritans became a chief political power because of the English Civil War
d. The Puritans' clergy mainly departed from the Church of England after 1662

36. Which of the following statements is *not* true about the Gilded Age in America?

a. The Gilded Age was the era of the "robber barons" in the business world
b. The Gilded Age got its name from the excesses of the wealthy upper class
c. The Gilded Age had philanthropy Carnegie called the "Gospel of Wealth"
d. The Gilded Age is a term whose origins have not been identified clearly

37. Which of the following is *not* true about Democracy and the formation of the United States?

    a. The founding fathers stated in the Constitution that the USA would be a democracy

    b. The Declaration of Independence did not dictate democracy but stated its principles

    c. The United States Constitution stipulated that government be elected by the people

    d. The United States Constitution had terms to protect some, but not all, of the people

38. Which of the following statements does *not* describe the average European diet BEFORE the expansion of trade routes?

    a. Europeans ate for survival, not enjoyment.

    b. They had an abundance of preservatives such as salt that could make food last longer.

    c. Grain-based foods such as porridge and bread were staple meals.

    d. Spices were unavailable.

39. Which of these is true concerning the French Revolution, America, and Europe?

    a. When France's revolution spread and they went to war with other European countries, George Washington allied with the French.

    b. During the time period around 1792, American merchants were conducting trading with countries on both sides of the war.

    c. American traders conducted business with various countries, profiting the most from the British West Indies.

    d. The Spanish navy retaliated against America for trading with the French by capturing American trading ships.

40. Which group overtook Rome in the mid-600s BC and established much of its infrastructure, including sewers, roads, and fortifications, only to be driven out of the city in 509 BC?

    a. Latins.

    b. Etruscans.

    c. Greeks.

    d. Persians.

41. The writers of The Federalist Papers published under the pen name "Publius." Who were the authors?

    a. James Madison, John Jay, and Alexander Hamilton

    b. George Washington, Thomas Jefferson, and James Madison

    c. Alexander Hamilton, Benjamin Franklin, and Thomas Jefferson

    d. Benjamin Franklin, John Jay, and Thomas Jefferson

42. Social studies education has many practical applications. Which of the following is the most direct application of teaching high school seniors the structure of the U.S. government?

    a. Knowledge of the fundamentals of federalism

    b. Informed participation in school elections

    c. Knowledge of a system of checks and balances

    d. Informed participation in U.S. political processes

43. The U.S. government is best understood as a federalist government because:

    a. the legislative branch consists of two representative bodies.

    b. it is a representative democracy rather than a direct democracy.

    c. political power is divided between the federal government and the states.

    d. a national Constitution shapes national legislation.

44. One reason the Articles of Confederation created a weak government was because it limited Congress's ability to do what?

    a. Declare war

    b. Conduct a census

    c. Vote

    d. Tax

45. The philosophy of the late 17th-18th centuries that influenced the Constitution was from the Age of:

    a. Enlightenment

    b. Empire

    c. Discovery

    d. Industry

46. The votes of how many states were needed to ratify the Constitution?

    a. Five

    b. Ten

    c. Nine

    d. Seven

47. Virginian _____ advocated a stronger central government and was influential at the Constitutional Convention.

    a. Benjamin Franklin

    b. James Madison

    c. George Mason

    d. Robert Yates

48. Power divided between local and central branches of government is a definition of what term?

    a. Bicameralism

    b. Checks and balances

    c. Legislative oversight

    d. Federalism

49. The Senate and the House of Representatives are an example of:

    a. Bicameralism

    b. Checks and balances

    c. Legislative oversight

    d. Federalism

50. The vice president succeeds the president in case of death, illness or impeachment. What is the order of succession for the next three successors, according to the Presidential Succession Act of 1947?

a. President pro tempore of the Senate, secretary of state, and secretary of defense
b. Speaker of the House, president pro tempore of the Senate, and secretary of state
c. President pro tempore of the Senate, Speaker of the House, and secretary of state
d. Secretary of state, secretary of defense, and Speaker of the House

51. The President has the power to veto legislation. How is this power limited?

I. Congress can override the veto
II. The President cannot line veto
III. The President cannot propose legislation

a. I and III
b. II only
c. I and II
d. I only

52. The civil rights act that outlawed segregation in schools and public places also:

a. Gave minorities the right to vote
b. Established women's right to vote
c. Outlawed unequal voter registration
d. Provided protection for children

53. Which of the following is a power held only by the federal government?

a. The power to levy taxes, borrow money, and spend money
b. The power to award copyrights and patents to people or groups
c. The power to establish the criteria that qualify a person to vote
d. The power to ratify proposed amendments to the Constitution

54. Of the following actions, which one requires a three-fourths majority?

a. State approval of a proposed amendment to the Constitution
b. Submitting a proposal for an amendment to the Constitution
c. Ratification for appointments to the Presidency in the Senate
d. The introduction of charges for an impeachment in the House

55. Which of the following statements is *not* correct about U.S. westward expansion and Manifest Destiny?

a. The idea that U.S. freedom and values should be shared with, even forced upon, as many people as possible had existed for many years.
b. The term "Manifest Destiny" and the idea it represented had been used for many years prior to the 1830s.
c. Many Americans believed that America as a nation should ultimately be extended to include Canada and Mexico.
d. Increased nationalism after the resolution of the War of 1812 and rapid population growth added to Manifest Destiny.

56. Presidential candidates are eligible for public funding if they raise $5,000 per state in how many states?

    a. Twenty
    b. Ten
    c. Twenty-five
    d. Seventeen

57. What judicial system did America borrow from England?

    a. Due process
    b. Federal law
    c. Commerce law
    d. Common law

58. Which of the following is a possible absolute location for New Orleans?

    a. 30° S, 90° E
    b. 30° N, 90° E
    c. 30° S, 90° W
    d. 30° N, 90° W

59. On which type of map are different countries represented in different colors, with no two adjacent countries sharing a color?

    a. Physical map
    b. Political map
    c. Climate map
    d. Contour map

60. Which of the following statements about the equator is true?

    a. It intersects four continents.
    b. It is to the north of both horse latitudes.
    c. It is located at 0° longitude.
    d. It is not very windy.

61. The apparent distance between Greenland and Norway is greatest on a(n)

    a. Mercator Map.
    b. Conic Projection Map.
    c. Contour Map.
    d. Equal-Area Projection Map.

62. Which of the following is *not* a method of representing relief on a physical map?

    a. Symbols
    b. Color
    c. Shading
    d. Contour Lines

63. Which map describes the movement of people, trends, or materials across a physical area?

    a. Political Map
    b. Cartogram
    c. Qualitative Map
    d. Flow-line Map

64. What is the most common type of volcano on earth?

    a. Lava dome
    b. Composite volcano
    c. Shield volcano
    d. Cinder cone

65. Water is continuously recycled in the hydrosphere. By which process does water return to the atmosphere after precipitation?

    a. Percolation
    b. Cohesion
    c. Evaporation
    d. Condensation

66. Which type of rock is formed by extreme heat and pressure?

    a. Limestone
    b. Metamorphic
    c. Sedimentary
    d. Igneous

67. Which part of a hurricane features the strongest winds and greatest rainfall?

    a. Eye wall
    b. Front
    c. Eye
    d. Outward spiral

68. Which of the following are not included in a geographical definition of Southeast Asia?

    a. Myanmar, Laos, Cambodia, and Thailand
    b. Vietnam, the Malay Peninsula, and Brunei
    c. East Malaysia, Indonesia, and the Philippines
    d. These are all geographical parts of Southeast Asia

69. Which of the following exemplifies the multiplier effect of large cities?

    a. The presence of specialized equipment for an industry attracts even more business.
    b. The large population lowers the price of goods.
    c. Public transportation means more people can commute to work.
    d. A local newspaper can afford to give away the Sunday edition.

70. For thousands of years, Africans have cultivated the grasslands south of the Sahara Desert, an area known as the

    a. Qattara Depression.
    b. Great Rift Valley.
    c. Congo Basin.
    d. Sahel.

71. Tracy needs to determine the shortest route between Lima and Lisbon. Which of the following maps should she use?

    a. Azimuthal projection with the North Pole at the center
    b. Azimuthal projection with Lisbon at the center
    c. Robinson projection of the Eastern Hemisphere
    d. Robinson projection of the Western Hemisphere

72. Which of the following countries are separated by a geometric border?

    a. Turkish Cyprus and Greek Cyprus
    b. North Korea and South Korea
    c. France and Spain
    d. England and Ireland

73. During one year in Grassley County, there are 750 births, 350 deaths, 80 immigrations, and 50 emigrations. What is the natural increase rate for this year?

    a. 400
    b. 830
    c. 430
    d. More information is required.

74. Which of the following is *not* one of the world's four major population agglomerations?

    a. North Africa
    b. Eastern North America
    c. South Asia
    d. Europe

75. Which of the following statements concerning choice theory are correct?

    I. Scarcity forces people, including producers, to make choices
    II. Producers make choices and, as a result, face trade-offs
    III. Opportunity cost is one way to measure the cost of a choice

    a. I only
    b. I and II only
    c. II and III only
    d. I, II, and III

76. John Maynard Keynes advocated what?

    a. Supply-side economics
    b. Demand-side economics
    c. Laissez faire economics
    d. The Laffer Curve

77. Proponents of legislating greater societal income equity, support which of the following:

    I. Impose a progressive income tax
    II. Impose high estate taxes
    III. Impose a gift tax

  a. I only
  b. II only
  c. I, II, and III
  d. II and III only

78. Which of the following best defines American GDP?

  a. The value, in American dollars, of all goods and services produced within American borders during one calendar year
  b. The value, in American dollars, of all goods and services produced by American companies during one calendar year
  c. The total value, in American dollars, of all American household incomes during one calendar year
  d. The value, in American dollars, of a "market basket" of goods and services in one year divided by the value of the same market basket in a previous year multiplied by 100

79. Ivy loses her job because her skills as a seamstress are no longer required due to a new piece of machinery that does the work of a seamstress more quickly and for less money. Which type of unemployment is this?

  a. Frictional
  b. Structural
  c. Cyclical
  d. Careless

80. Which is considered part of the natural rate of unemployment?

  a. Frictional unemployment only
  b. Cyclical unemployment and frictional unemployment
  c. Structural unemployment and cyclical unemployment
  d. Frictional unemployment and structural unemployment

81. Which of the following is a supply shock NOT likely to produce?

  a. An increase in input prices
  b. An increase in price levels
  c. An increase in employment
  d. A decrease in GDP

82. Which of the following are true of the demand curve?

    I. It is normally downward sloping
    II. It is normally upward sloping
    III. It is influenced by the law of diminishing marginal unity
    IV. It is unaffected by the law of diminishing marginal unity

  a. I and III only
  b. I and IV only
  c. II and III only
  d. II and IV only

83. **The price of fleece blankets goes up from $10 to $11. At the same time, demand goes down from 1,000 blankets to 800 blankets. Which of the following statements is true?**

    a. Demand is elastic
    b. Demand is inelastic
    c. The price elasticity quotient, or E_d, is less than 1
    d. The price elasticity quotient, or E_d, is equal to 1

84. **The price of oil drops dramatically, saving soda pop manufacturers great amounts of money spent on making soda pop and delivering their product to market. Prices for soda pop, however, stay the same. This is an example of what?**

    a. Sticky prices
    b. Sticky wages
    c. The multiplier effect
    d. Aggregate expenditure

85. **Which of the following will result if two nations use the theory of comparative advantage when making decisions of which goods to produce and trade?**

    a. Each nation will make all of their own goods
    b. Both nations will specialize in the production of the same specific goods
    c. Each nation will specialize in the production of different specific goods
    d. Neither nation will trade with one another

86. **Which of the following is most likely to benefit from inflation?**

    a. A bond investor who owns fixed-rate bonds
    b. A retired widow with no income other than fixed Social Security payments
    c. A person who has taken out a fixed-rate loan
    d. A local bank who has loaned money out at fixed rate

87. **What does the data in this table most directly describe?**

Inputs	1	2	3	4
Output	20	50	80	100

    a. The Law of Diminishing Marginal Returns
    b. Law of Increasing Opportunity Cost
    c. Law of Demand
    d. Consumer surplus

88. **How do banks create money?**

    a. By printing it
    b. By taking it out of the Federal Reserve
    c. By loaning it out
    d. By putting it into the Federal Reserve

89. **Which of the following correctly states the equation of exchange?**

    a. $MV = PQ$
    b. $MP \times VQ$
    c. MP/VQ
    d. $VP = MQ$

90. Economics is best defined as the study of what?
  a. Scarcity
  b. Business
  c. Trade
  d. Supply and demand

Answer Key and Explanations

1. D: Of those countries listed here, the two countries whose respective indigenous populations are not as large as the populations of the other countries are Argentina and Uruguay. Argentina's population is approximately 86.4% of European descent, roughly 8% of mestizo (of mixed European and Amerindian heritage), and an estimated 4% of Arab or East Asian ancestry. Uruguay's population is estimated to be 88% of European descent, 4% of African, and 2% of Asian, with 6% of mestizo ancestry in its rural northwest region. Guatemala and Peru (a) have larger indigenous populations. Guatemala, in Central America, has approximately over 40% of its population as indigenous peoples. Peru, in South America, is estimated to have 45% indigenous peoples and 37% partly indigenous peoples for a total of 82%. Ecuador and Bolivia (b) in South America still have indigenous peoples. The population of Ecuador has an estimated 25% indigenous and 65% partly indigenous peoples, for a total of 90%. Paraguay in South America and Mexico in North America (c) both have sizeable indigenous populations. Paraguay's population is estimated to include 95% partly indigenous peoples. Mexico is estimated to have 30% indigenous and 60% partly indigenous peoples in its population for a total of 90%.

2. A: It is not true that England's defeat of the Spanish Armada in 1588 ended their war with Spain. It did establish England's naval dominance and strengthened England's future colonization of the New World, but the actual war between England and Spain did not end until 1604. It is true that Henry VIII's desire to divorce Catherine of Aragon strengthened English expansionism (b). Catherine was Spanish, and Henry split from the Catholic Church because it prohibited divorce. Henry's rejection of his Spanish wife and his subsequent support of the Protestant movement angered King Philip II of Spain and destroyed the formerly close ties between the two countries. When Elizabeth became Queen of England, she supported the Reformation as a Protestant, which also contributed to English colonization (c). Sir Francis Drake, one of the best known English sea captains during this time period, would attack and plunder Spanish ships that had plundered Native Americans (d), adding to the enmity between Spain and England. Queen Elizabeth invested in Drake's voyages and gave him her support in claiming territories for England.

3. B: The Virginia Company of London was based in London, not Massachusetts. It had a charter to colonize American land between the Hudson and Cape Fear rivers (c). The other Virginia Company was the Virginia Company of Plymouth, which was based in the American colony of Plymouth, Massachusetts (a). It had a charter to colonize North America between the Potomac River and the northern boundary of Maine (d).

4. C: Hernando Cortes conquered the Mexican Aztecs in 1519. He had several advantages over the indigenous peoples, including horses, armor for his soldiers, and guns. In addition, Cortes' troops unknowingly transmitted smallpox to the Aztecs, which devastated their population as they had no immunity to this foreign illness. Vasco Nunez de Balboa (a) was the first European explorer to view the Pacific Ocean when he crossed the Isthmus of Panama in 1513. Juan Ponce de Leon (b) also visited and claimed Florida in Spain's name in 1513. Cabeza de Vaca (d) was one of only four men out of 400 to return from an expedition led by Panfilio de Narvaez in 1528, and was responsible for spreading the story of the Seven Cities of Cibola (the "cities of gold").

5. B: Peter Zenger was an 18th century journalist in New York who was charged with seditious libel after he published articles critical of New York governor William Cosby. His subsequent acquittal in 1735 established a precedent for American freedom of the press. Options A, C, and D can all be rejected because they do not accurately describe the historical significance of Peter Zenger's trial.

135

Although these options name other important freedoms or rights in American history, these rights or freedoms were not central to Peter Zenger's trial. In particular, note that while answers B, C, and D all list rights contained in the First Amendment to the United States Constitution, only B contains the particular right at issue in the Zenger case.

6. A: The attitudes of American colonists after the 1763 Treaty of Paris ended the French and Indian War were not a direct contributor to the American Revolution. American colonists had a supportive attitude toward Great Britain then, and were proud of the part they played in winning the war. Their good will was not returned by British leaders (b), who looked down on American colonials and sought to increase their imperial power over them. Even in 1761, a sign of Americans' objections to having their liberty curtailed by the British was seen when Boston attorney James Otis argued in court against the Writs of Assistance (c), search warrants to enforce England's mercantilist trade restrictions, as violating the kinds of natural laws espoused during the Enlightenment. Lord George Grenville's aggressive program to defend the North American frontier in the wake of Chief Pontiac's attacks included stricter enforcement of the Navigation Acts, the Proclamation of 1763, the Sugar Act (or Revenue Act), the Currency Act, and most of all the Stamp Act (d). Colonists objected to these as taxation without representation. Other events followed in this taxation dispute, which further eroded Americans' relationship with British government, including the Townshend Acts, the Massachusetts Circular Letter, the Boston Massacre, the Tea Act, and the resulting Boston Tea Party. Finally, with Britain's passage of the Intolerable Acts and the Americans' First Continental Congress, which was followed by Britain's military aggression against American resistance, actual warfare began in 1775. While not all of the colonies wanted war or independence by then, things changed by 1776, and Jefferson's Declaration of Independence was formalized.

7. C: Colonists did find that tea shipped directly by the British East India Company cost less than smuggled Dutch tea, even with tax. The colonists, however, did not buy it. They refused, despite its lower cost, on the principle that the British were taxing colonists without representation (d). It is true that the British East India Company lost money as a result of colonists buying tea smuggled from Holland (a). They sought to remedy this problem by getting concessions from Parliament to ship tea directly to the colonies instead of going through England (b) as the Navigation Acts normally required. Boston Governor Thomas Hutchinson, who sided with Britain, stopped tea ships from leaving the harbor, which after 20 days would cause the tea to be sold at auction. At that time, British taxes on the tea would be paid. On the 19th night after Hutchinson's action, American protestors held the Boston Tea Party, dressing as Native Americans and dumping all the tea into the harbor to destroy it so it could not be taxed and sold. Many American colonists disagreed with the Boston Tea Party because it involved destroying private property.

8. C: Massachusetts did set a valuable example for other states by stipulating that its constitution should be created via a special convention rather than via the legislature. This way, the constitution would take precedence over the legislature, which would be subject to the rules of the constitution. It is not true that twelve states had new constitutions by the end of 1777 (a). By this time, ten of the states had new constitutions. It is not true that Connecticut and Massachusetts retained their colonial charters minus the British parts (b). Connecticut and Rhode Island were the states that preserved their colonial charters. They simply removed any parts referring to British rule. Massachusetts did not formalize its new constitution in 1778 (d). This state did not actually finish the process of adopting its new constitution until 1780.

9. D: The Louisiana Purchase actually increased the U.S.'s territory by 100% overnight, not 50%. The Louisiana territory doubled the size of the nation. It is true that Jefferson initially sent a delegation to Paris to see if Napoleon would agree to sell only New Orleans to the United States (a).

It is also true that Napoleon, who expected America to encroach on Louisiana, decided to avoid this by offering to sell the entire territory to the U.S. (b). It is likewise true that America only had authority to buy New Orleans. Nevertheless, the delegation accepted Napoleon's offer of all of Louisiana (c).

10. B: Hamilton did not object to U.S. western expansionism, and Burr did not support it. There were certain Federalists other than Hamilton who opposed expansion to the west as a threat to their position within the Union, and these opponents did attempt to organize a movement to secede (a). To get Aaron Burr to champion their cause, they offered to help him run for Governor of New York (c). Hamilton did lead the opposition against Burr's campaign (d).

11. A: The U.S. did carry out a three-pronged invasion of Canada early in the war, but they did not succeed on two fronts. Instead, they lost on all three. Americans did win sea battles against the British early in the war, but were soon beaten back to their homeports and then blockaded by powerful British warships (b). Admiral Perry did defeat the British on Lake Erie on September 10, 1813 (c). Perry's victory allowed William Henry Harrison to invade Canada (d) in October of 1813, where he defeated British and Native Americans in the Battle of the Thames.

12. D: Political corruption was not an immediate effect of the rapid urban growth during this time. The accelerated growth of cities in America did soon result in services being unable to keep up with that growth. The results of this included deficiencies in clean water delivery and garbage collection, causing poor sanitation (a). That poor sanitation led to outbreaks of cholera and typhus, as well as typhoid fever epidemics (b). Police and fire fighting services could not keep up with the population increases, and were often inadequate (c).

13. D: All the laws (d) named were instrumental in spurring westward migration to the Great Plains. The Homestead Act (a), passed in 1862, gave settlers 160 acres of land at no monetary cost in exchange for a commitment to cultivating the land for five years. The Timber Culture Act (b), passed in 1873, gave the settlers 160 acres more of land in exchange for planting trees on one quarter of the acreage. The Desert Land Act (c), passed in 1877, allowed buyers who would irrigate the land to buy 640 acres for only 25 cents an acre. Thus, (d), all of these laws were instrumental in spurring westward migration to the Great Plains during that period, is correct.

14. B: Germany's declaration of war on Russia in 1914, following the assassination of Archduke Ferdinand (b), did not contribute to ending American neutrality in World War I. Once Germany declared war, England, France, Italy, Russia, and Japan joined as the Allied Powers against the Central Powers of Germany and Austria-Hungary, and US President Woodrow Wilson declared America's neutrality. When Germany designated the area surrounding the British Isles as a war zone in February 1913 (a), and warned all ships from neutral countries to stay out of the zone, an end to American neutrality was prompted. President Wilson's responded to Germany's declaration by proclaiming that America would hold Germany responsible for any American losses of life or property. When Germany sank the British passenger vessel *Lusitania*, 128 American passengers were killed (c). This further eroded Wilson's resolve to remain neutral. In February 1917, Germany declared unrestricted submarine warfare on any ship in the war zone (d); this signified that ships from any country would face German attack.

15. A: The postwar conference that brought US-Soviet differences to light was (a) the Potsdam conference in July of 1945. The conference at Yalta (b), in February of 1945, resulted in the division of Germany into Allied-controlled zones. The Dumbarton Oaks conference (c) (1944) established a Security Council, on which with the US, England, Soviet Union, France, and China served as the five permanent members. Each of the permanent members had veto power, and a General Assembly, with limited power, was also established. The Tehran conference (d) included FDR's proposal for a new international organization to take the place of the League of Nations. This idea would later be realized in the form of the United Nations.

16. D: In 1956, Egypt did not attack Israel. On October 29, 1956, Israel attacked Egypt. England and France did join this war within two days. It is true that Egyptian President Gamal Abdul Nasser refused to take America's side in the Cold War (a). In reaction to his refusal, President Eisenhower's administration pulled its funding from the Aswan Dam project in Egypt (b). Nasser then nationalized the British-owned Suez Canal (c).

17. C: The person or group not instrumental in advancing civil rights and desegregation immediately after WWII was (c), Congress. As African American soldiers came home from the war, racial discord increased. President Harry Truman (a) appointed a Presidential Committee on Civil Rights in 1946. This committee published a report recommending that segregation and lynching be outlawed by the federal government. However, Congress ignored this report and took no action. Truman then used his presidential powers to enforce desegregation of the military and policies of "fair employment" in federal civil service jobs. The National Association for the Advancement of Colored People (NAACP) (d) brought lawsuits against racist and discriminatory practices, and in resolving these suits, the Supreme Court (b) further eroded segregation. For example, the Supreme Court ruled that primaries allowing only whites would be illegal, and it ended the segregation of interstate bus lines. The landmark civil rights laws were not passed by Congress until the 1960s.

18. B: Of the programs enacted by Johnson, the one most closely related to JFK's legacy was (b), the Civil Rights Act, which Johnson pushed through Congress using allusions to Kennedy and his goals. While Kennedy received congressional backing for a raise in minimum wage and public housing improvements, his efforts regarding civil rights were thwarted by conservative Republicans and Southern Democrats in Congress. However, as the Civil Rights movement progressed through the campaigns of the Freedom Riders, Kennedy developed a strong commitment to the cause.

The Economic Opportunity Act gave almost $1 billion to wage Johnson's War on Poverty. The Great Society (c) was Johnson's name for his comprehensive reform program which included a variety of legislation (see also question #102).

19. B: The GATT countries did agree to abolish or decrease many of their tariffs, but this agreement did not include only 57 countries. It was much larger, including a total of 117 countries. The GATT was approved by Congress in 1994 (a). In addition to having 117 countries agree to increase free trade, the GATT also set up the World Trade Organization (WTO) for the purpose of settling any differences among nations related to trade (c). Another instance of free trade policy established in the 1990s was the Senate's ratification of NAFTA. The negotiation of this agreement was originally made by the first Bush administration, with President Bush and the leaders of Canada and Mexico signing it in 1992 (d), but it still needed to be ratified.

20. B: There was not a reduction in military spending after the war. Although the manufacturing demand for war supplies and the size of the military decreased, the government had increased military spending from $10 billion in 1947 to more than $50 billion by 1953—a more than fivefold increase. This increase strengthened the American economy. Other factors contributing to the strengthened economy included the significantly higher birth rates during the Baby Boom (a) from 1946 to 1957, which stimulated the growth of the building and automotive industries by increased demand. Government programs, such as the GI Bill (the Servicemen's Readjustment Act of 1944), other veterans' benefits, and the National Defense Education Act all encouraged college enrollments, which increased by nearly four times (c). Additionally, larger families, increased mobility and low-interest loans offered to veterans led to suburban development and growth (d) as well as an increased home construction.

21. D: The statement that the 1986 Immigration Reform and Control Act reduced illegal Mexican immigration is not true. This legislation punished employers with sanctions for hiring undocumented employees, but despite this the illegal immigration of Mexicans to America was largely unaffected by the law. It is true that twice as many people immigrated to America in the 1980s than in the 1970s (a): the number reached over nine million in the 80s. It is true that the majority of immigrants were Latin American (b). In addition to Latin Americans, other large groups of immigrants in the 1980s were Asians and Caribbean inhabitants (c).

22. C: The Mississippi Freedom Democratic Party did attend the 1964 Democratic convention; however, they were unable garner Johnson's support to unseat the regular delegation from Mississippi. A riot did break out in Watts in 1965 (a), and in the following three years, more riots occurred in Newark, N.J. (b) and in Detroit, Michigan (d). These riots were manifestations of the frustrations experienced by blacks regarding racial inequities in American society.

23. A: The earliest written language in Mesopotamia was Sumerian. Ancient Sumerians began writing this language around 3500 BC. Elamite, from Iran, was the language spoken by the ancient Elamites and was the official language of the Persian Empire from the 6th to 4th centuries BC. Written Linear Elamite was used for a very short time in the late 3rd century BC. The written Elamite cuneiform, used from about 2500 to 331 BC, was an adaptation of the Akkadian cuneiform. Akkadian is the earliest found Semitic language. Written Akkadian cuneiform first appeared in texts by circa 2800 BC, and full Akkadian texts appeared by circa 2500 BC. The Akkadian cuneiform writing system is ultimately a derivative of the ancient Sumerian cuneiform writing system, although these two spoken languages were not related linguistically. Aramaic is another Semitic language, but unlike Akkadian, Aramaic is not now extinct. Old Aramaic, the written language of the Old Testament and the spoken language used by Jesus Christ, was current from 1100 BC-200 AD Middle Aramaic, used from 200-1200 AD, included literary Syriac (Christian groups developed the writing system of Syriac in order to be able to write spoken Aramaic) and was the written language of the Jewish books of Biblical commentary (Namely, the Talmud, the Targum, and the Midrash). Modern Aramaic has been used from 1200 to the present.

24. C: The New Kingdom was the period during which no more pyramids were built in Egypt. The Pyramids were built between the years of 2630 and 1814 BC, and the New Kingdom spanned from circa 1550-1070 BC. As a result, the last pyramid was built approximately 264 years before the New Kingdom began. 2630 BC marked the beginning of the reign of the first Pharaoh, Djoser, who had the first pyramid built at Saqqara. 1814 BC marked the end of the reign of the last Pharaoh, Amenemhat III, who had the last pyramid built at Hawara. In between these years, a succession of pharaohs built many pyramids. The Old Kingdom encompasses both the Third and Fourth Dynasties; therefore, all three of these choices encompass pyramid-building periods. Djoser's had his first pyramid built during the Third Dynasty. The Pharaohs Kufu, Khafre, and Menkaure, respectively, build the famous Pyramids of Giza during the Fourth Dynasty during their reigns at different times between circa 2575 and 2467 BC, the period of the Fourth Dynasty. The Middle Kingdom encompassed the 11th through 14th Dynasties, from circa. 2080 to 1640 BC—also within the time period (2630-1814 BC) when pyramids were built by the Pharaohs.

25. B: It is not true that the Crusades succeeded at Christians' reclaiming the "holy land" (the Middle East) from Muslims. Despite their number (nine not counting the Northern Crusades) and longevity (1095-1291 not counting later similar campaigns), the Crusades never accomplished this purpose (a). While they did not take back the Middle East, the Crusades did succeed in exacerbating the decline of the Byzantine Empire (c), which lost more and more territory to the Ottoman Turks during this period. In addition, the Crusades resulted in Egypt's rise once again to become a major power (d) of the Middle East as it had been in the past.

26. D: After the Black Death killed a third of Europe's population (a), the survivors were mainly upper classes with more money to spend on art, architecture, and other luxuries. The plague deaths also resulted in a labor shortage, thereby creating more work opportunities for the surviving people in lower classes (b). As a result, these survivors' positions in society appreciated. Once plague deaths subsided and population growth in Europe began to reassert itself, a greater demand existed for products and services. At the same time, the number of people available to provide these products and services was still smaller than in the past. Consequently, more merchants, artisans, and bankers emerged in order to provide the services and products people wanted, thereby creating a class of citizens between the lower-class laborers and the upper-class elite (c). After the two major Italian banks collapsed, wealthy investors who would normally have reinvested their disposable income did not do this, since the economy did not favor it. Instead, they invested their money in artistic and cultural products.

27. B: In order to prosper, a nation should not try to increase its imports. Mercantilism is an economic theory including the idea that prosperity comes from a positive balance of international trade. For any one nation to prosper, that nation should increase its exports (c) but decrease its imports. Exporting more to other countries while importing less from them will give a country a positive trade balance. This theory assumes that money and wealth are identical (a) assets of a nation. Mercantilism dictates that a nation's government should apply a policy of economic protectionism (d) by stimulating more exports and suppressing imports. Some ways to accomplish this task have included granting subsidies for exports and imposing tariffs on imports. Mercantilism can be regarded as essentially the opposite of the free trade policies that have been encouraged in more recent years.

28. C: It is not true that the English Civil Wars between 1641 and 1651 legalized Parliament's consent as a requirement for a monarch to rule England. These wars did establish this idea as a precedent, but the later Glorious Revolution of 1688 actually made it legal that a monarch could not rule without Parliamentary consent. The wars from 1641-1651 were all fought between Royalists who supported an absolute monarchy and Parliamentarians who supported the joint government of a parliamentary monarchy (a). Parliament was the victor (b) in 1651 at the Battle of Worcester. As a result of this battle, King Charles I was executed, and King Charles II was exiled. In the first of these civil wars, from 1642-1646, and the second, from 1648-1649, supporters of King Charles I (d) fought against supporters of the Long Parliament.

29. D: Resentment against the Protestant Reformation was not a cause given for the French Revolution. Choices (a), (b), and (c) are just a few among many causes cited for the war. Famines caused malnutrition and even starvation among the poorest people (a). Escalating bread prices contributed greatly to the hunger. Louis XV had amassed a great amount of debt from spending money on many wars in addition to the American Revolution. Military failures as well as a lack of social services for veterans exacerbated these debts. In addition, the Court of Louis XVI and Marie Antoinette spent excessively and obviously on luxuries even while people in the country were starving, and France's monetary system was outdated, inefficient, and thus unable to manage the national debt (b). Much of the populace greatly resented the Catholic Church's control of the country (c). However, there was not great resentment against the Protestant Reformation (d); there were large minorities of Protestants in France, who not only exerted their influence on government institutions, but undoubtedly also contributed to the resentment of the Catholic Church.

30. A: In the 1780s, the French national debt was very high. The French nobility adamantly resisted attempts by King Louis XVI to reform tax laws, which led to a high tax burden on the French peasantry. The French government spent almost 50% of its national expenditures on debt-related payments during the 1780s; thus it could not and did not spend almost 60% to finance luxuries for the French nobility. This eliminates choice B. King Louis XVI temporarily banned the guild system to bolster, rather than stifle, free trade. Because this system gave skilled craftsmen economic advantages, journeymen opposed ending the system. This eliminates choice D. Regardless of the status of guilds before the French Revolution, French society did not offer many opportunities for upward social mobility. Few peasants were able to advance. This eliminates choice C.

31. C: The only accurate statement about the end of WWI is that President Wilson had proposed that the nations of the world form a coalition to prevent future world wars. While he did not give the coalition a name, he clearly expressed his proposal that such a group form in the fourteenth of his Fourteen Points. The Treaty of Versailles (1919) did not bring peace among all countries involved in the war (a); Germany and the United States arrived at a separate peace in 1921. Furthermore, the Treaty of Versailles did not contain a clause for establishing the United Nations (b); it contained a clause for establishing the League of Nations. The League of Nations was created as dictated by the treaty, but when the Second World War proved that this group had failed to prevent future world wars, it was replaced by the United Nations after World War II. President Wilson did not succeed in getting the USA to ratify the League of Nations (d).

32. A: Russian's involvement in World War I brought social tension in Russia to a head. Contributing factors included military defeats and civilian suffering. Prior to Russia entering the war, Russian factory workers could legally strike, but during the war, it was illegal for them to act collectively. This eliminates answer C. Protests continued during World War I, and the Russian government was overthrown in 1917. This eliminates answer D. Answer B can be rejected because World War I did not go well for the Russian Army; Nicholas III, therefore, had no successes upon which to capitalize.

33. A: The latest occurring decolonization event was the Eastern Bloc and Soviet Satellite states of Armenia, Azerbaijan, Estonia, Georgia, Kazakhstan, Kyrgyzstan, Latvia, Lithuania, Moldova, Russia, Tajikistan, Turkmenistan, Ukraine, and Uzbekistan, which all became independent from the Soviet Union in 1991. (Note: This was the last decolonization of the Cold War years, as the end of the Soviet Union marked the end of the Cold War.) Canada completed its independence from British Parliament via the Canada Act (b) in 1982. In the Caribbean, the Bahamas gained independence from the United Kingdom (c) in 1973. Algeria won its independence from France when the Algerian War of Independence, begun in 1954, ended in 1962 (d).

34. B: U.S. industrialization was confined to the Northeast until after the Civil War because the Northeast had faster-running rivers than the South. The earliest American factories used horse-drawn machines. When waterpower was developed and proved superior, the Northeast's faster rivers were more suited to water-powered mills than the South's slower rivers. The war did not delay the development of water power (a). Waterpower was developed before the Civil War in the late 1790s. Steam power, a more efficient alternative to water power, was developed after the Civil War and eventually replaced waterpower. With steam-powered engines, industry could spread to the South, since steam engines did not depend on rapidly running water like water-powered engines. While British emigré Samuel Slater's first cotton mill using horse-drawn production did lose a lot of money (c), this was not a reason for industrial delay. In fact, Slater's Beverly Cotton Manufactory in Massachusetts, the first American cotton mill, in spite of its financial problems, was successful in both its volume of cotton production and in developing the water-powered technology that ultimately would succeed the horse-drawn method. Slater's second cotton mill in Pawtucket,

Rhode Island, was water-powered. Industrial delay was not because milling technology had not yet been invented (d). Slater learned of new textile manufacturing techniques as a youth in England, and he brought this knowledge to America in 1789. Resistance of Southern owners of plantations and slaves did not slow the spread of industrialism. Rather, as seen in (b) above, the South did not have the geographic capability to sustain waterpower. Once steam power was developed, the South joined in industrialization.

35. A: The inaccurate statement is the Puritans unconditionally supported the English Reformation. While they agreed with the Reformation in principle, they felt that it had not pursued those principles far enough and should make greater reforms. Similarly, they felt that the Church of England (or Anglican Church), though it had separated from the Catholic Church in the Protestant Reformation, still allowed many practices they found too much like Catholicism (b). The Puritans did become a chief political power in England because of the first English Civil War (c) between Royalists and Parliamentarians. The Royalists had a profound suspicion of the radical Puritans. Among the Parliament's elements of resistance, the strongest was that of the Puritans. They joined in the battle initially for ostensibly political reasons as others had, but soon they brought more attention to religious issues. Following the Restoration in 1660 and the Uniformity Act of 1662, thereby restoring the Church of England to its pre-English Civil War status, the great majority of Puritan clergy defected from the Church of England (d).

36. D: It is not true that the Gilded Age is a term whose origins have not been identified clearly. In 1873, Mark Twain and Charles Dudley Warner co-authored a book entitled The Gilded Age: A Tale of Today. Twain and Warner first coined this term to describe the extravagance and excesses of America's wealthy upper class (b), who became richer than ever due to industrialization. Furthermore, the Gilded Age was the era of the "robber barons" (a) such as John D. Rockefeller, Cornelius Vanderbilt, J.P. Morgan, and others. Because they accumulated enormous wealth through extremely aggressive and occasionally unethical monetary manipulations, critics dubbed them "robber barons" because they seemed to be elite lords of robbery. While these business tycoons grasped huge fortunes, some of them—such as Andrew Carnegie and Andrew Mellon—were also philanthropists, using their wealth to support and further worthy causes such as literacy, education, health care, charities, and the arts. They donated millions of dollars to fund social improvements. Carnegie himself dubbed this large philanthropic movement the "Gospel of Wealth" (c).

37. A: It is not true that the founding fathers specifically stated in the Constitution that the USA would be a democracy. The founding fathers wanted the new United States to be founded on principles of liberty and equality, but they did not specifically describe these principles with the term "Democracy." Thus, the Declaration of Independence, like the Constitution after it, did not stipulate a democracy, although both did state the principles of equality and freedom (b). The Constitution also provided for the election of the new government (c), and for protection of the rights of some, but not all, of the people (d). Notable exceptions at the time were black people and women. Only later were laws passed to protect their rights over the years.

38. B: Preservatives such as salt were only introduced to the European diet after trade routes opened and these goods could be brought to Europe.

39. B: In 1792, when the French Revolution turned into European war, American traders conducted business with both sides. It is not true that Washington allied with the French (a) at this time. Washington issued a Proclamation of Neutrality in 1792 when the French went to war with European countries. While they did trade with both sides, American merchants profited the most from the French West Indies, not the British West Indies (c). The Spanish navy did not retaliate against America for trading with the French (d). Though Spain was an ally of Britain, it was the British who most often seized American ships and forced their crews to serve the British navy.

40. B: The Etruscans were from a kingdom to the north that seized control of Rome from the Latins in the mid-600s BC. They began urbanizing the settlement, improving roads, adding drainage systems, etc. They were driven out of the region in 509 BC during an uprising of the Latins.

41. A: James Madison, John Jay, and Alexander Hamilton published The Federalist in the Independent Journal in New York. It was a response to the Anti-Federalists in New York, who were slow to ratify the Constitution because they feared it gave the central government too much authority.

42. D: A practical application of content learned involves action, not merely knowledge. Options A and C, although they describe content that students would reasonably learn in a class or unit on the structure of the U.S. government, do not describe applications of content, or applications of a social studies education. Therefore options A and C can both be rejected. Option B does involve action and not merely the acquisition of knowledge. However, it is not as directly tied to learning the structure of the U.S. government as option D, informed participation in U.S. political processes. This is because informed participation in school elections is quite possible without knowing the structure of the U.S. government. Informed participation in U.S. political processes requires knowledge of the structure of the U.S. government (i.e., voting on an issue requires an understanding of where a given candidate stands on that issue).

43. C: A federalist system of government is a government under which power is shared by a central authority and sub-components of the federation. In the United States in particular, power is shared by the federal government and the individual states. Option A, that the legislative branch consists of two representative bodies (the House of Representatives and the Senate) is true, of course, but does not describe a uniquely federalist structure. Rather, it describes the concept of bicameralism. Option A may thus be eliminated. Option B, likewise, describes different types of democracy but not federalism. B can thus be eliminated. Regarding option D, this statement is also true (the U.S. Constitution shapes national legislation) but it is not a descriptive statement of the federalist system because the statement makes no mention that power is shared by the states.

44. D: Congress did not have the authority to levy taxes under the Articles of Confederation. Without the ability to levy taxes, there was no way to finance programs, which weakened the government.

45. A: The Age of Enlightenment was a time of scientific and philosophical achievement. Also called the Age of Reason, human thought and reason were prized.

46. C: The Constitution was not ratified immediately. Only five states accepted it in early 1788; Massachusetts, New York, Rhode Island, and Virginia were originally opposed to the Constitution. Rhode Island reluctantly accepted it in 1790.

47. B: James Madison was a close friend of Thomas Jefferson and supported a stronger central government. George Mason and Robert Yates were both against expanding federal authority over the states. Benjamin Franklin was a proponent of a strong federal government, but he was from Massachusetts.

48. D: Some of the men who helped frame the Constitution believed the central government needed to be stronger than what was established under the Articles of Confederation. Others were against this and feared a strong federal government. A system of checks and balances was established to prevent the central government from taking too much power. This arrangement is known as federalism.

49. A: The Senate and House of Representatives make up a bicameral legislature. The Great Compromise awarded seats in the Senate equally to each state, while the seats in the House of Representatives were based on population.

50. B: The Presidential Succession Act lists the Speaker of the House, president pro tempore of the Senate, and secretary of state next in succession after the vice president. However, anyone who succeeds as president must meet all of the legal qualifications.

51. C: The President has the power to veto legislation directly or use a pocket veto by not signing a bill within ten days after receiving it. Congress adjourns during this time period. A veto can be overridden if two-thirds of the House and the two-thirds of the Senate both agree. The President must veto a complete bill and does not have the authority to veto sections or lines.

52. C: The Civil Rights Act of 1964 affected the Jim Crow laws in the Southern states. Many minorities suffered under unfair voting laws and segregation. President Lyndon Johnson signed the Civil Rights Act of 1964 into law after the 1963 assassination of President Kennedy, who championed the reform.

53. B: Only the federal government has the power to give copyrights and patents to individuals or companies. The power to levy taxes, borrow money, and spend money (a) is a power shared by federal and state governments. The power to set the criteria that qualify individuals to vote (c) is a power given to state governments only. The power to ratify amendments proposed to the Constitution (d) is a power of only the state governments.

54. A: The action that needs a three-fourths majority vote is state approval of a proposed constitutional amendment. Proposing a constitutional amendment (b) requires a two-thirds majority vote. Ratifying presidential appointments in the Senate (c) also requires a two-thirds majority vote. Introducing charges for impeachment in the House of Representatives (d) requires a simple majority vote.

55. B: The term "Manifest Destiny" had not been used for many years before the 1830s. This term was coined in 1844. However, it is true that the idea this term expressed had been around for many years before that (a). It is also true that many Americans believed Manifest Destiny would mean America would ultimately encompass Canada and Mexico (c). Factors contributing to Manifest Destiny included the rise in nationalism that followed the War of 1812 and the population growth that increased that nationalism (d).

56. A: Presidential candidates are eligible for a match from the federal government (with a $250 per contribution limit) if they can privately raise $5,000 per state in twenty states. Candidates who accept public money agree to limit spending. Candidates who do not accept matching funds are free to use the money they raise privately.

57. D: America is a common law country because English common law was adopted in all states except Louisiana. Common law is based on precedent and changes over time. Each state develops its own common laws.

58. D: The only answer choice that represents a possible absolute location for New Orleans is 30° N, 90° W. When a location is described in terms of its placement on the global grid, it is customary to put the latitude before the longitude. New Orleans is north of the equator, so it has to be in the

Northern Hemisphere. In addition, it is west of the prime meridian, which runs through Greenwich, England, among other places. So, New Orleans must be in the Western Hemisphere. It is possible, then, to deduce that 30° N, 90° W is the only possible absolute location for New Orleans.

59. B: On a political map, countries are represented in different colors, and countries that share a border are not given the same color. This is so that the borders between countries will be distinct. Political maps are used to illustrate those aspects of a country that have been determined by people: the capital, the provincial and national borders, and the large cities. Political maps sometimes include major physical features like rivers and mountains, but they are not intended to display all such information. On a physical, climate, or contour map, however, the borders between nations are more incidental. Colors are used on these maps to represent physical features, areas with similar climate, etc. It is possible that colors will overrun the borders and be shared by adjacent countries.

60. D: Around the world, the area around the equator is known for a relative lack of wind. Indeed, the equatorial belt is sometimes called the doldrums because the constant warm water encourages the air to rise gently. To the north and south, however, there are trade winds that can become quite violent. The equator only intersects three continents: Asia, Africa, and South America. It is in between the north and south horse latitudes, which are belts known for calm winds. Finally, the equator is located at 0° latitude, not longitude, though the 0° line of longitude does intersect the equator.

61. A: The apparent distance between Greenland and Norway will be greatest on a Mercator map. The Mercator map is a type of cylindrical projection map in which lines of latitude and longitude are transferred onto a cylindrical shape, which is then cut vertically and laid flat. For this reason, distances around the poles will appear increasingly great. The Mercator map is excellent for navigation because a straight line drawn on it represents a single compass reading. In a conic projection map, on the other hand, a hemisphere of the globe is transposed onto a cone, which is then cut vertically (that is, from rim to tip) and laid flat. The apparent distances on a conic projection will be smallest at the 45th parallel. A contour map uses lines to illustrate the features of a geographic area. For example, the lines on an elevation contour map connect areas that have the same altitude. An equal-area projection map represents landmasses in their actual sizes. To make this possible, the shapes of the landmasses are manipulated slightly, and the map is interrupted (divided into more than one part).

62. A: Symbols are not used to represent relief on a physical map. A physical map is dedicated to illustrating the landmasses and bodies of water in a specific region, so symbols do not provide enough detail. Color, shading, and contour lines, on the other hand, are able to create a much more complicated picture of changes in elevation, precipitation, etc. Changes in elevation are known in geography as relief.

63. D: A flow-line map describes the movement of people, trends, or materials across a physical area. The movements depicted on a flow-line map are typically represented by arrows. In more advanced flow-line maps, the width of the arrow corresponds to the quantity of the motion. Flow-line maps usually declare the span of time that is being represented. A political map depicts the man-made aspects of geography, such as borders and cities. A cartogram adjusts the size of the areas represented according to some variable. For instance, a cartogram of wheat production would depict Iowa as being much larger than Alaska. A qualitative map uses lines, dots, and other symbols to illustrate a particular point. For example, a qualitative map might be used to demonstrate the greatest expansion of the Persian Empire.

64. B: The composite volcano, sometimes called the stratovolcano, is the most common type of volcano on earth. A composite volcano has steep sides, so the explosions of ash, pumice, and silica are often accompanied by treacherous mudslides. Indeed, it is these mudslides that cause most of the damage associated with composite volcano eruptions. Krakatoa and Mount Saint Helens are examples of composite volcanoes. A lava dome is a round volcano that emits thick lava very slowly. A shield volcano, one example of which is Mt. Kilauea in Hawaii, emits a small amount of lava over an extended period of time. Shield volcanoes are not known for violent eruptions. A cinder cone has steep sides made of fallen cinders, which themselves are made of the lava that intermittently shoots into the air.

65. C: After precipitation, the heat of the sun causes evaporation, a process by which water molecules change from a liquid to a gas, ultimately returning to the atmosphere. The other options describe processes that pertain to properties of water, but not to water's return to the atmosphere. Percolation is the process by which water moves down through soil. Cohesion (specifically, structural cohesion) is the property of matter by which the molecules in a single substance stay together. Condensation is the process by which matter changes from a gas to a liquid; after evaporation, molecules of water form rain droplets through condensation.

66. B: Metamorphic rock is formed by extreme heat and pressure. This type of rock is created when other rocks are somehow buried within the earth, where they are subject to a dramatic rise in pressure and temperature. Slate and marble are both metamorphic rocks. Metamorphic rocks are created by the other two main types of rock: sedimentary and igneous. Sedimentary rock is formed when dirt and other sediment is washed into a bed, covered over by subsequent sediment, and compacted into rock. Depending on how they are formed, sedimentary rocks are classified as organic, clastic, or chemical. Igneous rocks are composed of cooled magma, the molten rock that emerges from volcanoes. Basalt and granite are two common varieties of igneous rock.

67. A: The eye wall of a hurricane has the strongest winds and the greatest rainfall. The eye wall is the tower-like rim of the eye. It is from this wall that clouds extend out, which are seen from above as the classic outward spiral pattern. A hurricane front is the outermost edge of its influence; although there will be heavy winds and rain in this area, the intensity will be relatively small. The eye of a hurricane is actually a place of surprising peace. In this area, dry and cool air rushes down to the ground or sea. Once there, the air is caught up in the winds of the eye wall and is driven outward at a furious pace.

68. D: These are all geographically parts of Southeast Asia. The countries of Myanmar (Burma), Laos, Cambodia, and Thailand are considered Mainland Southeast Asia, as are Vietnam and the Malay Peninsula. Brunei, East Malaysia, Indonesia, and the Philippines are considered Maritime Southeast Asia, as are Singapore and Timor-Leste. The Seven Sister States of India are also considered to be part of Southeast Asia, geographically and culturally. (The Seven Sister States of India are Arunachal Pradesh, Assam, Nagaland, Meghalaya, Manipur, Tripura, and Mizoram, which all have contiguous borders in northeastern India.)

69. A: One example of the multiplier effect of large cities would be if the presence of specialized equipment for an industry attracted even more business. Large cities tend to grow even larger for a number of reasons: they have more skilled workers, they have greater concentrations of specialized equipment, and they have already-functioning markets. These factors all make it easier for a business to begin operations in a large city than elsewhere. Thus, the populations and economic productivity of large cities tend to grow quickly. Some governments have sought to mitigate this trend by clustering groups of similar industries in smaller cities.

70. D: The Sahel, a belt of grasslands just south of the Sahara Desert, has long been a focus of agricultural efforts in Africa. This semiarid region has provided sustenance to people and animals for thousands of years. In the last thousand years, stores of salt and gold were found there, giving rise to empires in Ghana and Mali. Changes in climate have expanded the Sahara, however, and pushed the Sahel farther south. The Qattara Depression is a low-lying desert in Egypt. The Great Rift Valley is a region of faults and rocky hills that extends along the southeastern coast of Africa. The Congo Basin is a repository of sediment from the Ubangi and Congo rivers. It is in the northern half of what is now called the Democratic Republic of the Congo.

71. B: To determine the shortest route between Lima and Lisbon, Tracy should use an azimuthal projection with Lisbon at the center. An azimuthal projection depicts one hemisphere of the globe as a circle. A straight line drawn from the center of the map to any point represents the shortest possible distance between those two points. Tracy could obtain her objective, then, with an azimuthal projection in which either Lisbon or Lima were at the center. If the North Pole were at the center, the map would not include Lima because this city is in the Southern Hemisphere. A Robinson projection approximates the sizes and shapes of landmasses but does distort in some ways, particularly near the poles.

72. B: North Korea and South Korea are separated by a geometric border, meaning that the boundary between the two nations is a straight line drawn on a map, without respect to landforms. Specifically, the boundary between the Koreas is the 38th parallel. Another example of a geometric border lies between the continental United States and Canada. The Turkish Cyprus–Greek Cyprus border is anthropogeographic, or drawn according to cultural reasons. The border between France and Spain is physiographic-political, a combination of the Pyrenees Mountains and European history. The Irish Sea separates England from Ireland.

73. D: More information is required to calculate the natural increase rate for Grassley County during this year. Natural increase rate is the growth in population measured as the surplus of live births over deaths for every thousand people. The calculation of natural increase rate does not take account of immigration or emigration. The natural increase rate for Grassley County cannot be calculated because the original population of the county is not given. As an example, if the beginning population of the county had been 10,000, the natural increase rate would be 40;

$$\frac{400 \times 1,000}{10,000} = 40$$

74. A: North Africa is not one of the world's four major population agglomerations. These are eastern North America, South Asia, East Asia, and Europe. The largest of these is East Asia, which encompasses Korea, Japan, and the major cities of China. The second-largest population agglomeration is South Asia, which includes India and Pakistan. Most of the population in this area is near the coasts. The European agglomeration is spread across the largest piece of land, while the much smaller agglomeration in eastern North America is primarily focused on the string of cities from Boston to Washington, DC.

75. D: It is true that scarcity causes producers (and other people) to make choices. Producers must choose what to produce with limited resources. It is also true that the choices a producer makes when faced with scarcity come with trade-offs. There are advantages and disadvantages to different production decisions. And, finally, calculating the opportunity cost of a choice provides a manner with which to measure the consequence of a choice and compare that against the consequence of other choices.

76. B: John Maynard Keynes argued that government could help revitalize a recessionary economy by increasing government spending and therefore increasing aggregate demand. This is known as demand-side economics.

77. C: If a society wants greater income equity, it will impose a progressive income tax, which taxes the wealthy at a higher rate; an inheritance tax, which prevents the wealthy from passing all their wealth on to the next generation; and a gift tax, which prevents the wealthy from simply giving their wealth away.

78. A: GDP (Gross Domestic Product) is restricted to value produced within borders, whereas GNP (Gross National Product) is focused on value produced by companies regardless of borders.

79. B: Structural unemployment is unemployment that results from a mismatch of job skills or location. In this case, Ivy's job skill—her ability to work as a seamstress—is no longer desired by employers. Frictional and cyclical are other forms of unemployment; economists do not use the term careless unemployment.

80. D: It is believed that some level of frictional and structural unemployment will always exist, and that the best economists (and politicians) can hope for is to reduce cyclical unemployment to zero. Therefore, frictional and structural unemployment are sometimes referred to as natural unemployment, meaning unemployment that naturally exists within an economy.

81. C: A supply shock is caused when there is a dramatic increase in input prices. This causes an increase in price levels and decreases in employment and GDP. A supply shock causes the AS curve to move to the left (in).

82. A: As people have more and more of something, they value it less and less. This is the law of diminishing marginal utility, and it is what causes the downward slope of the demand curve.

83. A: The change in demand is 20% (1,000 − 800 = 200), and the change in price is 10% ($11 − $10 = $1). Because the change in demand is greater than the change in price, the demand is considered elastic. In this case, the price elasticity quotient is greater than 1.

84. A: The phenomenon of "sticky prices" refers to prices that stay the same even though it seems they should change (either increasing or decreasing).

85. C: When a nation follows the theory of comparative advantage, it specializes in producing the goods and services it can make at a lower opportunity cost and then engages in trade to obtain other goods.

86. C: A person who has taken out a fixed-rate loan can benefit from inflation by paying back the loan with dollars that are less valuable than they were when the loan was taken out. In the other examples, inflation harms the individual or entity.

87. A: The input and output data illustrate the Law of Diminishing Marginal Returns, which states that as inputs are added during production, there eventually comes a time when increased inputs coincide with a decrease in marginal return.

88. C: Banks create money by giving out loans. For example, assume a person puts $100 into a bank. The bank will keep a percentage of that money in reserves because of the reserve requirement. If the reserve requirement is 10% then the bank will put $10 in reserves and then loan out $90 of it to a second person. The money total, which started at $100, now includes the original $100 plus the $90, or a total of $190. The bank creates $90 by loaning it.

89. A: The equation of exchange is MV = PQ. This means that M (a measure of the supply of money) multiplied by the velocity of money, V, (the average number of times a typical dollar is spent on final goods and services a year) = P, the average price level of final goods and services in GDP × real output, Q (the quantity of goods and services in GDP).

90. A: Economics is defined as the study of scarcity, the situation in which resources are limited and wants are unlimited.

How to Overcome Test Anxiety

Just the thought of taking a test is enough to make most people a little nervous. A test is an important event that can have a long-term impact on your future, so it's important to take it seriously and it's natural to feel anxious about performing well. But just because anxiety is normal, that doesn't mean that it's helpful in test taking, or that you should simply accept it as part of your life. Anxiety can have a variety of effects. These effects can be mild, like making you feel slightly nervous, or severe, like blocking your ability to focus or remember even a simple detail.

If you experience test anxiety—whether severe or mild—it's important to know how to beat it. To discover this, first you need to understand what causes test anxiety.

Causes of Test Anxiety

While we often think of anxiety as an uncontrollable emotional state, it can actually be caused by simple, practical things. One of the most common causes of test anxiety is that a person does not feel adequately prepared for their test. This feeling can be the result of many different issues such as poor study habits or lack of organization, but the most common culprit is time management. Starting to study too late, failing to organize your study time to cover all of the material, or being distracted while you study will mean that you're not well prepared for the test. This may lead to cramming the night before, which will cause you to be physically and mentally exhausted for the test. Poor time management also contributes to feelings of stress, fear, and hopelessness as you realize you are not well prepared but don't know what to do about it.

Other times, test anxiety is not related to your preparation for the test but comes from unresolved fear. This may be a past failure on a test, or poor performance on tests in general. It may come from comparing yourself to others who seem to be performing better or from the stress of living up to expectations. Anxiety may be driven by fears of the future—how failure on this test would affect your educational and career goals. These fears are often completely irrational, but they can still negatively impact your test performance.

> **Review Video: 3 Reasons You Have Test Anxiety**
> Visit mometrix.com/academy and enter code: 428468

Elements of Test Anxiety

As mentioned earlier, test anxiety is considered to be an emotional state, but it has physical and mental components as well. Sometimes you may not even realize that you are suffering from test anxiety until you notice the physical symptoms. These can include trembling hands, rapid heartbeat, sweating, nausea, and tense muscles. Extreme anxiety may lead to fainting or vomiting. Obviously, any of these symptoms can have a negative impact on testing. It is important to recognize them as soon as they begin to occur so that you can address the problem before it damages your performance.

> **Review Video: 3 Ways to Tell You Have Test Anxiety**
> Visit mometrix.com/academy and enter code: 927847

The mental components of test anxiety include trouble focusing and inability to remember learned information. During a test, your mind is on high alert, which can help you recall information and stay focused for an extended period of time. However, anxiety interferes with your mind's natural processes, causing you to blank out, even on the questions you know well. The strain of testing during anxiety makes it difficult to stay focused, especially on a test that may take several hours. Extreme anxiety can take a huge mental toll, making it difficult not only to recall test information but even to understand the test questions or pull your thoughts together.

> **Review Video: How Test Anxiety Affects Memory**
> Visit mometrix.com/academy and enter code: 609003

Effects of Test Anxiety

Test anxiety is like a disease—if left untreated, it will get progressively worse. Anxiety leads to poor performance, and this reinforces the feelings of fear and failure, which in turn lead to poor performances on subsequent tests. It can grow from a mild nervousness to a crippling condition. If allowed to progress, test anxiety can have a big impact on your schooling, and consequently on your future.

Test anxiety can spread to other parts of your life. Anxiety on tests can become anxiety in any stressful situation, and blanking on a test can turn into panicking in a job situation. But fortunately, you don't have to let anxiety rule your testing and determine your grades. There are a number of relatively simple steps you can take to move past anxiety and function normally on a test and in the rest of life.

> **Review Video: How Test Anxiety Impacts Your Grades**
> Visit mometrix.com/academy and enter code: 939819

Physical Steps for Beating Test Anxiety

While test anxiety is a serious problem, the good news is that it can be overcome. It doesn't have to control your ability to think and remember information. While it may take time, you can begin taking steps today to beat anxiety.

Just as your first hint that you may be struggling with anxiety comes from the physical symptoms, the first step to treating it is also physical. Rest is crucial for having a clear, strong mind. If you are tired, it is much easier to give in to anxiety. But if you establish good sleep habits, your body and mind will be ready to perform optimally, without the strain of exhaustion. Additionally, sleeping well helps you to retain information better, so you're more likely to recall the answers when you see the test questions.

Getting good sleep means more than going to bed on time. It's important to allow your brain time to relax. Take study breaks from time to time so it doesn't get overworked, and don't study right before bed. Take time to rest your mind before trying to rest your body, or you may find it difficult to fall asleep.

> **Review Video: The Importance of Sleep for Your Brain**
> Visit mometrix.com/academy and enter code: 319338

Along with sleep, other aspects of physical health are important in preparing for a test. Good nutrition is vital for good brain function. Sugary foods and drinks may give a burst of energy but this burst is followed by a crash, both physically and emotionally. Instead, fuel your body with protein and vitamin-rich foods.

Also, drink plenty of water. Dehydration can lead to headaches and exhaustion, especially if your brain is already under stress from the rigors of the test. Particularly if your test is a long one, drink water during the breaks. And if possible, take an energy-boosting snack to eat between sections.

> **Review Video: How Diet Can Affect your Mood**
> Visit mometrix.com/academy and enter code: 624317

Along with sleep and diet, a third important part of physical health is exercise. Maintaining a steady workout schedule is helpful, but even taking 5-minute study breaks to walk can help get your blood pumping faster and clear your head. Exercise also releases endorphins, which contribute to a positive feeling and can help combat test anxiety.

When you nurture your physical health, you are also contributing to your mental health. If your body is healthy, your mind is much more likely to be healthy as well. So take time to rest, nourish your body with healthy food and water, and get moving as much as possible. Taking these physical steps will make you stronger and more able to take the mental steps necessary to overcome test anxiety.

Mental Steps for Beating Test Anxiety

Working on the mental side of test anxiety can be more challenging, but as with the physical side, there are clear steps you can take to overcome it. As mentioned earlier, test anxiety often stems from lack of preparation, so the obvious solution is to prepare for the test. Effective studying may be the most important weapon you have for beating test anxiety, but you can and should employ several other mental tools to combat fear.

First, boost your confidence by reminding yourself of past success—tests or projects that you aced. If you're putting as much effort into preparing for this test as you did for those, there's no reason you should expect to fail here. Work hard to prepare; then trust your preparation.

Second, surround yourself with encouraging people. It can be helpful to find a study group, but be sure that the people you're around will encourage a positive attitude. If you spend time with others who are anxious or cynical, this will only contribute to your own anxiety. Look for others who are motivated to study hard from a desire to succeed, not from a fear of failure.

Third, reward yourself. A test is physically and mentally tiring, even without anxiety, and it can be helpful to have something to look forward to. Plan an activity following the test, regardless of the outcome, such as going to a movie or getting ice cream.

When you are taking the test, if you find yourself beginning to feel anxious, remind yourself that you know the material. Visualize successfully completing the test. Then take a few deep, relaxing breaths and return to it. Work through the questions carefully but with confidence, knowing that you are capable of succeeding.

Developing a healthy mental approach to test taking will also aid in other areas of life. Test anxiety affects more than just the actual test—it can be damaging to your mental health and even contribute to depression. It's important to beat test anxiety before it becomes a problem for more than testing.

> **Review Video: Test Anxiety and Depression**
> Visit mometrix.com/academy and enter code: 904704

Study Strategy

Being prepared for the test is necessary to combat anxiety, but what does being prepared look like? You may study for hours on end and still not feel prepared. What you need is a strategy for test prep. The next few pages outline our recommended steps to help you plan out and conquer the challenge of preparation.

STEP 1: SCOPE OUT THE TEST

Learn everything you can about the format (multiple choice, essay, etc.) and what will be on the test. Gather any study materials, course outlines, or sample exams that may be available. Not only will this help you to prepare, but knowing what to expect can help to alleviate test anxiety.

STEP 2: MAP OUT THE MATERIAL

Look through the textbook or study guide and make note of how many chapters or sections it has. Then divide these over the time you have. For example, if a book has 15 chapters and you have five days to study, you need to cover three chapters each day. Even better, if you have the time, leave an extra day at the end for overall review after you have gone through the material in depth.

If time is limited, you may need to prioritize the material. Look through it and make note of which sections you think you already have a good grasp on, and which need review. While you are studying, skim quickly through the familiar sections and take more time on the challenging parts. Write out your plan so you don't get lost as you go. Having a written plan also helps you feel more in control of the study, so anxiety is less likely to arise from feeling overwhelmed at the amount to cover.

STEP 3: GATHER YOUR TOOLS

Decide what study method works best for you. Do you prefer to highlight in the book as you study and then go back over the highlighted portions? Or do you type out notes of the important information? Or is it helpful to make flashcards that you can carry with you? Assemble the pens, index cards, highlighters, post-it notes, and any other materials you may need so you won't be distracted by getting up to find things while you study.

If you're having a hard time retaining the information or organizing your notes, experiment with different methods. For example, try color-coding by subject with colored pens, highlighters, or post-it notes. If you learn better by hearing, try recording yourself reading your notes so you can listen while in the car, working out, or simply sitting at your desk. Ask a friend to quiz you from your flashcards, or try teaching someone the material to solidify it in your mind.

STEP 4: CREATE YOUR ENVIRONMENT

It's important to avoid distractions while you study. This includes both the obvious distractions like visitors and the subtle distractions like an uncomfortable chair (or a too-comfortable couch that makes you want to fall asleep). Set up the best study environment possible: good lighting and a comfortable work area. If background music helps you focus, you may want to turn it on, but otherwise keep the room quiet. If you are using a computer to take notes, be sure you don't have any other windows open, especially applications like social media, games, or anything else that could distract you. Silence your phone and turn off notifications. Be sure to keep water close by so you stay hydrated while you study (but avoid unhealthy drinks and snacks).

Also, take into account the best time of day to study. Are you freshest first thing in the morning? Try to set aside some time then to work through the material. Is your mind clearer in the afternoon or evening? Schedule your study session then. Another method is to study at the same time of day that

154

you will take the test, so that your brain gets used to working on the material at that time and will be ready to focus at test time.

STEP 5: STUDY!

Once you have done all the study preparation, it's time to settle into the actual studying. Sit down, take a few moments to settle your mind so you can focus, and begin to follow your study plan. Don't give in to distractions or let yourself procrastinate. This is your time to prepare so you'll be ready to fearlessly approach the test. Make the most of the time and stay focused.

Of course, you don't want to burn out. If you study too long you may find that you're not retaining the information very well. Take regular study breaks. For example, taking five minutes out of every hour to walk briskly, breathing deeply and swinging your arms, can help your mind stay fresh.

As you get to the end of each chapter or section, it's a good idea to do a quick review. Remind yourself of what you learned and work on any difficult parts. When you feel that you've mastered the material, move on to the next part. At the end of your study session, briefly skim through your notes again.

But while review is helpful, cramming last minute is NOT. If at all possible, work ahead so that you won't need to fit all your study into the last day. Cramming overloads your brain with more information than it can process and retain, and your tired mind may struggle to recall even previously learned information when it is overwhelmed with last-minute study. Also, the urgent nature of cramming and the stress placed on your brain contribute to anxiety. You'll be more likely to go to the test feeling unprepared and having trouble thinking clearly.

So don't cram, and don't stay up late before the test, even just to review your notes at a leisurely pace. Your brain needs rest more than it needs to go over the information again. In fact, plan to finish your studies by noon or early afternoon the day before the test. Give your brain the rest of the day to relax or focus on other things, and get a good night's sleep. Then you will be fresh for the test and better able to recall what you've studied.

STEP 6: TAKE A PRACTICE TEST

Many courses offer sample tests, either online or in the study materials. This is an excellent resource to check whether you have mastered the material, as well as to prepare for the test format and environment.

Check the test format ahead of time: the number of questions, the type (multiple choice, free response, etc.), and the time limit. Then create a plan for working through them. For example, if you have 30 minutes to take a 60-question test, your limit is 30 seconds per question. Spend less time on the questions you know well so that you can take more time on the difficult ones.

If you have time to take several practice tests, take the first one open book, with no time limit. Work through the questions at your own pace and make sure you fully understand them. Gradually work up to taking a test under test conditions: sit at a desk with all study materials put away and set a timer. Pace yourself to make sure you finish the test with time to spare and go back to check your answers if you have time.

After each test, check your answers. On the questions you missed, be sure you understand why you missed them. Did you misread the question (tests can use tricky wording)? Did you forget the information? Or was it something you hadn't learned? Go back and study any shaky areas that the practice tests reveal.

Taking these tests not only helps with your grade, but also aids in combating test anxiety. If you're already used to the test conditions, you're less likely to worry about it, and working through tests until you're scoring well gives you a confidence boost. Go through the practice tests until you feel comfortable, and then you can go into the test knowing that you're ready for it.

Test Tips

On test day, you should be confident, knowing that you've prepared well and are ready to answer the questions. But aside from preparation, there are several test day strategies you can employ to maximize your performance.

First, as stated before, get a good night's sleep the night before the test (and for several nights before that, if possible). Go into the test with a fresh, alert mind rather than staying up late to study.

Try not to change too much about your normal routine on the day of the test. It's important to eat a nutritious breakfast, but if you normally don't eat breakfast at all, consider eating just a protein bar. If you're a coffee drinker, go ahead and have your normal coffee. Just make sure you time it so that the caffeine doesn't wear off right in the middle of your test. Avoid sugary beverages, and drink enough water to stay hydrated but not so much that you need a restroom break 10 minutes into the test. If your test isn't first thing in the morning, consider going for a walk or doing a light workout before the test to get your blood flowing.

Allow yourself enough time to get ready, and leave for the test with plenty of time to spare so you won't have the anxiety of scrambling to arrive in time. Another reason to be early is to select a good seat. It's helpful to sit away from doors and windows, which can be distracting. Find a good seat, get out your supplies, and settle your mind before the test begins.

When the test begins, start by going over the instructions carefully, even if you already know what to expect. Make sure you avoid any careless mistakes by following the directions.

Then begin working through the questions, pacing yourself as you've practiced. If you're not sure on an answer, don't spend too much time on it, and don't let it shake your confidence. Either skip it and come back later, or eliminate as many wrong answers as possible and guess among the remaining ones. Don't dwell on these questions as you continue—put them out of your mind and focus on what lies ahead.

Be sure to read all of the answer choices, even if you're sure the first one is the right answer. Sometimes you'll find a better one if you keep reading. But don't second-guess yourself if you do immediately know the answer. Your gut instinct is usually right. Don't let test anxiety rob you of the information you know.

If you have time at the end of the test (and if the test format allows), go back and review your answers. Be cautious about changing any, since your first instinct tends to be correct, but make sure you didn't misread any of the questions or accidentally mark the wrong answer choice. Look over any you skipped and make an educated guess.

At the end, leave the test feeling confident. You've done your best, so don't waste time worrying about your performance or wishing you could change anything. Instead, celebrate the successful completion of this test. And finally, use this test to learn how to deal with anxiety even better next time.

Important Qualification

Not all anxiety is created equal. If your test anxiety is causing major issues in your life beyond the classroom or testing center, or if you are experiencing troubling physical symptoms related to your anxiety, it may be a sign of a serious physiological or psychological condition. If this sounds like your situation, we strongly encourage you to seek professional help.

Thank You

We at Mometrix would like to extend our heartfelt thanks to you, our friend and patron, for allowing us to play a part in your journey. It is a privilege to serve people from all walks of life who are unified in their commitment to building the best future they can for themselves.

The preparation you devote to these important testing milestones may be the most valuable educational opportunity you have for making a real difference in your life. We encourage you to put your heart into it—that feeling of succeeding, overcoming, and yes, conquering will be well worth the hours you've invested.

We want to hear your story, your struggles and your successes, and if you see any opportunities for us to improve our materials so we can help others even more effectively in the future, please share that with us as well. **The team at Mometrix would be absolutely thrilled to hear from you!** So please, send us an email (support@mometrix.com) and let's stay in touch.

> **If you'd like some additional help, check out these other resources we offer for your exam:**
> **http://MometrixFlashcards.com/GACE**

Additional Bonus Material

Due to our efforts to try to keep this book to a manageable length, we've created a link that will give you access to all of your additional bonus material:

mometrix.com/bonus948/gacemgsocsci